W
3M

MW00424481

JESUS *of*
GALILEE

JESUS *of* GALILEE

CONTEXTUAL CHRISTOLOGY FOR THE 21ST CENTURY

——— ROBERT LASSALLE-KLEIN ———

PABLO ALONSO ❖ M. SHAWN COPELAND ❖ MARY DOAK ❖ VIRGILIO ELIZONDO

SEAN FREYNE ❖ ROBERTO S. GOIZUETA ❖ DANIEL GROODY ❖ GUSTAVO GUTIÉRREZ

MICHAEL E. LEE ❖ CAROLINE N. MBONU ❖ FRANCIS MINJ ❖ SOPHIA PARK

GIACOMO PEREGO ❖ JON SOBRINO ❖ JOSÉ SOLS

ORBIS BOOKS

Maryknoll, New York 10545

Founded in 1970, Orbis Books endeavors to publish works that enlighten the mind, nourish the spirit, and challenge the conscience. The publishing arm of the Maryknoll Fathers and Brothers, Orbis seeks to explore the global dimensions of the Christian faith and mission, to invite dialogue with diverse cultures and religious traditions, and to serve the cause of reconciliation and peace. The books published reflect the views of their authors and do not represent the official position of the Maryknoll Society. To learn more about Maryknoll and Orbis Books, please visit our website at www.maryknollsociety.org.

Copyright © 2011 by Robert Lassalle-Klein.

Published by Orbis Books, Maryknoll, New York 10545-0302.
Manufactured in the United States of America.

All rights reserved. No part of this publication may be reproduced or transmitted in any form or by any means, electronic or mechanical, including photocopying, recording or any information storage or retrieval system, without prior permission in writing from the publisher.

Queries regarding rights and permissions should be addressed to: Orbis Books, P.O. Box 302, Maryknoll, New York 10545-0302.

Library of Congress Cataloging-in-Publication Data

Jesus of Galilee : contextual christology for the 21st century / Robert Lassalle-Klein, editor.
    p. cm.
  Includes index.
  ISBN 978-1-57075-915-4 (pbk.)
  1. Jesus Christ—Person and offices. I. Lassalle-Klein, Robert Anthony.
  BT203.J4695 2011
  232'.8—dc22
                  2010053154

ISBN 978-1-57075-915-4

For Lynn, Kate, Rose, and Peter . . . life with you is a joy;
and for our dear friends,
Marina, José Antonio, Oscar, Elmer, Wil, and Elsi Zavala

CONTENTS

PART II
THE BIBLE

PART III
THEOLOGY

PART IV
SPIRITUALITY

ACKNOWLEDGMENTS

On behalf of all involved in *Jesus of Galilee: Contextual Christology for the 21st Century* I would like to thank Virgilio Elizondo, Gustavo Gutiérrez, and Jon Sobrino for their faithfulness in continuing to sow the seeds of intercultural theology and the preferential option for the poor around the globe and for drawing us back to Jesus of Galilee as the original sower. This book and the process that produced it owe much to their friendship, leadership, vision, and generosity. All the authors are also grateful to Orbis Books, which continues to play such a crucial role in connecting this vision with its audience, and to Susan Perry for her wise editorial assistance.

My own participation would not have been possible without the enthusiastic invitation and mentorship of Virgilio Elizondo and support from the University of Notre Dame and the Center for Latino Spirituality and Culture; the Wabash Center for Teaching and Learning in Theology and Religion; the Institut Catholique in Paris; the Centre for Liberation Theologies of the Katholieke Universiteit Leuven, Belgium; and faculty colleagues and students at Holy Names University in Oakland, California.

I am especially grateful to Santa Clara University and to the Ignatian Center for Jesuit Education for supporting me as the Bannan Fellow during the first half of 2010, and to the Department of Religious Studies who welcomed me and provided important feedback. Valuable input was provided by Paul Crowley, SJ, and Gary Macy from Santa Clara; Michael E. Lee; the 2010 Christology Group of the Catholic Theological Society of America; Raúl Fornet-Betancourt and the Fourth International Congress on Intercultural Philosophy in Buenos Aires, Argentina; William O'Neill, SJ, from the Jesuit School of Theology of Santa Clara; Don Gelpi, SJ, Rich Wood, Si Hendry, Chris Tirres, Frank Oppenheim, SJ, and other members of the John Courtney Murray Group; and the master's degree students in pastoral ministries of Holy Names University who read and offered helpful comments on my own contributions and the overall vision of the book.

Finally, thanks to Marina and José Antonio Zavala for the many years of friendship our families have shared. The projects come and go, but love and friendship remain. Thus my wife, Lynn, and I are humbly grateful for how the stories and friendships that have shaped this and other projects continue to weave their way into the fabric of our family life.

INTRODUCTION

FROM THE MARGINS OF GALILEE TO THE ENDS OF THE EARTH

Robert Lassalle-Klein

A Lover's Dream

Half a lifetime ago, while falling in love with my future wife, I had a dream. The earth appeared as a small, delicate, beautiful blue orb, set against the infinite black of deepest space. My heart was filled with wonder and love as I somehow saw, through heaven's eyes, the oceans and the continents with all their peoples, cultures, and infinite creativity pulsing with life. Then, suddenly, unexpectedly, the pulsing turned to pain. I was a lover watching the death of my beloved, or a parent watching the death of a child. Love and suffering poured from my broken heart. Then I awoke.

For me, the dream brought to consciousness my discovery of a love interest with the same First Love who created the garden before us, drawing us together in an exodus of awakening from the sleep of inhumanity. Some describe this God as a vigilant mother who worries as her children wander the desert of modernity, desperately seeking a better life. What cannot be denied is that vast changes are reshaping life in every corner of the globe, challenging the sacred beliefs and traditions of every people.

The planet faces ecological disaster within fifty years, driven by global warming and unsustainable consumption.[1] Roughly 40 percent of the people on the planet live in poverty,[2] while the annual income of the five hundred richest individuals exceeds that of the poorest 416 million people.[3] Globalization is accelerating cultural contacts and the scope of economic and environmental threats against weaker nations[4] that were once the province of a few hundred plundering Europeans.

In this context, followers of Jesus in the United States and other parts of the developed world are often puzzled by the hope, the hunger

1

for reconciliation, and the visions of a global ethic of respect for human rights and dignity that continue to emerge from such situations as apartheid in South Africa; the colonization of ancient civilizations in Africa, Asia, and Oceania; and the four hundred years of chattel slav- ery, genocide, and expropriation of native lands that defined the con- quest of the Americas.

Yet, since World War II the churches have produced from among survivors of these situations leaders like Desmond Tutu, Archbishop Oscar Romero, Mahatma Gandhi (a Hindu influenced by Jesus), Mar- tin Luther King, Jr., Mother Teresa, Dorothy Day, and countless others who have brought God close to us. They have participated in the struggles for justice and human dignity that we now understand to be a constitutive part of the gospel, and they have opened frontiers of inter- cultural and interreligious dialogue. Thanks in part to their leadership and the faithful service of others who have walked in the footsteps of Jesus, two billion Christians in light of the gospel make sense of the signs of the times that fill our newspapers. Countless women and men and churches of every denomination in Africa, Asia, the Americas, Oceania, Europe, and Antarctica struggle to meet the daily demands of Christian discipleship by asking, "Who was Jesus of Galilee, and what does it mean to follow Jesus Christ today?"

Some of the key theological figures associated with these leaders and their movements appear in these pages, together with a variety of newer voices that continue to emerge from the communities outlined above. Each essay asks, "Who was Jesus of Galilee?" and probes his sig- nificance for some corner of the world church that is global Christian- ity today. The latest scholarship from the great universities of Africa, the Americas, Asia, Europe, and Oceania is represented. More impor- tant, however, is the fact that the voices of many cultures and crucified peoples fill the pages that follow.

Some of the writers were born and raised in these communities, while others from the "developed" nations responded to the call of Jesus and his followers to "come and see." All the contributors know firsthand the pain of a planet in crisis. All have awakened from the sleep of inhumanity. And all find hope in a worldwide community of friendship that sustains and refreshes followers of Jesus, honoring and supporting their compassionate efforts to respond to the suffering of a broken world and to take the crucified peoples down from the cross.

In 2007 Pope Benedict XVI invited Christian believers and schol- ars to ponder a pointed question posed by an imaginary Jewish rabbi and brother: "So what has your 'Messiah' Jesus actually brought? He has not brought world peace, and he has not conquered the world's misery. So he can hardly be the true Messiah, who, after all, is supposed to do just that."[5] Benedict replies to his supposed Jewish interlocutor, "He has brought the God of Israel to the nations," and he "has brought the gift of universality, which was the one great definitive promise to Israel and the world." Benedict asserts that "the vehicle of this universalization is the new family, whose only admission requirement is communion with Jesus, communion in God's will." Speaking to Catholics, he notes, "This book is in no way an exercise of the magisterium, but is solely an expression of my personal search 'for the face of the Lord' (Psalm 27:8)."[6] He concludes, therefore, "Everyone is free, then, to contradict me. I would only ask my reader for that initial goodwill without which there can be no understanding."

Responding to Benedict's invitation, theologians from around the globe gathered in Galilee to dialogue about the significance of this unforgettable Jew for his followers among the nations of the world. This book is a small sample and outcome of that conversation, which has come to include many others. Each author writes about the role of Jesus of Galilee in the faith of a local Christian community, utilizing an intercultural approach grounded in a preferential option for the poor, and comparing and contrasting what he or she has found to the latest research on Jesus. The resulting essays introduce readers to some of the most recent research on Jesus of Galilee while exploring his significance for followers among the nations of Asia, Africa, Latin America, Europe, the Caribbean, and the United States. We get to see Jesus through the eyes of aboriginal Ādivāsi tribes from India; victims of the African slave trade and their descendants; refugees and immigrants from North Africa, Cuba, Puerto Rico, and mainland Latin America; U.S. Latino youth; Igbo tribeswomen from West Africa; immigrant families on the U.S./Mexico border; first world mothers and fathers troubled by the inequities of globalization; and church leaders from around the globe.

Each of the authors interprets membership in "the new family" through which Pope Benedict says Jesus "has brought the God of Israel to the nations" in the broadest sense of Matthew 25:40: "Truly I tell you, just as you did it to one of the least of these who are members of my family, you did it to me." All of the nations are God's children, and the God of compassion and mercy has a special concern for those who suffer. Thus, as Benedict himself has stated, echoing both Matthew 25:40 and the Great Command of Jesus (Mk 12:28–34, Mt 22:34–40, Lk 10:25–28), "Love of God and love of neighbor have become one: in the least of the brethren we find Jesus himself, and in Jesus we find God" (*Deus Caritas Est*, #15).

The Essays

Each essay in the volume explores the christological dimensions of some aspect of the faith of the nations in Jesus of Galilee, and the collection is organized to introduce readers to important methodological and disciplinary starting points for approaching Jesus. Thus, the book begins with six essays, each including an interpretive framework that Christian churches and scholars have found helpful and important for approaching Jesus. These include:

- *historical research on the Galilee of Jesus,*
- the *preferential option for the poor* of Jesus and the contemporary church,
- attention to *race, culture, and intercultural dynamics,*
- Jesus' belief that he was sent by the Father to initiate *the reign of God,* and *the crucifixion* as defining aspects of the life of Jesus, and
- the *historical reality of Jesus* as the object of the gospels and Christian faith.

After covering these starting points, the collection then moves to ten essays modeling a variety of approaches to Jesus from three disciplinary fields: biblical exegesis, theology and/or doctrine, and Christian spirituality. Ethical issues and methods run throughout the entire collection.

Jesus of Galilee: Starting Points

Sean Freyne introduces historical research on "*the cultural, social, economic, and religious context of first-century Galilee*" as a key starting point for understanding Jesus. Summarizing three centuries of quests for the historical Jesus, Freyne argues that "Jesus' actual career in Galilee informed the early Christian proclamation about him to a far greater extent than is often recognized." He begins by evaluating the impact of Hellenization in Jewish Galilee on the ministry of Jesus, accepting the claim of the synoptic gospels that Jesus first left, and then returned to the region in the wake of the arrest of John the Baptist.

Freyne then describes the "values revolution" embodied in the kingdom of God preached by Jesus, explaining his positions on wealth, power, and wisdom as part of Jesus' program for the renewal of Israel. He says these carry over to communities of followers that emerge in Jerusalem and Galilee soon after the death of Jesus. And he argues that profiles of these communities can be discerned from two of the earliest documents: the collection of Jesus' sayings (Q) and the Gospel of

Mark, which he asserts "can be plausibly attributed" to Galilean authorship. Thus Freyne helps us to see that, from beginning to end, Galilee proves to be crucial for placing the person and message of Jesus in their historical context, and for discerning their meaning today.

Fr. Gustavo Gutiérrez, OP, widely considered the father of liberation theology and a key voice in the "preferential option for the poor" of the Latin American bishops, introduces that option as a key building block for understanding the mission and message of Jesus of Galilee and the church. Gutiérrez explores the biblical basis for the preferential option for the poor in the parable of the Good Samaritan (Lk 10:30–37), showing how the story functions as the model for the Gospel of Luke and the 2007 meeting of the Latin American bishops at Aparecida, Brazil. Quoting Pope Benedict XVI, Gutiérrez asserts, "'Making ourselves neighbors,' ... means 'going as good Samaritans to meet the needs of the poor and those who suffer, and creating 'the just structures that are the condition without which a just social order is not possible'" (Benedict XVI, Address at Aparecida). And echoing both the Great Command of Jesus (Mk 12:28–34, Mt 22:34–40, Lk 10:25–28) and Benedict, Gutiérrez argues that love of God is love of neighbor expressed in the option for the poor, and love of neighbor expressed in the option for the poor is love of God.

Fr. Virgilio Elizondo adds *culture and intercultural theology* to the starting points already mentioned by Freyne and Gutiérrez: historical research on Galilee, and the preferential option for the poor. Variously described as the "founder"[7] or "herald of U.S. Hispanic theology"[8] and the creator of its "paradigm for theological scholarship,"[9] Elizondo introduces a key innovation with his use of the term *mestizo*, which Eduardo Fernández says "some might equate with 'half-breed,'"[10] in order to describe the intercultural character of U.S. Latino/a ethnicity, faith, and religious experience. Elizondo extended the term to Jesus of Galilee in his 1978 dissertation at the Institut Catholique in France and in his groundbreaking 1983 book, *Galilean Journey: The Mexican-American Promise*.[11] He then adds, "friends ... have been urging me to develop further the theme of the Galilean Jesus" ever since, particularly in relation to the following questions: 'How does Jesus of Galilee become the Christ to persons who feel doomed to exclusion and marginalization because of their mixed-race or mixed-ethnic origins? ... [And] is there something unsuspected in the humiliated Jesus that those of the dominant cultures have not detected?'" Elizondo addresses these questions and others, reprising themes addressed in more than thirty books as he reflects on a series of christological quotations from the Gospel of John (1:14, 8:32, 15:15, 16:13, 21) and Philippians 2:7.

M. Shawn Copeland, a leading African American theologian, adds *race* to culture and intercultural theology as key starting points for a contemporary approach to Jesus of Galilee. Seeking to develop "a theology accountable to the 'dangerous memory' of chattel slavery and the moral and social sin of racism" Copeland asserts, "betrayed, …captured, chained, and force-marched to the Atlantic coast; various peoples of West Africa including the Igbo, Bini, Fante, Mende, Yoruba, [and] BaKongo…endured filth, severe beatings, sexual assault, and immeasurable psychic trauma." Yet, "the enslaved people… found a way to reconfigure the African sacred cosmos" and to situate "Jesus of Nazareth within it" as a way of "asserting their humanity in the midst of a fundamentally inhuman situation."

Tracing this history, she describes the emergence of American "black religion" as an intercultural phenomenon, the African American "encounter…with the Bible," and the testimonial of spirituals and sorrow psalms "to the ways in which the enslaved people met God in the slave quarter, at the whipping post, on the auction block, in the hush arbor, in the midnight flight to freedom." She concludes with the warning, "If we would see him in Galilee, we must first meet him in excluded, despised, and poor children, women, and men of our time."

Fr. Jon Sobrino, SJ, adds the *reign of God* and *the cross* to our list of starting points for interpreting Jesus of Galilee. Beginning with the cross, Sobrino highlights the importance of Jesus' conflicts "with the priests, the doctors of the law, the Pharisees, and the powerful people of his day" in bringing about his crucifixion. He insists that, "consciously or unconsciously," the silence of church leaders about this aspect of the life of Jesus allows us "to avoid conflicts with those who continue oppressing the poor today…, the successors to those who killed Jesus."

Moving on the kingdom of God, Sobrino argues that, like all true followers of Jesus, "the Church must put itself clearly at the service of the Reign," which entails confronting "the reality of the anti-Reign" and being "ready to suffer the consequences." He says this means followers of Jesus must carry on not only "his *mercy* toward the oppressed, but also…his *anger* [toward their oppressors], which is most often forgotten." In the end, however, loving solidarity with the poor will be the most authentic witness to Christian discipleship, for "Latin America is a continent of 'crucified peoples' before whom the most important exigency for the Church—call it a 'mission' or a 'command' from God—is 'to take them down from the cross.'"

My article (**Robert Lassalle-Klein**) adds *the historical reality of Jesus* as a fifth and final dimension to our list of starting points for approaching Jesus of Galilee. The article begins by exploring the faith of Rosa Marina Zavala, a Salvadoran wife and mother who survived the 1981 Rio Lempa massacre by the U.S.–sponsored government of El Salvador, five years in a U.N.–sponsored refugee camp, and death threats back home, to eventually enter the United States in 1989 as an undocumented immigrant and become legalized as part of a landmark decision on political asylum for Salvadoran refugees.

I explain how suffering peasants like Marina and her family led Archbishop Romero to ask in what sense the crucified peasants of El Salvador are "the image" of the persecution and crucifixion of Jesus. I examine how Fr. Ignacio Ellacuría's work on the historical reality of Jesus helps to answer Romero's question, and identifies a new and different object from nearly three centuries of quests for the historical Jesus. I show that the historical realities of both Marina and Jesus are defined (in analogous but different ways) by their faith in a God of compassion who raises up new disciples and longs to give life to God's beloved children. And I argue that this God desires disciples who, moved by faith in the resurrection of Jesus and hope in the God of life, act in love to break the endless cycle of oppression and crucifixion by taking the crucified peoples down from the cross.

The Bible
Following this introduction to five interpretive frameworks for approaching Jesus (historical research on Galilee; the preferential option for the poor; race, culture, and intercultural dynamics; the reign of God and the cross; and the historical reality of Jesus), the collection then moves on to ten essays modeling disciplinary approaches to Jesus from biblical exegesis, theology and/or doctrine, and Christian spirituality. As noted earlier, ethical issues and methods run throughout.

Fr. Pablo Alonso, SJ, examines the intercultural encounter between Jesus the Jew and a Syrophoenician woman in the territory of the pagan city of Tyre northwest of Galilee (Mk 7:24–30). The encounter begins when the Syrophoenician woman begs Jesus "to cast the demon out of her daughter" and Jesus replies, "Let the children be fed first, for it is not fair to take the children's bread and throw it to the dogs." Alonso explains that Jesus' words betray "an assumption that Gentiles are excluded from his mission," and he cites Theissen's conviction that they manifest typically Galilean "prejudices, supported by economic dependency and legitimated by religious traditions."[12]

The author defends the historical plausibility of the encounter, and suggests that the woman leads Jesus to "change his mind" when she argues that even non-Jews can be included among the "children of God" (Mk 7:27–28, see Is 30:1). Alonso concludes by asserting that "the interaction of the Syrophoenician woman with Jesus reminds us that [we] …are called to take the lead in accepting foreigners, in working with migrants and refugees, and in intercultural and interreligious dialogue."

Sr. Caroline N. Mbonu is a member of the Igbo tribe listed by Shawn Copeland as one of the peoples kidnapped from West Africa and brought to the United States as slaves. Mbonu highlights the liberating implications of Mary's self-presentation in the annunciation (Lk 1:26–38) as a servant-leader who boldly accepts God's call to help liberate her people. The article follows Mary's transformation from an unnamed "virgin engaged to a man whose name was Joseph, of the house of David," to the self-possessed woman who responds to the angel Gabriel in the tradition of Israel's heroines and prophets, "Here am I, the servant of the Lord; let it be with me according to your word" (Lk 1: 38).

Sr. Caroline Mbonu highlights the importance of Mary's Galilean hearth for Igbo women, stating, "The seemingly mundane life of this Galilean maiden encourages women in Igbo society…to disallow depictions of themselves as naturally inferior, subordinate, eternal victims of male oppression." She boldly insists that, like Mary, "we are ready to engage the world as servants and leaders in our communities!" And, she concludes, "understood correctly, Luke's portrait of the Galilean Mary is an inspiration to Igbo women striving for abundant life in a society that continues to define us as the other."

Sr. Sophia Park, SNJM, was born and raised in South Korea and immigrated to the United States as an adult. She offers a proposal for the future of Korean *minjung* ("common people") theology based on her reading of Luke's account of the interaction of the disciples with the risen Jesus on the road to Emmaus (Lk 24:13–32). Approaching *minjung* theology as a contextual theology that arose during the struggle for liberation from military rule and successive repressive governments, she recalls that, "as a member of the generation of Korean *minjung* theology, I was baptized by the *minjung* Jesus of the oppressed, poor, and marginalized."

On the other hand, she observes, "now that Korea is an advanced and highly technical society, the *minjung* Jesus seems invisible." This leads her to ask, "Who, then, is the Jesus of this post-*minjung* period?"

and "Where can we again encounter the Jesus of the *minjung*?" Building on a close reading of Luke's account of the disciples who offer hospitality to the post-resurrection Jesus on the road to Emmaus, she suggests that the post-*minjung* Jesus will show his face to Koreans who offer hospitality to the stranger, and to the undocumented migrant worker, "for it is there that the community that gathers in His name continues to exclaim…after the breaking of the bread, 'Were not our hearts burning within" (24:32b)?'"

Fr. Giacomo Perego, SSP, from Italy is fascinated with a brief episode in Mark's account of the arrest of Jesus that has intrigued interpreters for centuries. At the moment of the arrest in Gethsemane, after all the disciples have fled, Mark informs us that "a certain young man was following him, wearing nothing but a linen cloth. They caught hold of him, but he left the linen cloth and ran off naked" (Mk 14:51–52). In response, Perego asks, "Who is this "young man?" and "Why is there such an insistence on what [he]…was wearing, and upon his nakedness?" Perego's article sheds light on this puzzle, noting that the young man, who is stripped of his clothing, prefigures both the stages of despoilment to which Jesus will be subjected, and the sad and humiliating flight of the disciples. He says that the latter captures Mark's conviction that "it is possible to follow the path of the Master only on the day following the experience of the paschal mystery" and that the stripping and the nakedness of the young man are unavoidable consequences of the decision to follow the path tread by Jesus of Galilee.

Theology

Roberto S. Goizueta was born in Cuba and grew up trying to assimilate into North American culture in various parts of the southeast United States as his father climbed the corporate ladder. Turning to Latin America for identity, he eventually realized, "I wasn't Latin American either."[13] Finally, Goizueta came to embrace the intercultural nature of his "both/and" existence, living in two worlds, and fully accepted in neither. Given this background, it is interesting that Goizueta resolves what he sees as a quandary regarding the preferential option for the poor in the thought of Gustavo Gutiérrez of Peru by turning to the work of U.S.–born Virgilio Elizondo of San Antonio, Texas.

Goizueta highlights the potential contradiction between universality and particularity in the claim by Gutiérrez that the two principal, overarching themes of scripture are the *universality* and graciousness of God's love, and the *particularity* of God's preferential love for the poor. He argues that Elizondo's U.S. Latino/a Christology, which emerges from the historical reality of the border, shows how the particularity of God's preferential love for the poor expresses and safeguards God's universal, gratuitous love. In the end, Goizueta argues that "it is precisely because the church is the church of the borderland and thrives among its inhabitants as the church of the margins, that the church can be present everywhere and to everyone."

Fr. Francis Minj, SJ, is an Indian Ādivāsi (aboriginal tribes that fall outside the Indian caste system like "untouchables") who serves as dean of the Tarunoday Regional Theology Centre, training Jesuits from the central tribal belt of India. His essay develops fundamental categories for the first contextualized Ādivāsi Christology utilizing a term of his own creation, *paramādivāsi*, to capture Christian teaching on the humanity and divinity of Jesus in a form intelligible to his people. The term combines *param* (supreme), *ādi* (primordial) and *vāsi* (dweller), and is designed to work as a metaphor uniting the human and the divine. Minj says the "term *paramādivāsi* echoes Karl Rahner's idea that God's self-revelation is universal, yet simultaneously local and specific to each time and people, thereby transcending the Hebrew-Christian Bible and its readers." Building on this insight, he develops "four Ādivāsi images for aspects of the mystery of Jesus Christ," including Jesus as Ancestor, Jesus as Messiah/Liberator, Jesus as High Priest (*Pahan, Naike*), and Jesus as Healer/Exorcist (*Deonra*). He ends these groundbreaking proposals by warning the reader that "the conclusions presented here are tenuous, and a fuller evaluation will come only with time for reflection and dialogue between and among Ādivāsi Christians and the larger church."

José Sols writes from his native Spain about the cultural matrix of secularization that he believes has reduced European Christianity to a shadow of itself. He regrets that European Catholicism has reacted defensively to the autonomy and freedom prized by modernity, and he finds parallels to the behavior of "Jewish religious authorities [who] betrayed the Alliance and suppressed freedom leading into the Babylonian exile and the exile-at-home under Roman rule at the time of Jesus." Arguing instead that "secularization presents an opportunity for renewal," he insists that just as "authentic freedom and love are grounded in responsible autonomy," so too, "European Christians are called as followers of Jesus and responsible adults to reform the structures of ecclesial and secular power that abrogate human freedom and autonomy." He offers a close analysis of scriptural accounts of the commitment of the Galilean Jesus to the responsible autonomy of his followers as a model for this approach.

Spirituality

Mary Doak, who lives and works in San Diego on the U.S. side of the Mexico border, wonders whether it is possible for hope to overcome the fear and selfishness driving the accelerating disparities of globalization. She writes, "As a Catholic theologian, an educated U.S. citizen, a wife, the Anglo mother of a Mexican daughter, and a feminist committed to an international ethic of care in service of the common good, I am deeply concerned with what might inspire those of us who benefit from the current global economy (yet seem none the happier for our privilege and wealth) to join those without adequate food and shelter to work together for a world of greater sharing rather than greater selfishness."

In search of an answer, she turns to "Christianity's origins in the hope brought by a Galilean rabbi to a people and a world marked by imperial domination, . . . a violent and oppressive situation in which there was much reason to despair." She argues this hope must be globalized today through forms of Christian praxis that influence international economics, communication, and politics. And she insists that contemporary hope must demonstrate concern for the sufferings of specific persons and peoples, especially those deemed insignificant by the power players of the global market and international politics.

Michael E. Lee was born of Puerto Rican parents in Miami, Florida. He begins with two childhood images of Jesus: the *pobre*, crucified, bleeding *Jesucristo* in La Catedral Dulce Nombre de Jesús near his grandparents' home in Humacao, Puerto Rico; and the resurrected Christ dressed in billowing white, hovering victoriously in front of the cross one thousand miles away in the chapel of St. Thomas the Apostle Church and elementary school in Miami, Florida. For Lee, these images capture the "in-between" "hybrid ways of negotiating selfhood and faith" of many young Hispanic-Latino/a adults "who feel forced to choose between the U.S. and Hispanic dimensions of our identity [and who] experience this dualistic either-or logic as inauthentic."

After examining current social-scientific data on young, native-born, second- and third-generation U.S. Latina/os, he turns to Nicodemus in John's gospel as a model for a richer, more nuanced way of understanding the possibilities for faith in a global scene of intercultural exchange. He concludes with the gospel idea that the followers of Jesus will find the Risen One in the borderland of Galilee, suggesting that "the life of the disciple is to be forged *in between* the two points on the journey," wherever they might be.

Finally, **Fr. Daniel Groody, CSC,** describes the social, political, economic, and spiritual struggles of immigrants along the U.S.–Mexico border as a contemporary form of crucifixion with strong parallels to the gospels. Groody writes: "They experience an economic crucifixion in their poverty, a political crucifixion in their marginality, a legal crucifixion in their undocumented status, a cultural crucifixion in their displacement, a social crucifixion in being separated from their families and loved ones, and, for those who die, an actual crucifixion." He says the "judgment of the nations" in Matthew 25 challenges followers of Jesus "to discern the face of Christ" among immigrants and sojourners. And he insists that the story is also about us, the reader, when the Son of Man declares, "Truly I tell you, just as you did it to one of the least of these . . . , you did it to me."

Groody asserts that immigrants make their hosts uncomfortable because they prompt us to weigh the source of our self-sufficiency, economic prosperity, and national security against the depth of their dependence on God and their willingness to rely on others in their time of need and vulnerability. This leads him to conclude, quoting Lydio Tomasi, that "it's not that the Church saves the immigrant, but that the immigrant saves the Church."[14]

After all is said and done, however, the question with which we began the volume still remains: "What has Jesus really brought . . . if he has not brought world peace, universal prosperity, and a better world?"[15] The essays in *Jesus of Galilee: Contextual Christology for the 21st Century* provide a partial answer, reflecting Jesus' significance for followers from the nations of Asia, Africa, Latin America, Europe, the Caribbean, and the United States. And though their perspectives may vary, one thing is clear. They have taken us to where Jesus lived, not to stay with him there, but so that we might follow him from the margins of Galilee to the ends of the earth.

Notes

1. Intergovernmental Panel on Climate Change, *Climate Change 2007: Synthesis Report* (New York: United Nations, November 17, 2007).

2. The 2010 Human Development Report states that 2.6 billion people live on less than $2.00 per day, and 1.75 billion are multidimensionally poor. *The Real Wealth of Nations: Pathways to Development, Human Development Report 2010* (New York: United Nations Development Programme, November 2010), 96.

3. *Beyond Scarcity: Power, Poverty and the Global Water Crisis, Human Development Report 2006* (New York: United Nations Development Programme, 2006), 269.

4. *Globalization with a Human Face, Human Development Report 1999* (New York: United Nations Human Development Programme, 1999), 2, 30–42.

5. Pope Benedict XVI, *Jesus of Nazareth: From the Baptism in the Jordan to the Transfiguration* (New York, Doubleday, 2007), 116–17.

6. Ibid., xxiii–xxiv.

7. Tim Matovina, *Virgilio Elizondo: Spiritual Writings*, Modern Spiritual Masters Series (Maryknoll, NY: Orbis Books, 2010), back cover.

8. Eduardo Fernández, *La Cosecha: Harvesting Contemporary United States Hispanic Theology (1972–1998)* (Collegeville, MN: Liturgical/Michael Glazier, 2000), 38.

9. Allan Figueroa Deck, SJ, *Frontiers of Hispanic Theology in the United States* (Maryknoll, NY: Orbis Books, 1992), xii–xv.

10. Fernández, *La Cosecha*, 39.

11. Virgilio Elizondo, *Galilean Journey: The Mexican-American Promise* (Maryknoll, NY: Orbis Books, 1983) is based on the author's doctoral dissertation *Mestissage, violence culturelle, annonce de l'Evangile*, presented at the Institut Catholique, Paris, 1978.

12. Gerd Theissen, *The Gospels in Context: Social and Political History in the Synoptic Tradition* (Minneapolis: Fortress Press, 1991), 78–79.

13. Dawn Gibeau, "Hispanic Theology Aims Church at Poor," *National Catholic Reporter* (September 11, 1992); cited in Fernández, *La Cosecha*, 54 notes 45, 54.

14. Lydio F. Tomasi, "The Other Catholics" (PhD diss., New York University, 1978), 301.

15. Pope Benedict XVI, *Jesus of Nazareth*, 44.

PART I

JESUS OF GALILEE: STARTING POINTS

1

JESUS IN CONTEXT

GALILEE AND GOSPEL

Sean Freyne

The fact that Jesus' early life and subsequent ministry can be firmly rooted in the cultural, social, economic, and religious environment of first-century Galilee gives a specific content to the claims associated with him in Christian belief. The rediscovery of the importance of the "synoptic Jesus" as distinct from the more highly theological account of the Fourth Gospel—an account that has dominated later christological debates and Western piety—is due in no small measure to the work of liberation theologians. Their retrieval of the reality of Jesus' ministry within a definite historical and geographical context has given specificity to the gospel claims that have for long been obscured by philosophical and theological abstractions. The Galilean Jesus is not just the presupposition for the Christian proclamation, as Rudolf Bultmann famously claimed. His Galilean ministry is an integral part of that proclamation.

At the same time, it is no easy task to locate Jesus and his ministry more precisely in the Galilean context. The gospel texts are still our best windows on that world. At the end of the exercise, however, one is reminded of Schweitzer's famous conclusion, namely, that the quest for *the* historical Jesus, that is, the figure who stands behind the synoptic versions of Jesus, is doomed to failure. Such provisionality, however, merely points to the incomplete and partial nature of all human searches for ultimate meaning, and the need for personal as well as academic humility on our part.

The present volume seeks to explore the Galilean Jesus as he is interpreted in communities of faith around the globe, communities that continue to read the gospel portraits in continuity with his first followers. These readings are informed by historical, archaeological, and literary reconstructions of the Jesus movement in its Galilean context, while also interpreting Jesus' message for intercultural communities of faith defined by the option for the poor.

In this article I would like to present my own provisional "reading" of the evidence in locating Jesus and his ministry in the cultural, social, economic, and religious context of first-century Galilee. My starting point is the claim that Jesus' actual career in Galilee informed the early Christian proclamation about him to a far greater extent than is often recognized in modern efforts to separate him from the earliest memories that the gospel writers have given us. While my "reading" is provisional, and likely to be revised in light of future discoveries, it is my hope that it may aid contemporary readers to understand the Galilean Jesus and his proclamation more adequately.

The Galilee of Jesus:
Overcoming the Legacy of Distorted Approaches
to the Role of Hellenization in Jewish Galilee

The Norwegian New Testament scholar Halvor Moxnes has analyzed the ways in which the question of "Galilee and Jesus" has played itself out over the three major phases of the quest for the historical Jesus. While this history is too complex to review in detail here, I will briefly summarize some of the findings of Moxnes, since they will assist in avoiding repetition of the mistakes of the past, mistakes that have a habit of recurring in recent construals of both Galilee and Jesus.

Perhaps his most important contribution is the manner in which Moxnes exposes the extent to which various nineteenth- and early twentieth-century European preoccupations and prejudices can be seen to have influenced the scholarly debates about both Galilee and Jesus. In particular the emergence of the idea of the nation state played a role in the manner in which the connection between land, people, and nation in first-century Galilee was understood. Likewise, widespread anti-Semitic attitudes were reflected in contemporaneous portrayals of Jesus, which undoubtedly played a role in the treatment of Jews in the Nazi period, with little or no active resistance from Christian scholars.

Thus, according to Moxnes, in the writing of Friedrich Schleiermacher, Galilee was deemed to be an integral part of the Jewish land, and its people were seen as constituting the Hebrew nation. David Friedrich Strauss, on the other hand, presented Galilee as different from and in opposition to Judea, the former representing freedom from political and religious domination, and the latter in thrall to Roman power and the bastion of conservative orthodoxy in religious matters. Such a representation reflected Strauss's own positions within liberal

German Protestantism and his opposition to state bureaucracy in the true spirit of the Reformation ideals. His influence on the ways that both Galilee and Jesus are understood continues to have an enduring appeal to the present day, as we shall see.

The French scholar Ernst Renan was to develop further this contrast between Galilee and Jerusalem/Judea, adding his own somewhat anti-Semitic perspective to the question of "Jesus and Galilee." His depiction of the Galilean landscape was highly romantic—and deeply flawed. Relying on contemporary ideas of a causal connection between natural environment and human characteristics, his idyllic picture of Galilee and Galileans is used to establish a sharp contrast between them and their Judean neighbors to the south. As Susannah Heschel explains, Renan argues that Jesus, though Jewish originally, was able to transcend Judaism's narrow confines. "After visiting Jerusalem Jesus was no longer a Jew," Renan declares. In an earlier work he had claimed that he was the first to recognize that the Semitic race was inferior intellectually and culturally to the Indo-Europeans/Aryans. Ideas of race were not as yet based on immutable characteristics such as blood lines. Thus Jesus' ability to transcend his Semitic/Jewish origins, thanks to his Galilean experiences, was seen as indicative of the superiority of the religion that he initiated—a monotheism that was less rigid and more mythological than that of either Jews or Muslims.

Some of these ideas and the arguments supporting them have had far too long a shelf-life, as we shall presently see, yet it is important to signal here alternative views from the period. In the English-speaking world, George Adam Smith's *Historical Geography of the Holy Land* went through twenty-five editions between 1894 and 1931. Smith, a pious Scottish Presbyterian, shares Renan's romantic views of the Galilean landscape, but he avoids the latter's deterministic ideas of human characteristics being shaped by the physical environment. In his view, purely moral and religious forces can overcome the temptations that different regions offer. In this regard Jesus did not succumb either to the more opulent life of the Hellenized lake region, nor to the lure of imperial power as this was represented in the district of Caesarea Philippi by the temple to Rome and Augustus of Herod the Great. Jesus' choice of simple Galilean fishermen for his permanent retinue shows how much he was able to transcend the dangers in his Hellenized homeland, where the road systems had brought even Nazareth into the mainstream of Mediterranean life.

In view of the dominance of German scholarship in the period, the Old Testament specialist Albrecht Alt is another example of someone who transcended the prevailing prejudices of his time. In a number of articles about Galilee and Jesus written between 1931 and 1949, Alt used archaeological data (insofar as any was then available) and Hebrew Bible research in countering reductionist hypotheses about Galilee grounded in the anti-Semitic attitudes of his contemporaries. His treatment of Jesus in Galilee comes in a 1949 essay that follows from a series dealing with the territorial/administrative history of the region from the Persian to the Roman periods. Alt did not succumb to the temptations of other German scholars, including his own teacher Gerhardt Kittel, of engaging in the de-Judaization of Jesus and the Hellenization of Galilee that was quite a feature of the period, most notably in the work of the Jena professor of New Testament Walter Grundmann. The latter had published his *Jesus der Galiläer* in 1941, in which he argued that with great probability Jesus was not a Jew, because Galilee "was heathen" (*heidnisch war*).

This conclusion was based on a long history of German scholarship, emanating from Strauss as we have seen, which claimed that the population of Galilee was heathen on the basis of the LXX translation of *galil ha-goyim* in Isaiah 8:23 as *galilaia tōn ethnōn* (Γαλιλαία των εθνων), variously translated in our English Bibles as "Galilee of the Nations" or "Galilee of the Gentiles." Either way the expression is deemed to have an ethno-centric connotation that sees other ethnic groups as hostile, even perverted, from an Israelite perspective. In an earlier article on the Isaian text, Alt had challenged the view that it could be taken as descriptive of the population of Galilee in Jesus' day, since even in its original setting of eighth century BCE Israel, it referred to the whole northern region of Palestine from the Mediterranean to the Euphrates, and not to the relatively small territory that was later identified as political Galilee. Isaiah was promising salvation to come for all the inhabitants of the region, Israelite and non-Israelite alike, who had come under the Assyrian yoke in 731 BCE.

In Alt's view, the account of the Assyrian invasion of Galilee in 2 Kings 15:29 did not suggest deportation of all the native Israelites, but only of the ruling class, unlike what occurred in Samaria ten years later (2 Kings 17:19–23). Therefore, he argues, despite the administrative changes of the Neo-Babylonian, Persian, and Greek regimes, there was a continued presence of an Israelite population in Galilee throughout the intervening centuries until the establishment of a native Judean state by the successors of the Maccabees, the Hasmoneans, in the mid-second century BCE. We shall discuss later the likelihood of this view in the light of current evidence, especially the vastly expanded pool of archaeological data, but here it is important to note that Alt, unlike many of his contemporaries, does not agree with the notion of a Gentile or pagan Galilee in the first century. In his opinion Galilee freely and of its own accord entered the Judean state as soon as it was feasible, because of the religious and cultural affinity its residual Israelite population had with its southern cousins.

In his discussion of Jesus in Galilee, Alt continues with his method of exploring the administrative history of the region, situating the various places that Jesus is said to have visited within their proper administrative districts. Five in all are postulated for Galilee on the basis of the literary evidence from the Hasmonean period. These range over the three traditional divisions of Galilee according to Jewish lore, namely, Upper Galilee to the north, Lower Galilee to the south, and the Valley, or lake district, to the east. In contrast to Smith, he suggests that Nazareth lay somewhat removed from its administrative center, which was not (as many take for granted) nearby Sepphoris, but rather Legio, situated to the south in the Great Plain. In Alt's view it was remote, rural, and backward, and from his upbringing there, Jesus would not have been inclined to participate in the more cosmopolitan Hellenistic culture of the cities.

Nevertheless, his main theater of operation was the lake region, where, according to Alt's view, the Israelite presence was most likely to have been eroded, due to more intensive signs of Hellenistic culture there. The parlous situation of the older way of life in this region may even have touched villages such as Capernaum and Corazin, explaining why Jesus moved the center of his operations from the interior to this "border" region. In contrast to Smith's views of simple fishermen, however, Alt correctly notes that one of the important signs of Hellenization was the development of the fish industry along the lakefront, especially at Magdala, whose Greek name, Tarichaea, suggests the salting of fish, a process that enabled their export, even to faraway Rome. Thus, Alt clearly breaks with the romantic views of the Galilean landscape and its influences on native characteristics, recognizing the importance of the social, economic, and cultural factors instead. As such his work is prescient of modern emphases in many important respects.

In this section, then, I have drawn on Moxnes's analysis of the distorting influence of reductionist and anti-Semitic approaches in past attempts to reconstruct the Galilee of Jesus. At the same time I have noted the importance of "the long view" as represented in Alt's work in describing the reality of Jesus' Galilee. I have argued that his work has provided a more nuanced understanding of both the Isaian text that has been so central to various reconstructions of Galilean life, and of

Galilee itself, by attending to the history of the region over the centuries. This complex situation and history constituted the inherited reality of Jesus, and his responses to its demands and opportunities represented part of his own historical reality, a reality that would continue after his death in and through the lives of his faithful followers who returned to Galilee after Easter, there to initiate their faithful remembrance of his praxis.

The Jesus of Galilee:
The Return of Jesus to Galilee after John's Arrest

How, then, can the longer view and more nuanced approach to Galilee marked out by Alt help us to develop a more balanced and adequate reconstruction of the Galilee of Jesus? I have argued elsewhere that the reconstruction of the Galilean social and cultural world is a separate, but overlapping enterprise to that of locating Jesus in Galilee, and that the former enterprise is best served by taking the long view of Alt. In this section I will briefly summarize my own hypotheses on those aspects of first-century Galilee that overlap with efforts to locate the ministry of Jesus in its cultural, social, economic, and religious contexts. While there is insufficient space in the present volume to present the detailed arguments for my position, these are set out more fully in a number of my recent publications that are listed in the bibliography at the end of this essay.

The synoptic gospels all agree that Jesus was returning to the region in the wake of John's arrest, thereby suggesting that he had spent some time elsewhere and was likely to have come under different influences (Mk 1:14f; Mt 4:12; Lk 4:14). By contrast, the Fourth Gospel does not highlight the Galilean aspect of Jesus' ministry in the narrative, since his main focus in that version is on Jerusalem/Judea. Accepting the synoptic viewpoint, Jesus' relationship with his homeland should not be construed as one of undifferentiated affirmation of the Galilean ethos in which he was reared. On his return there, both family and neighbors deemed him to be an errant son, whose wisdom and behavior was not consonant with the familial and village values that a son might be expected to uphold (see Mk 3:21, 31–34; 6:1–6). His return to the region, therefore, was not a homecoming but a mission with a prophetic and urgent message for his fellow Galileans.

In seeking to address the questions of what conditions Jesus was likely to have encountered on his return to Galilee and how these might have contributed to the shape of his ministry there, three issues seem to have repeatedly emerged in the previous discussion. These are:

- Hellenization in Galilee: To what extent was Galilee influenced by the Hellenistic ethos of the eastern Mediterranean, giving rise to an ethnically mixed population?
- Economic and social conditions in Galilee: What were the economic and social conditions that prevailed for different strata of the population, especially during the reign of Herod Antipas, coinciding as it did with the life and ministry of Jesus?
- Jesus and Judaism in first-century Galilee: What was the nature of Galilee-Jerusalem relations in religious matters, and is it appropriate to speak of a Galilean Judaism that was substantially distinct from that in Judea?

Hellenization in Jewish Galilee:
Distinct Communities in Close Proximity

The impact of Hellenization on Jewish belief and practice has in the past been discussed mostly in terms of two opposing and implacable cultural forces, *Hellenismos* and *Ioudaismos*. However, it is now generally recognized that the serious attempt to transform the Jerusalem cult center into a shrine of Zeus, the head of the Greek pantheon, by Antiochus IV Epiphanes in the mid-second century BCE was a brief interlude. The decline of both the Ptolemaic and the Seleucid dynasties, which had ruled the whole region since Alexander's conquest of the East in 333 BCE, meant that indigenous peoples like the Judeans, the Nabateans, and the Itureans were able to reclaim ethnic independence and continue to function as client kingdoms, even under Roman imperial rule.

That is not to suggest that the arrival of the Greeks in the east had no impact on the overall culture of the region. It meant that cultural change associated with the process of Hellenization was one of translation rather than wholesale change. Greek became the *lingua franca* of trade and commerce from the third century BCE, with inevitable consequences for the interior Galilean region also, bringing Greek technical expertise in fishing, pottery making, and other local industries. Thus Galilee was indeed encircled (as the actual name suggests) with evident signs of Greek culture during the Hellenistic age.

Yet this is by no means the whole story. Archaeology has helped considerably to fill in, and in some instances to correct, the rather partisan accounts of the literary sources. One incident from the immediate aftermath of the crisis generated by Antiochus's takeover of the temple, reported in 2 Maccabees 4:18–20, is indicative of a more general attitude. On the occasion of the quadrennial games at Tyre, Jason, the leader of the pro-Hellenistic party in Jerusalem, sent a delegation, described as "the Antiochian citizens from Jerusalem," that is, native Judeans with Greek cultural affiliations, with an offering of three hundred silver drachmas to honor the patron god of the games, Herakles. However, on arrival in Tyre the delegation decided that such use of the money was inappropriate. Religious belief, Greek culture, and economic realities all intermingle in this incident, and it is noteworthy that despite the way in which the delegation is given a decidedly Greek profile, they demur at appearing to worship the pagan god. In all probability this is indicative of the relationships that continued to prevail into the first century CE. Even those who might have benefitted from the new possibilities of the Greek world and its cosmopolitan ethos drew the line when it came to worshiping a god other than Yahweh.

The gradual emergence of an independent Jewish state during the late second and early first centuries BCE under the Hasmoneans, the descendants of the more militant Jewish resistance party, the Maccabees, did not involve turning back the clock with regard to the ongoing process of Hellenization. On the one hand, the Judean expansion to the north involved Greek military strategy and even the use of foreign mercenaries, while on the other it was aimed at reclaiming "ancestral lands" according to the author of 1 Maccabees 15:33. These settlers were of Judean origin. Despite their new situation, they availed themselves of the increased opportunities that Hellenization offered, while still remaining staunchly loyal to their Judean roots. This did not exclude at least some of the population from acquiring a proficiency in the Greek language in addition to the older Aramaic that had been the lingua franca since Persian times, so well exemplified in the case of the first-century Jewish historian, Josephus.

It could be argued that the Herodian period saw an even more intensified process of Hellenization, in that Roman imperial aspirations took on a decidedly Greek coloring in architecture, artistic representation, and other aspects of the luxurious lifestyle. When one compares the ways in which the Hasmonean and the Herodian elites in Palestine embraced aspects of the Greek way of life, it might be claimed that while the former "acted Greek without becoming Greek," as the issue has been pithily described, the latter embraced the Greek way of life with enthusiasm and alacrity. It must be remembered that the Herodians were client kings of Rome, and were therefore more likely to follow the trends that were set at the center. The three temples built by Herod in honor of Roma and Augustus were located outside recognized Jewish territory, namely, at the two Caesareas (Maritima on the coast

and Philippi in the north in the foothills of Mt. Hermon) and Se-
baste/Samaria in the center of the country. Thus any direct offence to
Jewish sensitivities was avoided. It was only with the advent of his son
Herod Antipas as tetrarch of Galilee that direct Herodian influence on
Galilee can be discerned from the archaeological record.

Jesus' ministry in Galilee coincided with the reign of Herod Antipas, yet, curiously, the tetrarch is a somewhat vague figure in the
background of the ministry. Jesus' encomium of his own mentor, reported in an early Q passage, suggests that he is much more impressed
by John's ascetic lifestyle than with those who are "dressed in fine garments and dwell in royal palaces"(Q/Lk 7:24–27/Mt 11:7-10). This al-
lusion could plausibly be seen as an oblique reference to Herod Antipas
and his royal residence in Tiberias. As a new foundation, Tiberias had a
more obvious Hellenistic ethos and allegedly was founded on a Jewish
burial ground in contravention to Jewish piety practices.

The suggestion that Jesus visited Sepphoris and participated in the
displays of Greco-Roman culture that might have been performed in
the theater there has won little support among modern scholars. Apart
from his apparently principled avoidance of Herodian centers, such an
assumption would entail his knowing Greek to some extent at least, a
supposition that is by no means certain. In assessing the extent to
which Jesus might have encountered aspects of Greek culture during
his public ministry in Galilee it is important to note that he is never
said to have visited either of the two most important Herodian centers.
Furthermore, in Mark's account, we hear of his journeying to the "borders" of Tyre, "the villages" of Caesarea Philippi, "the territory" of the
Gadarenes, and "the borders" of the Dekapolis. Yet he is never said to
have entered any of the actual cities where Greek language and culture
were undoubtedly more prominent than in the adjacent countryside.

It is on the borders of Tyre that Jesus meets the woman, Syro-
Phoenican by birth, but culturally a Greek (*Helene*). Thus, while retain-
ing her ethnic identity as a Syrian, she belongs to the class that participated in the larger cultural ethos. Most commentators see this story as a
later creation having to do with the beginnings of the mission to the
Gentiles. Yet this judgment overlooks the realistic character of both the
situation and the actors in the context of our knowledge of Tyre/Galilee
relations and ethnic tensions previously discussed. Far from depicting
Jesus as reflecting an open and universalist outlook, the passage presents
him as supporting a thoroughly ethno-centric point of view. His journeys to these outlying regions are not for the purpose of opening up his
mission but rather for gathering the "lost sheep of the house of Israel." It

is the woman who has the universal outlook, as befits a true Hellene, and because of this she is able to cross the prevailing boundaries—ethnic, religious, and gender—that separate the two characters.

This sketch of Hellenistic influences in Galilee based on archaeological as well as literary evidence does not suggest that Galilean society was mixed, or that more open attitudes toward the larger Mediterranean world prevailed there in contrast to those in Judea, as Renan and others had argued. Likewise, more recent efforts to describe Galilee as home to the Cynic movement (a type of anti-establishment, popular teaching characteristic of Greco-Roman cities at the time) seems highly implausible. What we encounter rather are the remains of the older Persian and Greek ethos at some sites from the second century BCE that had been abandoned and the emergence of many new settlements, which, on the basis of the material remains (such as pottery, evidence of specifically Jewish ritual practices such as *miqvaoth* or ritual baths, the absence of pig bones), indicate strong links with Jerusalem and Judea. It also seems improbable that Alt's position with regard to the continued Israelite presence remaining over the centuries can be sustained. Galilee was indeed encircled by Greek *poleis* or city-states, but the strong indications are that the new settlers resisted any encroachment into the interior.

The evidence points to the fact that religious as well as political factors played an important role in drawing the boundaries between the various zones of Jewish and non-Jewish settlements, even when some aspects of daily life, such as styles of domestic architecture, methods of wine-making, water collection, soil cultivation, and the like are shared. The story of the Syro-Phoenician woman shows that Jesus shared at least some of the prejudices concerning non-Jews. Unlike many of his fellow Galileans who participated from time to time in violent ethnic clashes with their neighbors, he was prepared to be challenged as to the basis for those values. Like other northern prophets such as Elijah, he would agree to offer his healing ministry to non-Jews also, succumbing to the woman's subtle suggestion that they both belonged in the same house and at the same table, despite the current pejorative classification of non-Jews by Jews, which his reference to "dogs" suggests that he shared. This and similar experiences in his journeys "into the surrounding region of Galilee" must have deepened and broadened his understanding of his messianic role, causing him to recognize that, at its best, as in the case of the prophet Isaiah, his own Jewish tradition could also envisage a place at the banquet which the Lord of Hosts was preparing for all peoples (Is 25:6–7).

Economy and Society in First-century Galilee:
Social Context for the "Values Revolution" of Jesus

As will already be evident, it is impossible to separate entirely religio-cultural and socio-economic realities, since they are both intertwined in the warp and woof of daily life, especially in ancient societies. Nevertheless, it is important to focus on the latter more directly since so much of Jesus' teaching deals with these aspects, giving rise to what has been described by Gerd Theissen as his "values revolution."

Cultural change in the sense of language, religion, art and architecture, and the like is related to population shifts, the arrival of new technologies, different needs, and changed communications with the outside world. The changes that occurred in the early Hellenistic period set the pattern for subsequent periods, including the reign of Herod Antipas. The land-owning patterns that were established by the Hellenistic period seem to have undergone little change under subsequent regimes.

Both the literary and archaeological records suggest that, at least from the time of the Hasmonean conquest of the north, the biblical pattern of private ownership of individual plots of land became the norm, a pattern subsequently continued by Herod the Great.

Broadly speaking, two differing views have emerged with regard to the economy of Galilee and its impact on the lives of the village-dwellers of Jesus' day. On the one hand there is the view of the ancient city as being parasitic on the countryside, and on the other the claim that increased urbanization and growth in population brought increased prosperity for all. The reign of Herod Antipas provides a useful focal point for testing the first scenario, since in a relatively short space of time two urban centers emerged within the heartland of lower Galilee, the afore-mentioned Sepphoris, rebuilt by Herod Antipas after it had been destroyed by the Roman general Varus in 4 BCE, and Tiberias, founded to honor Augustus' successor in 19 CE.

One proposal, for which I have considerable sympathy, is that both projects were not only an immediate and direct drain on the Galilean economy, giving rise to alienation among the rural peasants, but that they were also symbols of a power system that is typical of aristocratic empires. According to this pyramid-shaped model, drawn from cross-cultural examples, aristocratic empires concentrate all the power at the top, in the hands of a small ruling elite that is served by a retainer class of artisans, scribes, tax collectors, and other officials who are both sufficient and necessary to maintain order. At the base of the pyramid, and representing the majority of the population, are the poor, comprised of tenant farmers, landless peasants, displaced or rejected outsiders by virtue of bodily infirmity or some other affliction, and slaves. All these are excluded from any access to power and have no influence on the social realities.

In a similar vein, Richard Horsley, while focusing on the exercise of power rather than on economic realities directly, stresses the presence of Roman imperial structures as being the dominant and determining social reality in the Galilee of Herod Antipas. Horsley highlights its demands on subject peoples, demands that led to the "disintegration of the fundamental forms of social life that accompanied the economic burdens." For Horsley, therefore, Jesus should not be thought of as a wandering charismatic healer but as a prophet engaged in a program of renewal of village life that had come under severe pressure from a politically controlled economy.

Before opting for this apparent consensus in terms of both Galilee's social and economic conditions and Jesus' role there, it is important to consider the alternative claims of other scholars and the evidence that they bring to the discussion. To begin with the respective roles of Sepphoris and Tiberias, it is worth reconsidering the extent to which claims about the former's significance for first-century Galilean life as a whole are warranted. In fact the archaeological evidence from Tiberias suggests a decidedly more Roman character, something that also corresponds to Josephus's description of the founding of the place. Sepphoris, situated close to Nazareth, inevitably drew the attention of historians as to its possible influence on Jesus. Yet many of the more dramatic discoveries, such as the villas with mosaics, the synagogue, and even the theater (at least in its more expanded form), are to be dated to the second century and later when the name of the place was changed to Diocaesarea. And Sepphoris had a much more important role in the Roman administration of the region than was the case under Herod Antipas.

The implications of downgrading somewhat the role of Sepphoris in the reign of Herod Antipas would be to question whether it really fits the typology of a "consumer city," and whether it might not be better to judge its importance as one of the five places that acted as administrative and distributive centers for Galilee that are known from the literary sources. As such it still had an important role to play, especially for the surrounding associated villages. Thus, Josephus can declare that Sepphoris could have adopted a more independent stance in the first revolt against Rome had it chosen to do so, "situated in the centre of Galilee and surrounded by many villages" (*Life*, 346). This might suggest a mutuality between city and village, the former providing an outlet for the produce of the latter. Thus, for example, the village of Shikhin had a pottery-making industry and provided Sepphoris with most of its large vessels that would be used for transporting grain and oil.

In an important study of Herod Antipas's reign, Danish scholar Morten Jensen has examined the evidence from four recently excavated village sites in lower Galilee/Golan and claims that there is no evidence of decline in the first century at any of the sites excavated. In the early Roman period Galilean villages participated in the economic opportunities and dangers inherent in the Mediterranean system. In his opinion "it would be a mistake to assume that the Jesus movement operated in a cultural, political or economic isolation from major urban centres." The evidence for these claims comes from a more sophisticated approach to our understanding of the Galilean economy. Thus Douglas Edwards, who has excavated at two of the sites in question, sees evidence for the existence of varied and complex market conditions that cannot be subsumed under the general rubric of a "politically controlled economy."

Yet not everybody is so convinced by the inference of a "vibrant economic environment" based on this evidence alone. Generalized ideas about a "Mediterranean economy" in which Galilee could participate need to be tempered by local circumstances, where factors other than commercial ones do in fact seem to have impacted trade and commerce, at least to some extent. However, it does seem possible to find some middle ground between the two positions, just outlined, that could prove helpful in deciding the issue.

It would be highly unlikely that the immediacy of the Herodian presence signified by Herod Antipas's building projects did not cause problems for Galileans. Some degree of social stratification, with attendant benefits, undoubtedly occurred, as the evangelist Mark indicates in describing the guest list at Herod Antipas's birthday party: military officers, grandees, and leading men of Galilee (Mk 6:21), as well as his more general mention of the Herodians and tax collectors. The benefits of "the peace under Tiberius" of which Tacitus speaks may not have touched everybody in Galilee equally. Clearly, Galilee's social organization was mixed, as was its economy, and we cannot assume that all shared equally in the prosperity, if that is what we should call it, associated with the rule of Herod Antipas.

Despite the uncertainties, I would suggest the Jesus movement occupied an important social niche within this complex web of social and economic relationships. It is significant that in the lightly veiled reference to the Herodian court in Jesus' reference to those "dressed in fine garments" inhabiting "royal palaces" it is the opulence of the court rather than the abuse of power that is referred to (Q/Lk 7:25; Mt 11:8). While challenging the relative opulence of the better off, Jesus also addressed a series of blessings for the poor, the hungry, and the mourners, in contrast to the woes pronounced on the rich, the well-fed, and those who currently rejoice (Q/Lk 6:20–25; see Mt 5:2–10), reflecting, it would appear, the actual realities of Galilee of his day.

These blessings and woes fit into the larger pattern of Jesus' teaching and praxis that he attributed to the kingdom or reign of God, as present in and through his ministry now, not just a symbolic statement of hope for the future. His program touched every area of social life— the home, the village, the marketplace, the exercise of authority, even the temple itself in faraway Jerusalem. As noted above, German New Testament scholar Gerd Theissen has used the phrase "values revolution" to categorize the radical nature of this vision, confronted as he was with various systems of power and domination operating in first-century Galilee and Judea. Theissen singles out three areas, namely, the use of possessions, the deployment of power, and the identification of "true wisdom," as being particularly important in terms of Jesus' kingdom praxis, which contrasts radically with the ideals of kingship as these were understood in the period, coloring even Jewish hopes for an ideal Son of David to come (Psalms of Solomon 17).

As somebody whose activity gave rise to questions about his possible messianic status even outside the circle of his own immediate followers, Jesus had to be quite unequivocal with regard to the expectations people had of him. Thus, instead of advocating a philanthropic use of *wealth*, as even Herod the Great had done on occasion, Jesus actually demanded that the wealthy abandon their possessions entirely, trust in God's benevolent care of his creation, and follow him, thereby attaining the blessed status of the poor whose trust in a caring God had freed them from the burdens of anxiety that assail the rich, then and now (Q/Lk 12:22–31; Mt 6:25–33).

For him *power* consisted in service, not tyrannical domination and oppression, as was too often the case in Herodian Judea and in the Roman East generally (Mk 10:42–44). Nor did Jesus aspire to the *wisdom* of the learned scribes, who for centuries had acted as counsellors of the ruling elites, so graphically described two centuries earlier by his Jerusalem namesake, Jesus ben Sirah (Sir 38:24–39:11). Jesus of Galilee did cultivate wisdom, but it was the proverbial wisdom of the peasants that provided him with the images and paradoxes that were most appropriate for his message of proclaiming the advent of God's reign, despite all evidence to the contrary.

Judaism in Galilee and Judea:
Regional Diversity and the Craftsman of Galilee

As discussed in the earlier part of this paper, the de-Judaization of Jesus and the Hellenization of Galilee have often been closely linked in scholarly discussion. Yet it remains to be determined what is meant by a Jewish Galilee, and where the Galilean Jesus should be located within the spectrum of different forms of Jewish practice and belief of the period. It was E. P. Sanders who first challenged the way in which Judaism had been construed by Christian scholars, largely around the four philosophies (Pharisees, Sadducees, Essenes, and Zealots) described by Josephus. Sanders points out that the majority of first-century Jews were not members of any of these parties, but rather held a number of practices and beliefs in common, arising from a shared history that dates back to the return from the Babylonian exile. This is a highly significant clarification. But since Sanders does not resolve the issue of regional variations in terms of his notion of a Common Judaism, the question remains as to whether or not there was, as has been alleged, a radically different type of Jewish practice in Galilee. And if this was the case, how might it have impacted Jesus' own actualization of his inherited religious tradition there?

The archaeological record seems to rule out Alt's claims for a continued Israelite presence in Galilee over the centuries, even though Richard Horsley has built on Alt's claim, but with a very different understanding. Instead of the Galilean "Israelites" entering the Hasmonean state freely and by choice when the opportunity arose in the second century BCE, Horsley views the Judean immigration to the north that, as mentioned previously, began at that time, as a southern imposition on the old Israelite way of life. According to him, these people had over the centuries developed their own customs and habits that were quite independent of Jerusalem. Thus he views the newly arrived Judeans of the second/first centuries BCE as bearers of the great, or official tradition based in Jerusalem, seeking to impose this on "the little tradition" that had developed in Galilee. Like other Judean renewal movements of the first century BCE about which we hear from Josephus, Horsley then argues that the Jesus movement was also thoroughly grounded in older Israelite traditions regarding Israel's destiny and mission. Accordingly, he views the Jesus movement, as it can be accessed in the earliest sources, namely Q and Mark, as one of renewal of Galilean village life rather than a reform of Judean laws and customs, as these had been developed by Jerusalem-based scribes.

One can agree with Horsley that the restoration of Israel seems to have been central to Jesus' vision. Such a hope, probably dating back to the breakup of David's kingdom in the ninth century BCE with the secession of the northern tribes, was often couched in strong territorial claims on a "greater Israel" that stretched from the Mediterranean to the Euphrates. It is reflected in the Jerusalem based pre-exilic prophets such as Isaiah, Ezekiel, and Jeremiah, and further developed in several strands of the literature of the Second Temple period, no doubt fostered by the Judean experience of loss in the Babylonian exile. The symbolic selection of the Twelve at the center of the Jesus movement, as well as Jesus' journeys outside the political Galilee of his day, discussed previously, is indicative of its self-understanding in this regard. Thus it can be said to be an exercise of national retrieval of a lost or diminished identity, just as the return to the desert of some of the other movements, like the Qumran Essenes and John the Baptist and his followers, is also indicative of their espousal of those ancient hopes.

The significance of Jesus' links with this strand of dissident Judaism, all of it originating in the south, are sometimes overlooked or downplayed. Yet, even though his own ministry was to take on a very different and socially radical stance once he returned to Galilee from his sojourn with John, he never ceased to acknowledge John's greatness and the fact that his mission was from God (Q/Lk 7:28; Mt 11:11). I therefore disagree with those scholars who see Jesus' so-called "lament for Jerusalem" (Q/Lk 13:34f; Mt 23:37-39) as a rejection of Jerusalem and a distancing by Jesus of himself and his movement from the temple and its symbolic significance.

In *Jesus, a Jewish Galilean* (2005), I have suggested that as well as being motivated by Israel's stories of conquest and tribal settlement from the Pentateuch, Jesus was also deeply indebted to the prophet Isaiah, himself a Jerusalemite, whose composite work is highly critical of the triumphalist Zion ideology, to which the ruling elite were wont to appeal. Their opulent lifestyle (Isa 1:27–31; 2:5–8) is matched by the arrogant behavior of the "rebellious people." Yahweh's blessings will be transferred to his servants who suffer at the hands of the arrogant rulers, but who form a lifeline to the future reward promised to the suffering servant in Isaiah 53:10. This nameless figure's silent acceptance of his treatment at the hands of his violent persecutors, arising from his trust in God's justice, was to provide the model for all those subsequently persecuted unjustly in Judean society from the "wise ones" of the Book of Daniel (Dan 11:33–35; 2:1–3) to Jesus and his followers in first-century Galilee and beyond.

In the final section of the book of Isaiah (so-called Trito-Isaiah) a group described as "the servants of the Lord" emerge, whose life-style and treatment at the hands of the ruling elite is modeled on that of the servant figure described in Isaiah 53 (Isa 65:8–11; 66:14). This group is to be rewarded by God in language that is clearly echoed in Jesus' promise of blessedness to his own faithful followers who show a passion for justice and rejection of all violence (Is 65:13–14; 66:1–2). This verbal and contextual similarity suggests that Jesus saw his own group in the light of this movement, which is critical of the Jerusalem ruling elite, but which still clings to the symbolism of Jerusalem and its temple as a sign of God's abiding presence with his faithful people. Such a profile would explain why a group of Jesus-followers centered on James the brother of the Lord emerged in Jerusalem so soon after Jesus' violent execution there, an execution that involved complicity, if not collaboration, between the discredited guardians of the Jerusalem sanctuary and the Roman authorities of the day.

The fact that scribes from Jerusalem sought to discredit Jesus, claiming that he was in league with the prince of demons (Mk 3:22) shows the perceived ties between Jerusalem and Galilee, even when the official guardians of the tradition may well have been suspicious of northern-based movements and critical of Galilean laxity. These biases are reflected in the Fourth Gospel's account of Jesus at the Feast of Tabernacles, when he was accused of being a member of the Galilean 'am ha-aretz, that is, one who not only does not follow Pharisaic halakah with regard to purity, but who is ignorant of Torah and is therefore accursed (Jn 7:15, 49). Such a characterization of Galileans generally does raise the general question of how and how well the Torah and Torah observance were disseminated among the Galilean populace in Jesus' day. Apart from the synagogue building at Gamla and Josephus' reference to a prayer house at Tiberias, there are only the general references to the synagogues of Galilee in the gospel narratives. The impression is that these were to be found in the towns and villages that Jesus visited, but as far as Galilee is concerned we have to wait for several centuries before clear evidence of a network of such buildings emerges.

Yet the absence of material evidence does not necessarily suggest laxity, ignorance, or indifference to the rituals that had helped to maintain Jewish identity in Galilee as elsewhere over the centuries. As mentioned previously, the Judeans who settled in Galilee and their offspring have left a record of their attachment to Jerusalem's customs and practices in the material remains at various sites, such as the two miqvehs found in a large building on the acropolis at Sepphoris, as well as the communal one found at Qeren Nephtali on the borders between Galilee and Tyre, all dating to c.100 BCE.

To be sure, not all Galileans, as indeed not all Judeans, were likely to have been observant by the standards of Pharisaic piety as these were practiced and promulgated by their scribal masters. Yet this should not be interpreted as a sign of a more open or less engaged commitment, given the attachment of Galileans to the pilgrimage to Jerusalem, attested by both Josephus and the gospels. Like other country prophets before and after him, Jesus availed of such occasions to challenge the prevailing ideology in Jerusalem. His action in the temple in overthrowing the tables of the money-changers and his entry into the city riding on a beast of burden, not in glorious triumph, are symbolic actions intended to call Israel to a different type of social and religious organization that would represent the messianic community, based on Israel's sense of its ideal past, and reflected in Jesus' values revolution as already described.

Afterword:
Galilee and Gospel

It must be said that Jesus had little success convincing his contemporaries about the possibilities of realizing his vision and praxis, even among the Galilean villagers who had so enthusiastically received him as a healer and teacher. Nevertheless, the story of Galilee and Jesus did not end with his "failure" in Jerusalem. Just as a community of more observant followers emerged in Jerusalem, as we have seen, so also after his death groups of followers of Jesus also surfaced soon in Galilee. The profiles of these groups can be discerned at least in outline from two of the earliest documents: the putative Sayings Source (a collection of Jesus sayings designated simply by the letter Q) and the Gospel of Mark. Both documents can be plausibly attributed to a Galilean provenance, the former attributed to a small group who continued Jesus' lifestyle of itinerancy and charismatic actions in Galilee, and the latter emanating from a more settled community based on the living memory of the inclusive message of Jesus enacted at a moment of crisis during or in the immediate aftermath of the Jewish War and the destruction of the Jerusalem temple in 70 CE.

The historical reality of Jesus inspires both documents and the groups that lie behind them, which nonetheless reflect the lived realities of their audiences. The profile of Jesus and his ministry that each develops, one focusing on the sayings and the other on the deeds, corresponds well with the profile of Jesus that Josephus give us in *Jewish Antiquities* (18:63–64). More significantly, in terms of the continued importance of the historical Jesus for the shape of Christian praxis today, the manner in which each develops its respective profile of Jesus shows that throughout the first century CE Galilee continued to provide an appropriate context in which to carry forward Jesus' own understanding of his person and ministry. Thus, the Q profile builds on the teaching of Jesus, which was heavily indebted to gnomic wisdom and enriched by his observation of and participation in the everyday lives of ordinary Galileans in their homes and villages. For the Q people, the exalted Jesus is Wisdom incarnate, whose words are justified by her deeds (Q/Lk 7:35; Mt 11:19).

For Mark, on the other hand, the issue of the messiahship of Jesus had become pressing in the wake of the failed project of militant messianic pretenders represented by the Jewish revolt. Jesus never claimed to be the Messiah during his earthly life, though others seemed to want to cast him in this role. The issue was and is, what kind of messiah did he represent, given that the prevailing notion was that of a royal figure, a son of David. A number of factors gave urgency to the need for a new understanding of messiahship, and Mark was able to forge a credible image from the Jesus traditions he had inherited.

Mark's dramatic narrative is dominated by the strangeness of Jesus' movements and his commands to silence just when it would appear that the truth about his messiahship would be about to emerge. This gives a sense of awe and mystery to the person of Jesus, so that he cannot be categorized by any of the accepted roles. At the same time, Mark's willingness to show Jesus learning from a Gentile woman about the true scope of his messianic mission legitimates the inclusion of Gentiles along with Jews in the new and egalitarian family that is being gathered in his name (Mk 3:31–35). Jewish members are reassured that the symbols of their belief are still intact, since the divine presence is still active in the world, despite the fall of the temple (Mk 13:14–27; 15, 38). Gentile converts, on the other hand, will no longer be seen as dogs, since they now share at the *same* table and from the one *bread* that represents Jesus (Mk 8:1–21). Thus, for Mark, the crucifixion of Jesus and the destruction of the temple may indeed be separated by decades, but theologically speaking, they are of a single piece. Both are signs of the implications of the collaboration of the temple leadership with, and facilitation of, the abuse of Roman imperial power. Ironically, however, their acts of injustice both lead to and set in motion a new vision of human community, built on the pillars of justice, forgiveness, and love.

Select Bibliography by Topic

Locating Jesus in Galilee

Alt, Albrecht. "Die Stätten des Wirkens Jesu in Galiläa territorialgeschichtlich betrachtet" (1949). In *Kleine Schriften des Geschichte Israels*. Vol. 2 of 3, 436-55. Munich: C. H. Beck, 1953–64.

Alt, Albrecht. "Jesaja 8:23-9, 6. Befreiungsnacht und Krönungstag." *Kleine Schriften*. Vol. 2, 206–25.

Freyne, Sean. "Galilee, Jesus and the Contribution of Archaeology," *The Expository Times* 119 (2008): 573–81.

Grundmann, Walter. *Jesus der Galiläer und das Judentum*. Leipzig: Verlag Georg Wigand, 1941.

Heschel, Suzannah. *The Aryan Jesus: Christian Theologians and the Bible in Nazi Germany*. Princeton: Princeton University Press, 2008.

Moxnes, Halvor. "The Construction of Galilee as Place for the Historical Jesus," *Biblical Theology Bulletin* 31 (2001): 26–37 and 64–77.

Moxnes, Halvor. "George Adam Smith and the Historical Geography of Galilee." In *A Wandering Galilean: Essays in Honour of Sean Freyne*, edited by Zuleika Rodgers, Margaret Daly-Denton, and Anne McKinley Fitzpatrick, 237–57. Leiden: Brill, 2009.

Moxnes, Halvor. "The Historical Jesus: From Master Narrative to Cultural Context," *Biblical Theology Bulletin* 28 (1999): 135–39.

Renan, Ernst. *The Life of Jesus*. New York: Prometheus Books, 1991. English edition of *La Vie de Jésus*. Paris: Michael Levy, 1863.

Smith, George Adam. *Historical Geography of the Holy Land*. 4th ed. New York: Harper & Row, 1966. First published 1896, London.

Hellenization in Galilee

Aviam, Mordechai. "Distribution Maps of Archaeological Data from the Galilee: An Attempt to Establish Zones Indicative of Ethnicity and Religious Affiliation." In *Religion, Ethnicity and Identity*, edited by Jurgen Zangenberg, Harold W. Attridge and Dale B. Martin, 115–32. Tübingen: Mohr Siebeck, 2006.

Chancey, Mark A. *Greco-Roman Culture and the Galilee of Jesus*. Society for New Testament Studies monograph series, 134. Cambridge: Cambridge University Press, 2005.

Collins, John J. and Sterling, Gregory E. eds. *Hellenism in the Land of Israel*. Notre Dame: University of Notre Dame Press, 2001.

Freyne, Sean. "Galilean Studies: Old Issues and New Questions." In *Religion, Ethnicity and Identity*, edited by Jurgen Zangenberg, Harold W. Attridge and Dale B. Martin, 33–52. Tübingen: Mohr Siebeck, 2006.

Hengel, Martin. *Jews, Greeks and Barbarians*. Philadelphia: Fortress Press, 1980.

Levine, Lee I. *Judaism and Hellenism in Antiquity: Conflict or Confluence?* Peabody, MA: Hendrickson, 1998.

Reed, Jonathan L. *Archaeology and the Galilean Jesus: A Re-examination of the Evidence.* Harrisburg, PA: Trinity Press International, 2000.

Rocca, Samuel. *Herod's Judea: A Mediterranean State in the Classical World.* Texts and Studies in Ancient Judaism, 122. Tübingen: Mohr Siebeck, 2008.

Economic and Social Realities

Batey, Richard A. *Jesus and the Forgotten City: New Light on Sepphoris and the Urban World of Jesus.* Grand Rapids: Baker Books, 1991.

Edwards, Douglas R. "Identity and Social Location in Roman Villages." In *Religion, Ethnicity and Identity*, edited by Jurgen Zangenberg, Harold W. Attridge and Dale B. Martin, 357–74. Tübingen: Mohr Siebeck, 2006.

Edwards, Douglas R. "The Socio-Economic and Cultural Ethos of the Lower Galilee in the First Century: Implications for the Nascent Jesus Movement." In *The Galilee in Late Antiquity*, edited by Lee Levine, 53–74. New York: The Jewish Theological Seminary of America, 1992.

Edwards, Douglas R. "Walking the Roman Landscape in Lower Galilee: Sepphoris, Jotapata and Khirbet Qana." In *A Wandering Galilean: Essays in Honour of Sean Freyne*, edited by Zuleika Rodgers, Margaret Daly-Denton, and Anne McKinley Fitzpatrick, 219–36. Leiden: Brill, 2009.

Fiensy, David A. *The Social History of Palestine in the Herodian Period: The Land Is Mine.* Lewiston, NY and Queenston, Ontario: The Edwin Mellen Press, 1991.

Finley, Moses. *The Ancient City: From Fustel de Coulanges to Max Weber and beyond.* Berkeley: The University of California Press, 1973.

Freyne, Sean. *Galilee from Alexander the Great to Hadrian: A Study of Second Temple Judaism.* Wilmington/Notre Dame: Michael Glazier and Notre Dame University Press, 1980. Reprint, Edinburgh: T and T Clark, 2000.

Freyne, Sean. *Galilee and Gospel: Collected Essays.* Wissenschaftliche Untersuchungen zum Neuen Testament, 125. Tübingen: Mohr Siebeck, 2000.

Hanson, K.C., and Oakman, Douglas E. *Palestine in the Time of Jesus: Social Structures and Social Conflicts.* Minneapolis: Fortress, 2008, 63-98 and 161–63.

Horsley, Richard. *Archaeology, History and Society in Galilee: The Social Context of Jesus and the Rabbis.* Valley Forge, PA: Trinity Press International, 1996.

Horsley, Richard. *Galilee: History, Politics, People.* Valley Forge, PA: Trinity Press International, 1995.

Horsley, Richard. "Jesus and Galilee: The Contingencies of a Renewal Movement." In *Galilee through the Centuries: Confluence of Cultures*, edited by E. Meyers. Winona Lake: Eisenbrauns, 1999.

Jensen, Morten Horning. *Herod Antipas in Galilee.* Wissenschaftliche Untersuchungen Zum Neuen Testament 2.Reihe, 215. Tübingen: Mohr Siebeck, 2006.

Theissen, Gerd. *The Gospels in Context: Social and Political History in the Synoptic Gospels.* Edinburgh: T and T Clark, 1992.

A Jewish Galilee

Berlin, Andrea M. "Jewish Life before the Revolt: The Archaeological Evidence," *Journal for the Study of Judaism*, 36 (2005): 417-69.

Chilton, Bruce D. *A Galilean Rabbi and His Bible: Jesus' Use of the Interpreted Scripture of His Time.* Wilmington, DE: Michael Glazier, 1984.

Freyne, Sean. *Jesus, a Jewish Galilean: A New Reading of the Jesus Story.* Edinburgh: T and T Clark International/Continuum, 2004.

Freyne, Sean. *Retrieving James/Yakov, the Brother of Jesus: From Legend to History.* Annadale, NY: Bard College, 2008.

Miller, Stuart S. "Stepped Pools, Stone Vessels and Other Identity Markers of a 'Complex Common Judaism.'" *Journal for the Study of Judaism* 41 (2010): 214-43.

Sanders, E. P. *Jesus and Judaism.* London: SCM Press, 1985.

Sanders, E. P. *Judaism, Practice and Belief 63 B.C.E.-66 C.E.* London: SCM Press, 1992.

Theissen, Gerd. "Die Jesusbewegung als charismatische Werterevolution." *New Testament Studies* 35 (1989): 343-60.

Afterward: Galilee and Gospel

Berlin, Andrea M., and Overman, J. Andrew, eds. *The First Jewish Revolt: History and Archaeology.* London and New York: Routledge, 2002.

Collins, John Joseph. *The Scepter and the Star: Jewish Messianism in Light of the Dead Sea Scrolls.* New York: Doubleday, 1995.

Freyne, Sean. "The Galilean Jesus and a Contemporary Christology." In "The Galilean Jesus," edited by Robert Lassalle-Klein. *Theological Studies* 70 (2009): 281-97.

Freyne, Sean. "The Geography of Restoration: Galilee-Jerusalem Relations in Early Judaism and Early Christianity." *New Testament Studies* 47 (2001): 289-311.

Freyne, Sean. "The Messiah in the Herodian Period." In *Redemption and Resistance: The Messianic Hopes of Jews and Christians in Antiquity*, edited by Markus Bockmuehl and James Carlton Paget, 29-43. London and New York: T and T Clark International/Continuum, 2007.

Kloppenborg, John S. *Excavating Q: The History and Setting of the Sayings Gospel.* Minneapolis: Fortress Press, 2000.

2

GOING TO MEET THE OTHER

Gustavo Gutiérrez

The realm of the poor and insignificant looks like the world of the Other when viewed from the perspective of the groups, the people, the opinions, and the concepts that dominate our life today. The poor and those who enter into solidarity with them are increasingly aware of this unjust situation.

However the so-called parable of the Good Samaritan (Lk 10:3–37), which has so greatly influenced Christian memory and inspired so many artistic expressions, emphasizes the primacy of the Other and the necessity of going to meet them.[1] If that is the attitude we must have toward all persons, it becomes even more exigent in regard to those who live in a situation of social insignificance. It is fascinating to read and re-read this gospel passage in this light.

The parable is composed of two closely related parts. Each begins with a question. After examining each part, I will reflect on the call of the parable to go to meet the Other.

What Must We Do to Inherit Eternal Life?

The story begins with the question posed by a lawyer: What must I do to inherit eternal life (Lk 10:25b)? The question concerns the relationship between daily conduct and eternal life, understood as the ultimate meaning of human existence.

The Question

The question assumes the need to do something in order to gain eternal life, for we are in the realm of the practical and of works, which provides a more concrete and personal approach to the great commandment than that offered by the parallel passages in Mark (12:18) and Matthew (22:36). The lawyer's question provides the first mention of the verb "to do" (Greek: *poieo*), which appears three other times framing the development of the narrative: two are found at the beginning (Lk 10:25, 27), and two others in the final verse (10:37). Practice is one of the axes on which the story turns.

Jesus responds by bringing up the issue of the interpretation of the law, and as happens so many times in the gospels, he formulates it in the form of a question: "What is written in the law" (Lk 10:26)? Acknowledging his interlocutor as someone trained to interpret the law, he adds, with a certain amount of deference, "What do you read there?" (10:26). The parable, which follows shortly, is dedicated to deepening our understanding of the answer.

The scribe responds correctly that love ought to inspire the believer's behavior. For that reason the text in Luke, unlike the parallel texts in Mark and Matthew, combines the two biblical passages cited from the Old Testament into one sentence (10:27). The first passage, which is preceded in the text of Deuteronomy by the solemn expression, "Hear, O Israel," says, "You shall love the Lord your God with all your heart, and with all your soul, and with all your strength" (see Deut 6:5). The phrase asks us, without repeating the verb *love*, to immediately connect all our human energies to the second passage which follows, "you shall love your neighbor as yourself: I am the LORD" (Lev 19:18). This combined formulation is thus an interpretation of the law.

Toward a Single Commandment

Some clarifications regarding these texts and the relationship that exists between them will help us to sketch the framework and the meaning of the parable that follows, which constitutes the second part of the pericope.

1. The first observation pertains to the scope of the *idea of neighbor*. It is important to note that in the text of Leviticus (19:18) the Hebrew term is *rea*, translated as neighbor (in Greek, *plesion*, or near), which has the narrow meaning of an associate or companion (moreover verse 18 identifies it with "your countrymen," literally "the children of your people").[2] The context clearly says the same thing since, a little later in the same chapter of Leviticus, we are called to see the immigrant (*ger*: guest, stranger) who resides "with you" as though such a person were native born, and we are told once again, "you shall love the alien as yourself" (10:33–34).

Here it is important to recall two other mentions of Leviticus 18:19 in the New Testament. For Paul, "the whole law is summed up in a single commandment, 'You shall love your neighbor as yourself'" (Gal 5:14; see Rom 13:8–9 and 15:2). For his part, James affirms that "the royal law according to the scripture" demands that "You shall love your neighbor as yourself" (Jas 2:8). These two verses connect love of neighbor with the fulfillment of the law to which Luke alludes. And the references to the law that immediately follow use the significant terms, "the whole law" and "the royal law." Both underline the importance of love of neighbor in the Christian life as a verifiable practice. Neither explicitly mentions the love of God, but the context does not require it, for it is precisely the love of God that is verified.

2. The expression "as yourself" is contested. One can read it literally, "as you love yourself," the most frequent translation, which is largely influenced by the Greek version of the Septuagint. But the Hebrew terms are open to another translation. Some Jewish scholars (Buber among them) suggest the expression: "love your neighbor who is like you," "your likeness"; "love your neighbor who does the same works that you do," or simply, "love your neighbor."[3] Norbert Lohfink proposes a reading that follows these lines, but goes further. For him, the expression "as yourself" is "a Semitism that is equivalent to 'my family' [which implies that] loving someone as yourself means . . . treating them as if they were a member of your family. And this love must also be extended to the neighbor, that is, to those who are not part of your family."[4] This means, "love your neighbor as you love your own," as you love your family, as you love your community.

In truth, the translation "love your neighbor as yourself" does not avoid the risk of an individualistic reading and a shortsighted view. The aforementioned versions certainly require clarifications, but they are interesting clues (particularly Lohfink's) that permit us to locate this expression in a wider horizon in which the Other clearly occupies the central place.

The neighbor is someone who is close to me, but who is also different and irreducibly other. His or her otherness helps me to step outside myself, and my recognition of him or her is a necessary aspect of my own personal affirmation. The parable will make it clear that love is not simply understood as an abstract feeling, but rather signifies doing something for the Other.

3. The third observation speaks to the way in which Luke presents the issue. The parallel texts in Mark and Matthew insist on the close relationship between love of God and love of neighbor. But Luke, as we have already said, goes in a direction that seems to merge the two precepts into one, which we will have to consider in analyzing the parable.

This is the same unity to which Benedict XVI draws our attention in his first encyclical: "Love of God and love of neighbor are thus insepa-rable, they form a *single* commandment" (*Deus Caritas Est*, 18, my em-phasis).[5] We also find it in Matthew 25:31–46, which provides an illu-minating perspective from which to the read the parable of the Good Samaritan: we find Jesus in the Other, in the poor.

The first part of the verse that we are considering ends—as will occur at the conclusion of the parable itself—with a response from Jesus that goes beyond his approval of the answer provided by the scribe. Jesus tells the scribe to put this single commandment into prac-tice: "do this and you will live" (10:28). "Do the truth," he could have said in Johannine terms (Jn 3:21); the act of love is the source of life, it is truth put in practice.

The scribe has responded to his own question, and Jesus has given his assent. At this point it is about moving on to what is most impor-tant, translating this precept into concrete gestures of love toward both God and his neighbor, thereby taking part in "eternal life," in the reign of God. In this way the scribe will become worthy of the beatitudes that Luke will offer in the following chapter, and which further emphasize the importance of practice. In response to the woman's shouted greet-ing, "Blessed is the womb that bore you," Jesus replies, "Blessed rather are those who hear the word of God and obey it" (Lk 11: 27–28)!

The dialogue with the doctor of the law is thus crucial for under-standing the message of the parable. The exchange not only illustrates the word that calls us to love of God and love of neighbor, but it also provides clarifications that underline the unity and universality of that love, and that draw our attention to the context in which that love has life: the context of practice.

Who Is My Neighbor?

The lawyer insists on clarifications; he wants to know exactly who his neighbor is. But instead of responding with an abstract definition, Jesus replies with a story.

From the Side of the Road

The crucial question, "Who is my neighbor?" (10:29), situates the per-son asking the question, the "I," in a space where the neighbor would probably refer to those nearby, people on his or her property, or those living in close proximity. These are people who, in one way or another, surround me and to whose needs I must attend, which in this case would include the man who was robbed. The scribe is not stepping out of his own little world if at the beginning of the conversation he asks, "What should *I* do," immediately adding "for *my* neighbor?" Perhaps this is why the text says he wanted to "justify himself" (10:29). But the gospel of Jesus consists in a call to abandon a world focused on the I—a world that is literally egocentric—and to enter into the world of the Other.

For this reason, after telling the story Jesus turns the tables on his questioner, responding with a question of his own that provides the key to the meaning of the story: Who behaved like a good neighbor to *the wounded man* found by the side of the road? In other words, who became a neighbor to the other, to the thou? Here we must see that a shift has taken place, the axis of the story has been moved. We are invited to realize that becoming a neighbor to the Other involves getting close to them. This is something that the first travelers did not do, and that only the Samaritan understood. Jesus' question changes the scenario: the heart of the problem resides not in the I of the questioner, but in the thou of the one who has been violated and forgotten. The performance of the travelers is judged in relation to him; as a result, the lawyer who is Jesus' interlocutor moves from the center to the periphery of our concerns, which seems to have been the location of the victim of the attack in the lawyer's original question.

Thus, there is a movement from the *I* of the lawyer to the *thou* of the wounded man, from my world to the world of the Other, a movement that is at the heart of the parable. We have moved from seeing the neighbor as an object, or recipient of our help, to considering him or her as a subject of a personal approach, of *fellowship*, which is more than an expression of simple physical and cultural neighborliness. This transition is in many ways Copernican: it inverts two worlds. The world of the lawyer gives way to the world of the person who was attacked (*his neighbor*). This move is particularly significant in a gospel like Luke's, which emphasizes the historical changes brought about by the Messiah.

For this reason, and contrary to our expectations, the key actor in the story is not the Samaritan, but rather the person identified as "a man" (*anthropós tis*, 10:30), the victim, the helpless one, the one with no name or standing. Nothing is said about him; he is an insignificant, anonymous person. We don't know if he is Jewish or Samaritan, the nature of his trade, or what he is doing there. He is the Other and he will define all the other characters in the narrative. His battered and abandoned condition calls out to people immersed in their everyday routines, and their response is to find any excuse to get away. The road to Jericho is an image of everyday life then and now. There we constantly cross paths with others, acquaintances and strangers. And what the Samaritan did happens among us today, as is also unfortunately true of what the Levite and the priest did.

Each of the characters in the story— including the robbers and the innkeeper—is designated by his religious identity or social location. The insignificance of the victim is captured by his anonymity and social nakedness. He is left with just one characteristic: his humanity, his face, which, according to Levinas, says, "Don't let me die." The presence of the victim touches every aspect of the story. We must read the text from the side of the road where the person was left beaten and "half dead," avoided by some and noticed by one whose heart was moved by the cruelty and injustice of the victim's condition.

The story calls us to a change of course, to take responsibility for what is implied by an authentic life for a human and a believer. The scribe has no choice but to recognize that the Samaritan was the one who acted with compassion by giving life to the injured, unlike the Levite and the priest who, by avoiding him, abandoned him to his fate and to death, thus becoming factual accomplices of the assailants.

The parable makes us understand that we must go beyond nationality, beyond religious or ethnic ties, and attend to the needy, whatever his or her social or religious status, with no one excluded. We are called to a universal questioning that pushes beyond existing categories and recognizes the priority of those who suffer abandonment and injustice. This is what Luke means when he talks about love of enemies and says "do good to those who hate you" (6:27).[6] This vision is underscored by the action of the Samaritan, who can be considered an "enemy" to those hearing the parable.

Nonetheless, it is important to note that the story of the Good Samaritan is not so much a rejection of the law as it is an innovative reinterpretation of it. The parable offers a hermeneutical key for understanding the law as Torah, as a teaching or path. Jesus does not respond to the lawyer with a formal definition of the notion of neighbor, which could lead to a touchy debate on the law. Rather, for Jesus it is about a dynamic category that presupposes getting closer to the Other, depending on our creativity. The neighbor is not defined *a priori*, for we can all be neighbors if we draw close to the Other. The model is set and the story invites us to behave like this in our daily lives. There is no mention, nor is there need for it at the moment, of a final judgment at the end of time. The focus is here and now.

Becoming a Neighbor

Thus, a neighbor is not the person we chance to meet in our neighborhood or in our daily travels, but rather the person whose acquaintance we choose to make, to the extent that we step out of our usual route and take that of the Other, entering into their world.[7] It is about becoming a neighbor to the Other, even the foreigner, to the one who is not a part of our own geographical, social, or cultural world. In a way, we could say that we do not "have" neighbors, but rather we "make them" through our own initiatives, gestures, and actions that bring us close to those we consider distant. Moving closer to the Other has a two-way effect: we become their neighbor and the Other becomes ours; it's a coming and going. This is the point of the aforementioned question of Jesus at the end of the story: "Which of these three, do you think, was (*gegonénai*) to the man who fell into the hands of the robbers" (10:36)?

Jesus' question replaces the earlier question posed by the doctor of the law, redirecting it to its roots: what must one do to inherit eternal life? The lawyer answers: act like the Samaritan ["The one who showed him mercy" (10:37)]. The verbal form *gegonénai* is often misleadingly translated as "had been," or "was," but could be more precisely translated as "made himself" or "became a neighbor," or "acted like a neighbor." This translation is important for the meaning of the text, since *being a neighbor* is not simply a given, but must be constructed or created.

This perspective is emphasized by the contrast between the first two travelers and the Samaritan, a touch that gives a particular bite to the story. Here we encounter another reversal of roles, in the style of Luke. Both the priest and the Levite—respected people connected to the cult, but whose behavior is disapproved by Jesus—see the man, but they cross to "the other side" of the road in order to avoid someone who is half dead. It is the Samaritan—a member of a rejected community—who leaves his path when he sees the injured man, comes close to him, and shows compassion. He makes his decision without being asked, without having any particular connection to the man who was attacked. His view (a view of mercy) is different from that of the first two travelers. Perhaps the victim is from the Jewish people, a foreigner to the Samaritan. What is important is that he has been assaulted and needs help. The Samaritan is not looking for reciprocity and does not expect a reward for his gesture. He acts out of generosity and gratuity, out of a kind of righteousness that "exceeds that of the scribes" (Mt 5:20) both then and now.

Neither does the Samaritan act out of observance of a cold and impersonal sense of duty (like Nazarín, the character in the movie by Buñuel, who excels in gestures of assistance acting out of duty rather than love[8]). Rather, he acts from the feeling provoked by the situation of the person who has been assaulted. What motivates the action of the Samaritan is compassion—in the sense of sharing the pain of the other—which he experiences personally. Luke chooses a strong term to describe this feeling, *splanknizomai*, which means to stir one's entrails.[9] Speaking at the beginning of the gospel through Zechariah, Luke talks about the "tender (*splankna*) mercy" of God (Lk 1:78), a love that literally becomes flesh, and which is neither ethereal or neutral. It is the presence of charity, the grace of God, incarnated in human love in the many ways in which human beings express their love, and which do not otherwise exist.[10] The physical repercussion of compassion (felt in the entrails) is an aspect of how charity is experienced in the human person, a radical unity of flesh and spirit. Without affective closeness, without friendship with the poor and insignificant, there is no solidarity with them. The Samaritan was capable of responding appropriately because he made the painful situation of the wounded person into his own.

Hospitality is a profound and frequent theme in scripture, a theme that illuminates our understanding of "being a neighbor." The Samaritan leaves his own road, his world, in order to enter in the life of the wounded stranger, the Other. He makes the stranger his guest because he hosts him in his own life, a gesture that he prolongs by entrusting the man to the care of the innkeeper, making the latter a participant in the gesture of hospitality. Hospitality, like nearness, involves reciprocity. It is interesting that the Spanish word for *guest* refers both to the one who receives hospitality and to the one who gives it. Hospitality does not make the personal reality of the one being accommodated in our world disappear; rather, it implies respecting that reality in its otherness, and being enriched by it. The God of the Bible takes hospice in our history, and in so doing makes us guests of his reign.[11]

Go and Do Likewise

The parable of the Good Samaritan does not explicitly mention the reign of God, but it describes the situation by which the reign should be characterized: the brotherhood/sisterhood of humankind. This brotherhood/sisterhood is rooted in the gift of relationship, in our nature as daughters and sons of the God announced by Jesus Christ, whose love surpasses all borders and which we build gesture by gesture.

The Samaritan, Image of Jesus

Our parable has been frequently allegorized, sometimes excessively, making each of the characters into figures from human history, or persons from the First or Second Testaments. Unfortunately this has sometimes removed them from the newness of good news of the Gospel of Luke, which forces us to be discerning. It is good to move away from the abuse of the allegorical interpretation of scripture, but abandoning it completely would be to lose a rich tradition with its spiritual impact on Christian life. Given that the Samaritan is presented as a model for Christian conduct, the insistence of the great pastors and theologians of the Patristic era or its importance serves to highlight the christological dimension of the story. This view, I believe, provides us with the ultimate meaning of the Samaritan's behavior: putting into practice the single commandment of love of God and love of neighbor, a summary of the ethics of the gospel.

The gospels in fact show us a Jesus who is sensitive to injustice and suffering, who practices compassion, and who has given his heart to the abandoned and the miserable. Caring for the victim, the Samaritan bandages "his wounds, having poured oil and wine on them" (10:34), and entrusts him to the innkeeper (10:34). Jesus approaches the needy and despised, whoever they might be, taking no account of national, cultural, or religious barriers. Elsewhere Luke describes Jesus' attitude of compassion for the widow whose only son has died (7:13), and for the father in the parable of the Prodigal Son (15:20). Both texts support the view that the Samaritan represents Jesus. The gospels each describe different expressions of kindness and even tenderness by Jesus, his preoccupation with alleviating the suffering of the marginated, his desire to appreciate the poor as persons, and his rejection of those who mistreat the vulnerable. It is impossible not to be moved by the Samaritan's actions, and not to think of him as a representative of Jesus, the Son of God.

As a result, it is clear that to be a disciple of Jesus is to act as he did and to love as he did. In this case that means acting like the Samaritan, becoming a neighbor to the one who is suffering and marginated. This means recognizing what was done by the Samaritan, not only that he was moved, but that he put mercy into practice, he attended to the wounded, and, preoccupied with what would happen to him, placed the wounded man into the care of the innkeeper (10:35). Then, for the second time in the story, Jesus tells the scribe, "go and do likewise" (10:37). This constitutes almost a commission for mission, something like "give your life, practice mercy"—without partiality—in the best and most fundamental sense of the term: give your heart through concrete gestures to the poor and forsaken. A foreigner considered ignorant of the law demonstrates the correct action for those who wish to inherit "eternal life" (10:25), which is to put the reign of God into practice. This is an idea that, despite appearances, dominates the pericope and provides a permanent standard for our own conduct.

It has been argued that the emphasis of this text on loving the stranger is complemented by the story of Martha and Mary, which highlights the love of God and follows the story of the Samaritan.[12] But I think this unfairly reduces the message of the parable, which is complex and rich and does not require this annotation. To behave like the Samaritan, drawing near to the needy, already squarely situates us in love of God. This is what it means to fulfill the single commandment. On the other hand, the pericope of Martha and Mary has its own coherence and meaning.

Our understanding of the parable of the Good Samaritan becomes clearer and more insistent if we start from the face of the Other. The text cannot be separated from the scene of the last judgment in Matthew 25, which gives it a permanent connection to history. The Latin American bishops have stated this clearly on a variety of occasions. Indeed, at its last three meetings, the Conference of Latin America Bishops has restated this and offered concrete examples of this gospel horizon, including lists describing the faces of the poor on the continent in whose faces we must learn to recognize the face of Christ.

A Samaritan Church

Reflecting on the reality of Latin America and the Caribbean, the 2007 Conference of Latin American bishops at Aparecida, Brazil, reaffirmed the preferential option for the poor and took the Samaritan as the model for the work of evangelization and humanization. "Illuminated by Christ," the Conference declares, "the suffering, the injustice, and the cross [of our people] call us to live like a Samaritan Church (cf. Luke 10:25-37)" (#27), adding the clarification, following Luke and citing the address by Pope Benedict XVI, "we are reminded that 'evangelization has always been united with human development and authentic Christian liberation.'" Evangelization is the good news of God's gratuitous love, which calls us to commit ourselves to the promotion of justice and to liberation from every kind of oppression. Evangelization and the good news are as inseparable as love of God and love of neighbor.

This approach, which strengthens Aparecida's conclusions, appears in a variety of places in the final document. The bishops argue that responding to Jesus who calls us to follow in his footsteps "demands that we join the good Samaritan (Lk 10:29–37) who commands us, following the practice of Jesus, to make ourselves into neighbors, most especially with those who suffer, and to create a society in which no one is excluded" (#135). "Making ourselves neighbors," taking the initiative to draw close to the Other, as we saw in the parable, means "going as good Samaritans to meet the needs of the poor and those who suffer, and creating 'the just structures that are the condition without which a just social order is not possible" (Benedict XVI, Address at Aparecida) so that the continent might become "our common home" (Aparecida, #537). This is a practice that reveals the identity Jesus and the *ecclesia* of his followers (Mt 11:2–6).[13]

The expression *Samaritan Church* is beautiful and evocative, but it also draws our attention to the paths we must follow in order to announce the initial presence of the reign of God in history. Beginning with Medellín and inspired by Vatican II, this was the position taken by the church in Latin America. The church understood that the proclamation of the good news to every person leads us to place a priority on solidarity with the poor and oppressed and to reject the unjust situation in which they are forced to live as contrary to the will of the God of love. This process not only led to Aparecida, but was also strengthened and opened itself to new perspectives there.

The primacy of the Other—and no one represents the condition of otherness more clearly than the poor and excluded—is an important aspect of the liberating word of the gospel. The option for solidarity with the forgotten and mistreated implies putting ourselves on their path, making them our guests, seeing them not only as needy or victims, but rather as equals, no matter how different from us they might be. It implies complete respect for their personal dignity and for their rights to be the agents of their own history. It also means making their demands for justice and their struggles for a more human life into our own.[14] The final basis of all conduct for the Christian is the following of Jesus.[15]

It is possible to understand the different dimensions of the preferential option for the poor—spiritual, theological, evangelical—only from the world of the poor, through the process of stepping out of our own path, without taking detours to avoid coming face to face with the injustice and suffering that afflict the poor. Living with these aspects of the option for the poor in their complexity and interactions implies what the gospel calls a conversion, a *metanoia*, which in the Bible means leaving one path and taking another.

This is the point of departure and the essential condition for accepting the reign of God and walking in the steps of the Christ of our faith. "Convert and believe in the good news" is what it says at the beginning of the earliest gospel (Mk 1:15). This is what the parable of the Good Samaritan invites us to do.

(Translated by Robert Lassalle-Klein and Salvador Leavitt-Alcántara)

Notes

1. In his memorable discourse at the end of the Vatican Council, Paul VI said: "The ancient story of the Samaritan has been the spiritual model for the Council. An immense compassion has penetrated everything. The discovery of human needs…has absorbed the attention of our Synod" (December 7, 1965). The parable of the Good Samaritan is found only in Luke and it bears his redactional and theological imprint.

2. This is the way it was read by the Qumran community, which was contemporary with Jesus.

3. For a brief presentation of the different positions regarding this term see Rodney S. Sadler, Jr., "Who Is My Neighbor? Introductory Explorations," in *Interpretation* (April 2008): 116–22.

4. "Reino de Dios y Economía en la Biblia," *Communio* 2 (March–April 1986): 112–24.

5. In another paragraph Benedict states, "Love of God and love of neighbor merge to become one" (*Deus Caritas Est*, 15).

6. Freud believed that it is utopian to speak of a love with universal scope, which he believes goes against the natural inclination of human beings: "If I love someone, it is necessary," he wrote, "that he or she deserves it for whatever reason" (Sigmund Freud, *El Malestar de la Cultura*, Obras Completas (Madrid: Editorial Biblioteca Nueva, 1981), 3044.

7. A neighbor "is not just someone that I encounter in my path, but rather someone in whose path I place myself (Gustavo Gutiérrez, *Teología de la Liberación* [Lima: CEP, 1971], 245).

8. Ibid., 246–48.

9. This term is used in Matthew 9:36, 14:4, 15:32, and 20:34. Mark uses it in 1:41, 5:19, 6:34, and 8:2. In Luke it appears only in 7:13 and 15:20, as we will see below.

10. "There is no charity outside of human love…Charity does not compare to human love" (Gustavo Gutiérrez, *Caridad y amor humano* [Lima: Unec, 1965], 9).

11. Claudio Monge, Dieu Hôte: Recherche Historique et Théologique sur les Rituels de L'Hospitalité (Bucharest: Zeta Books, 2008).

12. This is the case with John Nolland, who thinks that the parable speaks only about love of neighbor, and is complemented by the episode with Martha

and Mary, which refers to love of God (John Nolland, *Luke 9:21–18:34*, Word Biblical Commentary [Dallas: Word Books Publisher, 1993], 597).

13. Hugo Echegaray, *La Práctica de Jesús* (Lima: CEP, 1980).

14. Naim Ateek, who writes a commentary on this parable in Palestine, thinking about the Jewish-Palestinian conflict, underscores its message of an "unconditional love" (Naim Ateek, "Who Is My Neighbor?" *Interpretation* [April 2008]: 165).

15. Barnard Häring stated this clearly in his book, *La loi du Christ*, vol. 3 (Tournai: Desclee y Cie, 1959), which helped renew moral theology several decades ago in the period leading up to and following Vatican II.

3

MESTIZO JESUS

Virgilio Elizondo

A Family Friend

"I have called you friends"—John 15:15
I grew up in the Mexican tradition of Christianity, which is based on two principal icons: *Jesús Nazareno*, suffering for us on the cross and with us in our struggles, and *Nuestra Señora de Guadalupe*, reigning majestically in the temple of our hearts while offering us all her love, defense, and protection. They never appeared as doctrines to be believed or abstract truths to be memorized, but as beloved persons to converse with as they walked with us on the journey of life. From my earliest childhood I grew up with the assurance that I could place complete confidence in them, for they would never fail me, deceive me, or abandon me. I grew up knowing that in them and through them I would find responses to the many questions and enigmas of life. After a long life and many studies in various disciplines, I have no reason to begin doubting this today. I have reflected a lot and written a little on both Our Lady of Guadalupe and the Galilean Jesus, but now I want to probe deeper into the mystery and gift of the Word made flesh who walks among us today—a series of the most incredible surprises anyone would ever dare to imagine.

In our *barrios*, we never heard anything about the christological doctrines of the church, but we knew Jesus of Galilee very well. From the earliest days of my life, I have known him as a close friend and companion. He was very present in the tabernacle as *Jesús Sacramentado*, and we easily and frequently visited with him as our most trusted confidant. Vivid images of him were found throughout our homes, barrios, and churches. Simple songs, like the *corridos* of our people, kept him alive among us. Ritual celebrations from the *posadas* (Joseph and Mary seeking a place to stay where Jesus could be born), the *acostada del niño Dios* (the laying down of the "Baby God"), and the *levantada* (presentation of the Child Jesus) of February 2 to the vivid reenactments of *Semana Santa* (Holy Week) have kept the human Jesus very much present in our lives and communities.

From the baby in the crib or in the arms of his mother to the one calming the fishermen on the boat, to the one feeding the multitudes or enjoying himself at table with all kinds of people, to the man washing the feet of others, to the man in deep agony in the garden, to the one scourged and crowned with thorns and crucified, the Jesus of the gospel narratives has been alive and well among us. On the cross he was no angelic figure or solemn high priest, but a beaten, bleeding, suffering human victim of injustice dying a painful death—just like people who have been and are victims of injustice. In his unimaginable weakness, humiliation, and apparent defeat, he empowered us to accept whatever came to us in life and to never give in. This very real and very carnal Jesus is my Savior. He is not a teaching of the church, but one of our own in whom our own lives take on meaning. I have no problem with the christological teachings of our church, but the Jesus I know and seek to follow cannot be reduced to a mere doctrine any more than you or I can be reduced to a mere definition about our identity. We are much more. The Jesus who accompanies us throughout our lives and suffers with us in our afflictions has been a tremendous source of strength in our culture. *Jesús Salvador* is such a popular figure among us that we often name our children Jesús, Jesusita, Salvador, Encarnación, Crúz, and other such names.

As much as we knew about *Jesús Salvador*, we were equally very aware of the destructive force of sin all around us. Even our games, like the *piñata*, made us aware of the presence of the deceiving devil. The *piñatas* were always made in the form of devils or wrecking balls with seven peaks (seven capital sins). We were blindfolded and given a rod to break the *piñata*. The lesson: in life the devil would come at us from many different directions and disguised in many different ways. It was our task to fight against evil so that the glory of God would come upon everyone. The prize was inside the *piñata*, so no matter who broke it, the prize would be shared by all.

Unfortunately it wasn't only our games that made us aware of the presence of evil forces all around us. We knew of robbery, crime, cheating, vengeance, malicious lies, racial and ethnic slurs, beatings, humiliating insults, and even murder. But even more than that, we were well aware of the ugly prejudices people had against our African American neighbors and us. People called us ugly names, kept us out of many places because of our skin color, ridiculed us because of our accents, told us we could not make it in school or in society because we were not smart enough, and kept us out of seminaries and convents because we were not ethnically pure or holy enough to be there.

Our own were never present in positions of leadership in our church, schools, or society—as if God himself did not trust us. We were to be docile servants of the dominant society. In our hearts we knew this was not right, and since many of the people who treated us as if we were inferior and unworthy apparently were good people, we could only conclude that their ugliness toward us was not malice but rather a result of a much deeper evil. In time I would come to recognize this deeper evil as structural sin, as structural violence, which leads "good people" to do bad and horrible things while being convinced they are doing good. It is this structural evil that distorts, confuses, and sometimes even perverts our image and appreciation of others, of God, and worst of all, ourselves. It is this structural evil that blinds people to seeing the truth (Mt 23:1626, Catechism, 399). Wasn't this exactly what happened to the good and holy people who condemned Jesus as diabolically possessed, as a blasphemer and a common criminal, while being convinced they were speaking for God? Wasn't this the very "sin of the world" (Jn 1:29) that Jesus came to demolish, the very structures of society that could not appreciate him and ultimately killed him? How did Jesus respond to all this? How does he respond today?

The quest to know this *Jesús Salvador* better, as I long to know my own close friends better, has been with me as far back as I can remember, but it has continued to intensify as I have grown older. To know him simply as divine is no problem, for the divine will always be a mystery that is too far beyond us to fully comprehend; but to know him as a human being is a terrific adventure. One could never follow a purely divine Jesus, since we are not divine, but we could follow the human Jesus who came into our lives precisely to show us the way. Yet it is precisely in his humanity that his divinity is made manifest (*Catechism*, 515) and in following his way our humanity becomes divinized. To many, Jesus of Nazareth will continue to be as much of a scandal as he was in his own time and for early Christianity. It was so difficult for the scandal of Jesus of Nazareth to be appreciated for what it truly was that St. Paul would dare to write: "And no one can say, 'Jesus is Lord,' except by the Holy Spirit" (1 Cor 12:3). Who really is Jesus the Galilean, and just why did God become such a man to reveal the heart and face of God to us?

The idea of continuing my reflections about Jesus of Galilee has been brewing in my mind and heart for several years but, for some reason or another, I had not been moved to write about it, as if the theme needed more time to evolve and develop. It was while taking care of my slowly dying mother that I felt the energy to rekindle this project. It was as if her sleeping presence was giving me the inspiration and strength to get going.

Ever since the publication of my *Galilean Journey: The Mexican American Promise* in 1983, friends of mine have been urging me to develop further the theme of the Galilean Jesus. How does Jesus of Galilee become the Christ to persons who feel doomed to exclusion and marginalization because of their mixed race or mixed ethnic origins? Why has he been such a strong salvific figure for the poor and marginalized of Latin America, especially in his final humiliation, suffering, and crucifixion? Is there something unsuspected in the humiliated Jesus that those of the dominant cultures have not detected? Is there something in the colonized identity of the Galilean that people who have never been colonized do not recognize? Is there something that the poor and exploited, the broken and humiliated, the ridiculed and separated of the world have perceived that the powerful of this world have missed? Has the scandal of the human Jesus been too much, too ridiculous, too "far out" for the good and nice people of this world—this world as structured by sin and injustice?

"The spirit of truth, he will guide you to all truth"—John 16:13

In his book *Jesus through the Centuries: His Place in the History of Culture* Jaroslav Pelikan has demonstrated masterfully how different cultures in different ages have elaborated various images of Jesus that have allowed people of that place and time to recognize Jesus as their healer, as their liberator, and as their savior. Moreover, in seeking to write about Jesus of Galilee, each culture has in effect produced a self-image of its own ideal self. In seeking to know Jesus of Galilee they have come to know themselves, not as others say that they are, but as they truly are. This does not mean that they have written a new gospel or merely adjusted the gospel to fit their needs, but that they discovered aspects of the gospel that others have not noticed or emphasized.

Because Jesus was born and raised in circumstances very similar to our own Mexican American experience, we truly encounter him and know him in a very personal way. And who can better understand us than those born and raised among us, or at least in similar circumstances? They have insights into us like nobody else. Such is the story of Jesus who was raised in Nazareth, a rural town in the multiethnic Roman colony of Galilee. As the French language so beautifully brings out, only when we can *connaître*—be born with—can we know another. The verb "*connaître*" in French, which means to know a person, is a combination of the roots for the words "with" and "born."

Because of the many struggles for identity and belonging in my own life and, as I have discovered, in the lives of other mixed-race persons of ethnic and racial minorities, the issue of the social perception of Jesus' earthly identity is of the greatest importance for us today. I have asked myself the question with greater and greater intensity: Just what man did God become? With what accent did he speak? Did he mix the various languages of his region the way we do today—a sort of "Aramgreek" like our own Spanglish? Did he have elegant mainstream speech? How was he regarded by mainstream society? What passport would he have carried, what visas would he have been denied? How would people have reacted to his looks and ethnicity?

Because of the incarnation, as John Paul II pointed out in his first encyclical, *Redemptor Hominis*, every detail of the life of Jesus is part of the revelation. The question keeps pounding within my head and in my heart: Who, humanly speaking, was Jesus of Nazareth, and why did God become this very particular, stereotypically marked human being in order to be the savior of the world? What is the saving element of his earthly identity? After all, God did not begin the salvation of humanity by belonging to the great conquering and colonizing empires of this world, but through the marginal poor of the colonized peoples of the world. Yet he did not convert the colonized into colonizers but allowed them to initiate something new that would go beyond the categories of colonizer/colonized.

"The truth will set you free"—John 8:32

The more I reflect upon the human Jesus of the gospels, the more I discover how much he has to offer men and women of today who are struggling under the weight of low self-esteem, internalized notions of inadequacy, inferiority, and even ugliness. At the same time, others fail to appreciate the beauty and goodness of God because they stereotype others as ugly, inferior, and unwanted. It is amazing, especially among minorities, how often people think of themselves as less human, less deserving, less capable of achievement, and less beautiful than those of the dominant group. This low self-image along with the expectations that one will not do as well as the others are among the most destructive and oppressive elements that many people live with. It is this type of separating categorization of others that keeps people from entering into the unity of the human race intended by the Creator. This leads those who have been victimized by the sin of the world to commit the very destructive sin of not believing in themselves—as if God had created trash!

During my many years of teaching in various universities and especially during my work in San Fernando Cathedral, which is most of all a cathedral of the poor of San Antonio, I have become very aware of how deeply the elements of self-image and self-identity affect people's lives, condition their social behavior, and limit or enhance their possibilities. With Timothy Matovina I have written about this in *San Fernando Cathedral: Soul of the City*. Many students do not speak up in class discussions because of a deep inner fear that they know less than the other students or even that they are inferior to them. The fear is even more intense among students from oppressed minorities. They are often silent, not because they are not thinking but because they fear their manner of speaking might not be acceptable, beautiful enough to be listened to, or, even worse, that they have nothing of value to contribute. In fact, they usually have the most powerful insights to offer.

It has become increasingly evident over the years that one of the most demoralizing and enslaving factors in the lives of people of mixed race, or mixed ethnicities, is the constant feeling of "not belonging fully" to either one of the parent groups, of not being as beautiful as those of the dominant group. This engenders deep feelings of shame regarding one's looks, a sense of the impurity of one's soul, the unworthiness of one's being, and disregard for one's new cultural identity. Quite often, the beauty, creativity, and potential brought about by the new pool of customs and genes (cultural, linguistic, religious, and biological) that have come together in the *mestizo*, the person of mixed races, are not appreciated and are even disdained.

I have found that exposing *mestizos* and other marginal peoples to the Galilean Jesus has not only been very exciting but also very healing, liberating, and life giving. Out of his Galilean mixture, Jesus was able to transgress the segregating limits of purity of his people and begin a new universal fellowship that offered real hope to a humanity torn apart by tribal, ethnic, religious, and racial barriers. Closed identities lead to barriers of separation that are often, as is evident today, the basis of hatred, gangs, enslavements, segregation, wars, and even holocausts.

It is my growing conviction that the greatest thing Christianity has to offer the world is the Galilean Jesus who, out of marginalization, offers a new universal fellowship: a unity in diversity and a new humanity in the loving mixture of peoples. This is the Jesus who transgresses humanly made barriers of separation, no matter how sacred they appear to be, for the sake of human unity, and who transgresses humanly created systems of purity of body and blood for the sake of the true purity of God; this is love beyond all limits. After all, are we not all invited to share in his own body and blood so that our own bodies and blood might no longer be a basis of separation and death? The resurrection is precisely the rising above the death-bearing segregating factors of the world. The risen body is no longer bound by the earthly stereotypes of race, ethnicity, class, or even clothing. Thus the risen Lord, as those that arise with him, is no longer this or that (in the limiting sense in which these terms have functioned), but fully human, fully alive.

The human Jesus reveals both the lies of the world and the truth of God about human beings and even about the selfhood of God. It is true that Jesus reveals a very beautiful and loving God to us, but I think it is even more important and more revolutionary that Jesus reveals the truth, the good, and the beauty about us to ourselves and to others and in so doing reveals the true countenance and heart of God in whose image we have been created. He who was a scandal to the world from the very moment of his conception and who died condemned as a criminal is the greatest revelation of who is really a true, a good, and a beautiful human being. In him we discover the whole and life-giving truth about ourselves. In him, with him, and through him, we can disregard the stereotypes we have lived under and shout from our most innermost being: I AM! I am a true human being, a beautiful human being, a good human being—so much so that God was willing to send his son to give his life for me!

It is amazing to me how in the midst of the most vulnerable moments in the life of Jesus and in his most scandalous actions, the deepest truths about our humanity and about God are revealed. As you accompany me through the remainder of this essay, reflect upon your own experiences of suffering and struggle so that the truth of the Galilean may heal you, make you free, and bring you to the fullness of your humanity.

It is through the Galilean Jesus that shame is transformed into a new and triumphant life. It is no longer shame, but pride, gratitude, and even a sense of mission, no longer mere compliance to the dominant status quo, but a new creative spirit with new vision and values. As Pelikan wrote, "The way any particular age has depicted Jesus is often the key to the genius of that age" (*Jesus through the Centuries*, p. 3). In *nuestro amigo Jesús* a new humanity will emerge that will leave behind the destructive racial, ethnic, and religious barriers that destroyed so much of humanity in past generations and in many ways continue to do so today. This is indeed a new creation.

So Human, He Must Be Divine

"And the word became flesh and made his dwelling place among us" (Jn 1:14). Isn't this an incredible affirmation? The eternal God became human in a determined and limited time. The infinite God became a person in a very specific and particular space. The universal God became a culturally conditioned human being. The all-powerful God became completely vulnerable in Jesus, the man from Galilee, the son of Mary. And what is even more incredible is that I and many others know him personally.

Because I believe Jesus of Nazareth to be my savior and acknowledge how, in many ways, he has been my healer and liberator (as I describe in *The Future Is Mestizo: Life Where Cultures Meet*), I want to know more about him as a human being; it is precisely through his humanity that he has redeemed our own humanity and has rehabilitated us to our original beauty and dignity as created in the image and likeness of God. My own church in its renewed interest in evangelization has emphasized the personal encounter with Jesus of Nazareth as the core of evangelization. But just who is this human being Jesus of Nazareth, and why did God become in Jesus the very particular and socially situated person that he became? What is the salvific meaning of the very person that God became when God became flesh?

I remember quite well the great biblical scholar Luis Alonso Schökel, vice rector of the Pontifical Biblical Institute in Rome, saying, "Because throughout the Bible, and most of all through the Word made Flesh, God chose to reveal himself through the human, only to the degree that we appreciate the humanity of the Scriptures will we appreciate their divinity." So to probe the human dimension of the scriptures is to probe the ways of God as revealed through the struggles of human beings to become fully human. The entire Bible is a witness of the revelation of a loving and caring God through the struggles of the enslaved for freedom, of the marginalized for inclusion, of the shamed for positive recognition, of the imprisoned for liberty, of the rejected for acceptance, of the nobodies to become somebodies. Biblical revelation is about the God who hears the cries of the people, sees their suffering, and comes to save his people. The God of the Bible is the God of the struggles of humanity for freedom, dignity, and belonging (Ex 3:7–8).

The amazing thing about our Christian faith is that we believe that it is through the humanity of Jesus that we come to know God personally. In *Jesus Christ Liberator* Brazilian theologian Leonardo Boff brings this out beautifully when he states that at the end of the nagging question about who Jesus of Nazareth really was, the early Christians finally arrived at the insight that he was so completely human, he must have been divine! Thus the human and everything about his human situation become essential elements of the revelation, essential constituents of the redemptive process (*Catechism*, 515–518).

I do not know of any religion that so respects and exalts the human as our Hellenistic-Judeo-Christian faith. In Jesus, the true image of the human will be revealed. We are created in the image and likeness of God, but it is the man Jesus who is the definitive revelation of God and of true humanity as created by God. In Jesus of Nazareth we discover the truth of God and the truth of the human—who God truly is and what it truly means to be a human being. No one human group or religion has an exclusive monopoly on the truth about God and about the human. In fact, as humans in search of absolutes, we quickly create idols! In his life and message, Jesus offers a synthesis of the most humanizing elements of the various ethnic traditions circulating in his home region of Galilee— the great circle of Gentiles. Out of Galilee, the land of the darkness, of ignorance, and the mixture of various peoples, will emerge the great light to all nations (Mt 4:15–16). Another of God's surprises.

In our *mestizo* Christianity of Latin America, it is neither the defleshed images of a risen Christ nor the great christological titles that appeal to the people, but rather the figures depicting the very human Jesus of Nazareth, whether as a baby, as a boy, or most especially as the man of sorrows. At no time is his divinity more apparent to us than during our popular rituals of Good Friday. It is in his very ability to endure suffering, even to the extreme of scourging, thorns, and crucifixion, that he best reveals his divinity. The ordinary Latino poor seem to have an inspired instinct allowing his divinity to shine through that which, according to our modern standards of greatness, success, and beauty, we would consider a failure and a disgrace.

In the last few years, many fine scholarly works on the historical Jesus, the earthly Jesus, the real Jesus, the Jewish and even the Greco-Roman Jesus have been written. I have studied all of them, have enjoyed them all, and have learned a tremendous amount about the culture, society, and religion of Jesus. The work of these magnificent scholars has taken me a long way, but they all seem to fall short of asking the incarnational-theological question: Why did God become the very particular human flesh that God became in Jesus of Nazareth in Galilee in order to redeem humanity?

It seems that these studies lead down a fascinating path but fall short of arriving at the core of the issue. Just what did this "redemptive incarnation" redeem humanity from? Why was it necessary precisely in the particular way that it happened? Why are the social and cultural details examined important to God's salvific process? What is their salvific value to men and women today? How do they make a difference in the lives of those who wish to follow in the steps of the Master, those who wish to follow The Way?

These studies have definitely helped me to see and appreciate Jesus the Galilean in his socio-cultural milieu, but it is the dehumanized poor people struggling to be recognized as human beings and allowed to belong to the human race who have led me to the theological insights regarding the salvific aspects of the marginal peasant from Galilee going out to invite everyone into the reign of God. Yes, he was a great miracle worker, teacher, and prophet, but there were others around. He could not be easily classified by the ordinary categories of judgment. So who was he? It is crucial to know not just that Jesus invited everyone into his company but, even more important, who this Jesus was that was doing the inviting! To us today, he is the Son of God, but who was he to the people of his region and times? After all, it is not just what is said that is important, but who the person saying it is. What are his credentials? With what authority does he speak? Does he speak well and correctly?

Statements by important and well-recognized persons are listened to attentively while remarks by persons like Genoveva Martinez, the cafeteria cook, or Eusebio Perez, the undocumented immigrant, are easily ignored and even ridiculed, no matter how intelligent and profound their statements might be. The reputation or social status of the person who speaks is basic to the reception of any communication. People presuppose that words coming from a famous person will be important, while they usually don't even pay attention to the voices of those who are considered to be insignificant.

The gospel writers were not great scholars or academics but simply followers of Jesus who wrote for their own congregations out of what they remembered and tried to transmit to others (*Catechism*, 515). They were not writing doctoral dissertations but memories of a person who had transformed their lives, of one who had given them a completely new way of perceiving themselves, others, and society. They were simply writing about the one who had opened their eyes to see in a new way, their minds to a new understanding, and most of all their hearts to love in ways previously unheard of (Lk 23:13–53).

They were very much like modern-day *cursillistas* writing the memories of their *cursillo* experience so as to communicate to others the joy and excitement of what they experienced, of what totally transformed their lives. (A *cursillo* is an intensive, emotionally packed weekend experience that brings participants into a very personal encounter with Jesus as the Lord and savior of their lives. It often produces a very profound conversion and change of life in the participants.) They may not write with scholarly precision, but the depth of their thought shines through the very simplicity of their expression. They may not all recount the experience of the *cursillo* in the same way, but they are definitely speaking about the same *cursillo*.

Jesus came into a world whose cultures, structures, values, priorities, ways of thinking, and even religions had been contaminated and deformed by sin. His own people had been enslaved, exiled, and colonized. They struggled with the many contradictions and conflicting tensions and aspirations of a colonized people. Should they fight for freedom? Should they simply assimilate to the more dominant and attractive Greco-Roman culture? Should they retreat to an ethnic enclave? There was another way no one else had thought about. Jesus did not come to put a bandage on a messed-up humanity but to initiate a totally new creation. And he would start his work through an identity and a social location that not even the devil, much less anyone else, would suspect anything good could come from! As the late biblical scholar Raymond Brown used to say, the God of the Bible is a God of incredible surprises.

"We have found the Messiah"—John 21

Since my earliest childhood, I have known *Jesús de Nazaret*. Still, appreciating the incredible ways in which he brings salvation to humanity continues to be a fabulous adventure. In seeking the divine meaning of the human events and circumstances, the simplicity of the Jesus stories as recorded in the gospels, I use several sources that have helped me to appreciate in a very personal way just what Jesus was saving us from, what he was liberating us from. Since God became human so that through his humanity he could lead us to the divine, or as St. Augustine puts it, "God was born human so that we humans could be reborn divine," I try to read the gospels as a human story that brings out aspects of our own human story that we have not suspected or that, because of sin, we do not want to hear. It is the human story of Jesus that illuminates our own story, revealing aspects of grace we have not perceived and of sinfulness we have not recognized.

As a pastor of forty years, I use some of the marvelous insights that I have gained over the years in gospel-reading groups with the poor Mexican American people of the great frontier between Mexico and the United States—the *mestizo* people of *la frontera*. I also use the *Jesús Nazareno* who is alive in the popular traditions of the people. As one who loves art and who likes to contemplate God as the supreme and most creative artist, I want not just to read the gospels but to try to look at the portraits of human reality that they present to us. I want to pay close attention to the picture presented by the words of the gospels, for I believe that the gospel pictures put living flesh on the realities presented by the words of the gospel stories.

As a Catholic I want to refer to the new catechism of the Catholic Church and other church documents as an anchor to help me establish some basic points. These documents bring together the wisdom of many generations of searching. As a scholar, I make use of the well-recognized critical works that have come out recently on the culture, society, religion, and philosophical trends of the time and land of Jesus. These works have provided a fascinating and invaluable stage-setting for reflections on Jesus of Nazareth.

Beyond all these marvelous sources, I have tried to rely deeply not on my own work but on the illuminating power of prayer and contemplation, for it is precisely in the silence before *El Santísimo* (the Blessed Sacrament), in the deep awareness of my own inadequacies in relation to the mystery of infinite love and wisdom, that the most beautiful insights have emerged, often too beautiful to find the words adequate to express them.

Finally, in reflecting upon some of the basic texts of the New Testament that have been especially powerful in my pastoral work, I want to state clearly what Third World, African American, and feminist biblical scholars present as basic to all serious historical and theological Jesus research: the critical articulation of the author's social location and how this affects and determines the historical-theological reconstruction of Jesus. I study, work, and reflect theologically from within my lifetime experience of being a *mestizo* Mexican American living and working in the predominantly poor Mexican sections of my city of San Antonio and among the Latin American poor of the United States. As a child growing up speaking Spanish in the United States, I was often ridiculed and laughed at because of the way I spoke English. I often felt shame in the many demeaning ways in which the mainline society and even our religion portrayed us. We had to live with the many ugly stereotypes that were promulgated in the jokes, slurs, social studies textbooks, and media. Many of our people were kept out of public places and refused service because of the color of our skin. For a full presentation of my social location I suggest you read my autobiographical account in *The Future Is Mestizo: Life Where Cultures Meet*.

"Emptied himself, taking the form of a servant"—Philippians 2:7

The more I read the New Testament narratives from the perspective of socially wounded men and women, the more I appreciate the words of Jesus: "No one has greater love than this: to lay down one's life for one's friends" (Jn 15:13). From his very conception, Jesus loved us so much that he totally laid down his life in many ways. He put aside all the prerogatives of his divine life and even of social life so as to totally enter into the disfigurement, degradation, and suffering caused by the sin of the world.

In becoming human, the Son of God simply became one among the many (Phil 2:6). We learn from Paul's first epistle to the Corinthians that most of the early Christians were not from the wise or well-born of this world. Studies on the first Christians indicate that they were mostly from the poor, servants, and disenfranchised of society. They who were considered nothing by the world, looked upon as the scum of society, found a new sense of dignity and fellowship in their fellow "nothing" who was now seen as the Lord of heaven and earth. God had installed as the Lord and savior of the world the very one who had been maligned and rejected by the builders of this world, by the powerful elites of society, and by the leaders of his religion. The rejected had become the founding stone of the new building.

In inspired hymns preceding any of the written pages of the New Testament, the first Christians joyfully and triumphantly proclaimed this fact. In what is considered one of the earliest inspired hymns of the Christian community (Phil 2:6ff.), the true earthly identity of Jesus is proclaimed. So as to enter into flesh and blood solidarity with the victims of the sin of the world, that is, with the slaves, servants, and "nobodies" of this world, he who was by nature of divine condition empties himself of all social rank and status and enters humanity in the form of a slave.

The various English translations state "in the likeness of man." I personally prefer the translation of the *Nueva Biblia Española*, which, after stating that he took on the condition of a slave, states "he became one among so many"—in other words, one of the multitude of slaves and servants of the world, one of those without dignity and considered of inferior human condition by the dominant sector of society. The one who had freely humbled himself by being born among the nobodies was further humiliated by his scandalous death on the cross. Yet because of his obedient resolve to live his entire life in an entirely new way, totally different from the ways of sin, every knee would bend at the mention of his name and proclaim that Jesus Christ is Lord and the glory of God (Phil 2:10–11). Only the power of love can defeat the powers of evil without introducing an even greater evil. Jesus was obedient in loving humanity until the bitter end, no matter the cost, no matter the sacrifice.

This "humiliation," which was recognized and proclaimed by the earliest followers of Jesus, is key to understanding how the life of Jesus functioned in a redeeming way from the very instant of his conception. The victims of sin are humiliated and ridiculed in various ways. They are robbed of their basic humanity. They are made to feel inferior and impure. Stereotypes are created to justify their subjugation, enslavement, and exploitation. They are often made to think that the only way to freedom and the fullness of human life is to become like the very people who have sinned against them. They think that the only way out of domination is to dominate others; the only way out of slavery is to enslave others; the only way out of exploitation is to exploit others; the only way to come out of inferiority is to make others inferior; the only way out of oppression is to become an oppressor. Thus the chain of sin is not broken, and evil continues to develop and spiral in the world.

In the man from Galilee, God becomes the exploited, inferior, impure, enslaved human being—not to approve of this condition and just make us feel good because we are crushed, but to lead us out of this destructive spiral of evil. His message is not a call to arms and revolution, for that will only produce new forms of violence. Rather, he becomes the victim of sin to break the bondage of sin, and it is out of the victims, the "stones rejected by the builders," that the new creation, the true humanity, will come about: "God was born human so that we humans might be reborn divine."—St. Augustine

(This article is a slightly revised version of chapters 1 and 2 of my *A God of Incredible Surprises: Jesus of Galilee* [New York: Rowman & Littlefield Publishers, Inc., 2003] and is printed with permission of publisher.)

Bibliography

Boff, Leonardo. *Jesus Christ Liberator: A Critical Christology for Our Time.* Maryknoll, NY: Orbis Books, 1979.

Catechism of the Catholic Church, 2nd ed. New York: Doubleday, 2003.

Elizondo, Virgilio. *The Future Is Mestizo: Life Where Cultures Meet.* Boulder: University of Colorado Press, 2000.

———. *Galilean Journey.* Maryknoll, NY: Orbis Books, 2000.

———. *Guadalupe: Mother of the New Creation.* Maryknoll, NY: Orbis Books, 1997.

———. *The Way of the Cross: The Passion of Christ in the Americas.* Maryknoll, NY: Orbis Books, 1992.

——— and Timothy Matovina. *San Fernando Cathedral: Soul of the City.* Maryknoll, NY: Orbis Books, 1998.

John Paul II. *Redemptor Hominis.* Papal Encyclical Letter, March 4, 1979. Vatican City: Editrice Vaticana, 1979.

Pelikan, Jaroslav. *Jesus through the Centuries: His Place in the History of Culture.* New York: Perennial Library, 1987.

Schokel, Luis Alonso. *The Literary Language of the Bible: The Collected Essays of Luis Alonso Schökel.* Bibal Collected Essays, vol. 3. N. Richland Hills, TX: D & F Scott, 2001.

4

MEETING AND SEEING JESUS

THE WITNESS OF AFRICAN AMERICAN RELIGIOUS EXPERIENCE

M. Shawn Copeland

The story of Jesus of Nazareth, his life, ministry, and brutal murder, formed a key text for enslaved Africans in reconfiguring their religio-cultural life. Betrayed either by members of their own communities or hostile neighbors, and captured, chained, and force-marched to the Atlantic coast, various peoples of West Africa including the Igbo, Bini, Fante, Mende, Yoruba, and BaKongo found themselves first in dark, foul dungeons and then on board ships bound for another world.[1] Once the vessels set out to sea, the Africans endured filth, severe beatings, sexual assault, and immeasurable psychic trauma. Statistics suggest that from 15 to 30 percent of the captives died in "the middle passage."[2]

"From Boston in New England to Montevideo in the Viceroyalty of La Plata," the Africans found themselves scattered throughout the Americas:

> in gold-mining towns in central Brazil; on sugar cane planta-
> tions in Jamaica and Cuba; in the coffee-producing hills of
> Venezuela; on cotton and indigo estates in the southern re-
> gions of the USA; and in homes, streets, rivers, fields and even
> small factories everywhere in between, Africans and their de-
> scendants, in generations of bondage, encountered and helped
> create the New World.[3]

Denied inclusion in the category of "person," the enslaved people had neither legal nor political rights and endured the constant threat of psychological, bodily, and familial violation. The various forms of slavery that they confronted aimed to control, possess, and dominate, but just as often sought to reduce incarnate spirit to property, commodity, and object.[4] "This expectation, violently enforced, was in unremitting tension with the Africans' own sense of who they actually were."[5]

To negotiate this tension, the enslaved people reconfigured their religio-cultural world, thus asserting their humanity in the midst of a fundamentally inhuman situation. They found a way to reconfigure the African sacred cosmos.

This essay is about that reconfiguration and the meaning of Jesus of Nazareth within it. While Christianity never exhausted historical black or African American religious faith, sensibilities, and practices, it offered a protean path for individual and communal survival and remains an avenue with which to reckon. The first and lengthiest section considers the collapse or fragmentation of the African sacred cosmos, that is, the collapse or fragmenting of an interpretative order of values and meanings that constituted and explained peoples and their worldviews to themselves and to others. The encounter of culturally diverse African religious consciousness and dominative European and American interpretations of Christianity yielded black religion. The phrase "black religion" serves as a heuristic in grappling with religious exchange, change, adaptation, and reconfiguration among the enslaved peoples.[6] Thus, as a phenomenon, black religion emerges from culturally diverse creative engagement as well as from interculturality as the brutal encounter of African cultures with Christianized cultures of the Americas.

The second section attends to the encounter of the enslaved people with the Bible and adverts to their process of canonization or producing an "oral text." The third section sketches the origin of the spirituals or sorrow psalms, the "oldest extant religio-cultural form in Black North American life."[7] These songs are simple, yet not simplistic, possessing what African American Catholic liturgist Clarence Rivers called "magnitude."[8] Further, historian Sterling Stuckey cautions against detaching the spirituals from their life setting or religio-cultural context; these psalms form an integral part of the larger and complex matrix of black religious experience and expression.[9]

The first three sections of this essay are archaeological in that they retrieve the past in order to allow us to tease out some meanings of Jesus of Nazareth from the spirituals in the fourth section.

Collapse and Reconfiguration: "Black" Religion

Precise figures will never be known, but several million Africans were betrayed, kidnapped, and sold into slavery during the four centuries of the transatlantic trade in the bodies of children, women, and men. Each of these human beings was a member of a specific cultural-linguistic group. Each of these human beings was wrapped tightly in a religio-cultural web that governed rites of passage, festivals, kinship, marriage, social status, birth, funeral rites, relation to environment and topography, land, ethical concerns and behavior, healing practices, didactic and oral traditions, arts, trades, crafts, responsibilities, and authority. Each of these groups manifested the richness of human diversity on the continent of Africa.

At the same time, members of these particular groups intermarried, conducted trade and commerce, and cooperated (or not) in various social, cultural, and practical activities. Beneath and in the midst of diversity lay common or similar modes of religious and moral apprehension, patterns of worship, and aesthetic values—intercultural engagement. Thus, it is possible to speak of African religion in the singular and to emphasize a common outlook regarding the cosmos.[10] Indeed, Ghanaian Africanist Dale Massiasta argues that African religion constitutes a body of truths founded on the spiritual experiences, ideas, beliefs, and practices of African wisdom, mysticism, and humanism.[11]

The African cosmos was in every aspect sacred. Religion permeated every dimension of human life. The whole of the universe radiated the forces of the sacred—the Supreme Deity, lesser divinities, the Ancestors, and spirits. Ordinary and extraordinary daily activities, human encounters and relationships as well as natural phenomena were suffused with religious understandings and meanings. Ritual observances celebrated and commemorated various moments of human existence and accorded the highest expression to communal life. Above all, the African sacred cosmos accorded a most esteemed and honored place to the Ancestors, who in death remain intimately and actively connected to the living—intervening in daily affairs and dispensing blessings or punishments.

For enslaved Africans, the unraveling of the religio-cultural web and the collapse of the sacred cosmos began with seizure. The captives were described by whites, who saw them as "sad, depressed, in shock," showing "every sign of affliction," despondency, despair, and "torpid insensibility."[12] En route, the people would have been compelled to transgress religio-cultural laws and customs that regulated personal modesty, contact between men and women, care of children. They would have had to endure handling, beatings, torture, and sexual assault.

Slavery was not uniform but, rather, in each place it was shaped by necessity, economics, topography, climate, and human temperament. In the United States, slavery was never exclusively southern; slaveholding was practiced in Connecticut, Massachusetts, New York, and New Jersey, and slave shipbuilding thrived in Newport, Rhode Island, just as it did in Liverpool, England.[13] Slaveholders interrupted and controlled any gesture of psychic or interpersonal or cultural independence. They named their human chattel, denied them use of their languages, forbade them to honor their customs or worship their gods. Few slaveholders permitted stable marriages, toddlers were as likely to be sold as adults, and pregnant women were not exempt from beatings. On some geographically isolated farms or plantations, the enslaved people exerted some control over the affairs of their daily living, although not over their *lives* and *persons*. Workdays, whether spent in fields or in house settings, were long and enervating. Still, the people shared and shaped, preserved and transmitted practices and attitudes reflective of their African-derived social structures and religio-cultural traditions.

Historians Albert Raboteau, Mechal Sobel, and John Blassingame[14] have documented the ambiguous attitudes and behavior of slaveholders toward the religious lives of the enslaved people. Spanish colonists, who established a foothold in 1565 in what is now northern Florida, routinely baptized enslaved Africans into the Roman Catholic Church and prepared them for the reception of sacraments. Less than a century later, despite the objections of clergy, Anglo-American Protestant slaveholders demonstrated considerable reluctance at the notion of baptizing enslaved people. On some plantations, the enslaved people attended white churches, sitting or standing in designated areas; on other plantations, they were punished severely for praying and singing. On other plantations, a white minister was assigned to preach to the enslaved people, while on still other plantations they were permitted to hold unsupervised praise meetings that were sometimes led by a "slave" preacher. In other situations, the people withdrew to woods, gullies, and thickets (called brush arbors or "hush arbors") to pray and sing. In such tentative and tensive privacy, the enslaved people created the spirituals; reconfigured and adapted African customs and spiritual practices of shouting, moaning, spirit possession, and dance, and, not infrequently, prepared for escape and strategized for rebellion.

Yet, Anglo-American Christianity, as the preaching of salvation in Jesus, had a decisive impact on the enslaved people. In turn, these men and women shaped and "fitted" Christian practices, rituals, symbols, myths, and values to their own particular social experiences, expectations, and needs.[15] At the same time, because so much of the intimate life of the enslaved people—their feelings and hopes, desires and aspirations—were hidden from the master class, indeed, from nearly all whites, it is not possible to pronounce with any certainty the burial of the African gods and the complete disappearance of African religion. However, what the people came to pass on to their descendants may be named "black" or African American religion.

The term "black religion" expresses the enslaved people's creative blending and fusing of remembered wholes or fragments of various rituals and practices from the canons of African religion. Black religion manifested a refined mystical grasp of the forms and the presence of the sacred on this side of the Atlantic, profound sorrow over loss of contact with the Ancestors who could not travel across the boundary, and adaptation of symbols from Anglo-American Christianity. While the extent to which enslaved peoples preserved and transmitted their religio-cultural traditions and practices remains controversial, scholars acknowledge that African-derived religio-cultural traditions, rituals, and practices form the bedrock of African American cultural and religious expression. Black religion, then, is a phenomenological rather than a denominational heuristic. Africa and African retentions hold a more or less normative status, while Christianity furnished language, images, and symbols by which the enslaved peoples interpreted their condition and its meanings.[16]

Further, the word "black" is *not deployed* as an adjective; it neither modifies nor adorns. Rather it demarcates a dense horizon of meaning and value—a black worldview. Thus, the term, "black" is retrieved from negatory usage; and, although the term connotes "opaqueness," the transcendent reality as grasped and experienced *is* awe-filled, holy, mystery; the reality as expressed *is* ecstatic, joyous, creative.[17] At the same time, black religion is a quite modern term. Its poignant advent was heralded by exploration, enslavement, coloniality; its provenance is modernity. It insinuates alienation, erosion, and rupture, even as it signifies restoration, recollection of "root paradigms,"[18] and cultural re-memory or continuity of meaning, world, and identity[19] in order to nurture and sustain black religious consciousness and to ground a new black sacred cosmos.

The Bible: Forming an "Oral" Text

Prior to the preaching associated with the Great Awakening and the evangelizing mission of the Baptists and Methodists, enslaved people demonstrated interest in Christianity. In the early eighteenth century, slaveholders began to argue that Christian baptism might better equip the enslaved people to accept their fate. In this effort, the Bible was used to legitimate and to sacralize perpetual bondage. Womanist ethicist Katie Cannon argues that three ideological notions supported the exegetical strategies of slaveholding apologists: (1) the charge that the enslaved Africans were not human, (2) the claim that God

had foreordained black people to a life of subjugation and servitude
to white people, and (3) the assumption that because the Bible does
not expressly prohibit the buying and selling of human flesh, slavery
was not a breach of divine law.[20]

Theologian Riggins Earl writes that some plantation clerics, such
as Bishop Meade, presented Jesus to slave masters as the servant-of-servants. Meade declared that Jesus "chose the form of a servant and became the servant-of-servants, illustrating [the] blessed doctrine [of slav-
ery] by his own meek, patient, suffering life."[21] Since Jesus was
"faultless in word and deed toward those in bondage," slaveholders
were to imitate him by perfect behavior toward those whom they held
in slavery. Further, since Jesus was presented as meek and humble, enslaved women and men were urged to imitate him by accepting their
enslavement meekly and humbly, without protest, for it was by God's
divine will that were to be slaves. In this way, the person of Jesus was
used to legitimate slavery.

Yet, their massive and protracted suffering and utter poverty—dispossessed of their very bodies—accorded the enslaved people a privileged hermeneutical stance. They turned a critical eye on the Christianity of the slaveholders.[22] In the slave narratives, one former enslaved
man offers this report:

> I often heard select portions of the Scriptures read...On Sun-
> day we always had one sermon prepared expressly for the
> coloured people...So great was the similarity of texts that
> they are always fresh in memory: "Servants, be obedient to
> your masters, not with eye-service, as men-pleasers." "He that
> knoweth his master's will and doeth it not, shall be beaten
> with many stripes"; and [verses] of this [type]...One very
> kind-hearted clergyman...was very popular with the coloured
> people. But after he had preached a sermon from the Bible that
> it was the will of Heaven from all eternity that we should be
> slaves, and our masters be our owners many of us left...consid-
> ering, like the doubting disciple of old, "This is a hard saying,
> who can hear it."[23]

Despite such frequent eisegesis, the Bible came to occupy a central
place in the religions of the African diaspora. In the religious experience and practices of the enslaved people and in the historic and independent black churches of the Americas and the Caribbean, biblical
stories, themes, characters, sayings, and images have given meaning

and hope to the struggle of black women and men for emancipation, liberation, and self-realization in this world and triumphant life in the next.

Since enslaved Africans were prohibited *de jure* and *de facto* from learning to read and/or to write, they gained knowledge of the content, message, and meaning of the Bible through public readings and sermons.[24] Slaves caught or reported as writing or reading were penalized and sometimes mutilated by having a finger cut off.[25] Still, the people persisted, often with the help of someone who had learned to read surreptitiously or someone who was willing to breach the laws against their literacy. But with or without such help, the people took confidence in their own determination and skill, and some among them memorized chapters or portions of the Bible. These spoken fragments or passages became the subject of meditation, reflection, and sermonic interpretation. Indeed, biblical revelation provided the enslaved people with material for the singular mystical and political mediation of their condition—the spirituals.[26]

The oral transmission of the Bible contributed to the reconfiguring of the religious and cultural lives of the enslaved people and the Bible came under their creative rhetorical and poetic genius. Through prayer, sermon, and song, the enslaved Africans discerned their communal exegetical situation and unmasked the exegetical situation of members of the plantocracy, the master class. Thus, the enslaved people developed a tradition of African American interpretation. As Hebrew Bible scholar Renita Weems observes:

> since slave communities were illiterate, they were, therefore, without allegiance to any official text, translation, or interpretation; hence once they heard biblical passages read and interpreted to them, they in turn were free to remember and repeat in accordance with their own interests and tastes... [F]or those raised within an aural culture retelling the Bible became one hermeneutical strategy, and resistance to the Bible, or portions of it, would become another.[27]

The people formed what womanist theologian Delores Williams calls an "oral text," a life-affirming canon. The composition of the oral text was a communal process. From among biblical texts preached in sermons or passages read aloud at (white) family prayers, members of the enslaved community apprehended, evaluated, judged, and selected life-affirming texts. These were memorized, repeated, and reshaped;

purged of malicious meanings, these passages became the subject of meditation, reflection, and sermonic interpretation among the enslaved people. As Weems pointed out, the people were not tied intellectually or morally to any particular written text or translation or interpretation; the oral text they developed revealed affinities with the prophetic and apocalyptic traditions of the Hebrew and Christian Scriptures. These passages or stories or sayings were handed down from generation to generation, through story and song and moral prescription. These texts were judged as the *true* word of God in the Bible.

In the context of enslavement and colonialism, the Bible became a site of contestation about the religious, cultural, and social meaning of Africans and their descendants in the Americas.[28] At the same time, because they were a people dispossessed of land, the Bible as oral text became for them what historian of religions Charles Long calls a *topos*. In other words, the Bible became for the enslaved people and their descendants in the Americas "an intimate and familiar place . . . a place that one's ancestors [knew and] humanized," "a [place of] wisdom for coming generations."[29] The Bible became a place where they might meet and see Jesus.[30]

The Spirituals

Poet and literary critic James Weldon Johnson believed that many spirituals were the work of highly gifted individuals. On the other hand, novelist and folklorist Zora Neale Hurston maintained that the spirituals are "Negro religious songs, sung by a group, and a group bent on expression of feelings and not on sound effects."[31] When asked about the composition of their religious songs, enslaved men and women often replied: "The Lord just puts the song in our mouth. We are not schooled, and the Lord puts every word we sing in our mouth."[32] When this question was put to a freedwoman from Kentucky, she insisted that the words of the spirituals were sung to traditional African tunes and familiar songs.

> We older folks would make them up on the spur of the moment, after we wrestled with the Spirit and come through. But the tunes were brought from Africa by our grandfathers. They were just familiar songs. They called them spirituals because the Holy Spirit revealed them to us. Some folks say that Master Jesus taught them to us, but I have seen them start in [prayer] meetings. We would all be in the praise house on Sunday and the white preacher would explain the word and read

where Ezekiel says, "Dry bones going to live again." And, honey, the Lord would come shining through those pages and revive this old woman's heart. I would jump up then and there and shout and sing and clap and the others would catch the words and they all take up the words and keep adding to it and then it would be a spiritual.[33]

A spiritual took form in the moaned or sung utterance of an enslaved African in the Americas in response to or about a given social or religious experience that had communal and/or universal application.[34] In and through song, one man's or one woman's experience of sorrow or shout of jubilation became that of a people. And, without a doubt, the spirituals are gifts of the Spirit.

In creation and performance, the spirituals are marked by flexibility, spontaneity, and improvisation. The pattern of call-response allowed for the rhythmic weaving or manipulation of time, text, and pitch, while the response or repetitive chorus provided a recognizable and stable foundation for the extemporized lines of the soloist or leader.[35] Moreover, the creation and performance of the spirituals were nourished by the African disposition for aesthetic performance—for *doing* the beautiful—in dance and song.

The spirituals give access to the "experience[s], expression[s], motivations, intentions, behaviors, styles, and rhythms" of black religio-cultural life.[36] They are a window on the religious, social, aesthetic, and psychological worldview of a people. They are best appreciated when we imagine them, not concertized with dissonances "ironed out," but moaned in jagged irregular harmony, falsetto breaking in and keys changing with emotion.[37] Further, the spiritual is linked most intimately to the staid shuffling of the ring-shout. A distinct form of worship, the ring-shout is basically a dancing-singing phenomenon in which the song is *danced* with the whole body—hands, feet, shoulders, hips. When the spiritual is sounded, the ring-shout begins. The dancers form a circle and move counter-clockwise in a ring, first by walking slowly, then literally by shuffling—the foot just slightly lifted from the floor. Sometimes the people danced silently; most often they sang the chorus of the spiritual as they shuffled; at other times, the dancers themselves sang the song. Frequently, a group of the best singers stood at the side of the room to "base" the others, singing the stanzas of the song and clapping their hands. The dancing and singing would increase in intensity and energy and sometimes went on for hours.[38]

The language employed in the spirituals is intensely poetic and expressive, decorative and poignant. The vocabulary is filled with vivid simile, creative and effective juxtaposition of images and metaphor. Rooted in the historical experience of oppression, this highly charged symbolic language is most fundamentally a language of joy and mysticism in the midst of survival and resistance. The singers drew selectively on material from the Old and New Testaments, the Hebrew and Christian Scriptures. In the spirituals, salvation history takes place before our very eyes and we are included in it. The spirituals dialogue with the Scriptures, laying the cultural, religious, and social experiences of the enslaved peoples beside those of the Hebrews, with the same expectation that the Lord God of Hosts would deliver and comfort them. In the mode of midrash, the spirituals reshape, re-tell, and associate characters and stories, parables, events, and miracles from discrete books and passages of the Hebrew and Christian Scriptures. The songs tell the mercy of God and testify to the ways in which the enslaved people met God in the slave quarter, at the whipping post, on the auction block, in the hush arbor, in the midnight flight to freedom.

"Meeting and Seeing" Jesus

Given the brutal and brutalizing conditions of enslavement, the people's appeals to supernatural power or divine omnipotence are not surprising. Indeed, the story of the deliverance of the people of Israel from Egyptian enslavement "became an archetype which enabled the [enslaved people] to live with promise."[39] Over time, the enslaved people came to understand the Christian God as an omnipotent and moral deity who is responsible for creation and who intervenes in history; at the same time, they came to respond to formal Christian Trinitarian discourse with an experiential distinction.[40] While praising the "Great Supreme Being, who stood by them in the past days of slavery,"[41] the enslaved people and their descendants found a friend, companion, and fellow sufferer in Jesus Christ. He embodied the "notion of the deity as companion and creator, a deity related more to the human condition than deities of the sky, and the subjection of this deity in the hands of human beings."[42]

Thus, in the encounter with Christianity, the story of Jesus gripped the imaginations of the enslaved peoples. They took Jesus to themselves; the innocence, the agony, and the cruelty of his suffering were like their own. They met Jesus' compassion with compassion, they met his love with love; in the paradox and promise of his life, they found a means to express the paradox and promise of their own lives. To borrow a compelling image offered by one freed man, perhaps, we may say that Jesus "hooked [them] in the heart."[43]

Jesus stands at the center of the "oral text": touching, healing, and accompanying the enslaved people. They sang: He is "rock in a weary land," a "shelter in a storm," and "a little talk with Jesus makes it right." Jesus was the fellow sufferer whose healing touch soothed the burning ache of their salted wounds; he was the companion who wrapped his arms tightly around bodies drenched in sweat from hard work; he was the friend who kissed their hands torn and bruised from cutting sugar cane or picking cotton. Jesus consoled mothers whose children were sold away; he stood in seething anger beside men whose wives and daughters were raped; he wept hot tears with children whose parents were humiliated. Jesus was the companion who stood by them in the midst of affliction and restored their dignity. No wonder the maker of the spiritual sang: "I want Jesus to walk with me / All along my pilgrim journey / Lord, I want Jesus to walk with me. In my trials, Lord walk with me / When my heart is almost breaking, Lord, I want Jesus to walk with me." Jesus is the comforter in time of trouble and in the most intimate moments of anguish. Thus the spiritual cries, "Give me Jesus, Give me Jesus, You may have all this world, Give me Jesus."

Like the excluded, despised, and poor who crowd the pages of the gospels, the enslaved folk relied on, leaned on Jesus. Like African sacred medicine (*Kongo nkisi*), the very name of Jesus brought relief and delight: "I love Jesus for his name's so sweet / I'm just now from the fountain, His name's so sweet"; "Jesus Christ is first and last, No man works like him"; "Fix me, Jesus, fix me"; "I know the Lord has laid his hands on me." The enslaved people saw themselves, read themselves, or inscribed themselves on the pages of the Bible. Jesus was for them! Jesus placed his very body between the despised, excluded, and poor and the powers and principalities of the world. The excluded sensed the "otherness" of Jesus; he too was a stranger in a world of death and oppression.

The Gullah-speaking people of the Sea Islands, which extend along the coast of South Carolina and Georgia, exemplify the African tradition in the Americas of determined creativity, shaping, preservation, and transmission of religio-cultural life. Their Moving Star Hall Singers have recorded "Meet Me in Galilee" in a manner consonant with the original singing.[44] The biblical text of the song comes from the post-resurrection scene in Matthew 28:1–10. The women disciples who have followed Jesus make their way to the tomb of Jesus. Mary Magdalene and "the other Mary" see an angel who tells them that Jesus "has been raised from the dead, and indeed he is going ahead of you to Galilee; there you will see him" (vv. 5–7). The angel urges the women to go quickly and tell the men. When Jesus himself meets the two women he tells them, "Do not be afraid. Go and tell my brothers to go to Galilee; there they will see me" (vv. 9–10).

The singers work the song as a conditional dialogue:

Oh Mary, O Lord, if you want to see me / Meet me in Galilee.
Oh, tell me Mary / Ay Lord / If you want to see me / Meet me
    in Galilee. Oh Just roll the stone away / Oh Lord / If you
    want to see me / Meet me in Galilee.
Oh, he promised us / Oh Lord / Tell my disciples / Meet me
    in Galilee.
If you want to meet me / Ay Lord / Want to see me / Meet me
    in Galilee.

Faith in and friendship with Jesus are conditions for the journey, conditions for seeing him.

In the context of the spirituals, Galilee is the "home country of Jesus and his friends—slaves in the front ranks—and the meeting place of the faithful."[45] If, as scholars have concluded, Galilee was a place of mixed race and ethnicity, of startling cultural diversity, then the enslaved people and their descendants would be reassured. They too were and are women and men of mixed race and ethnicity, of startling cultural diversity.[46] If, as scholars suggest, the villagers of lower Galilee were skilled artisans, carpenters, blacksmiths, and stonemasons; laborers and workers, small farmers or sharecroppers, and fishermen; often large and extended families, kinfolk, and friends, then the enslaved people and their descendants would feel quite secure: they too were and are people of many and diverse skills, talents, interests, and forms of training; they too were and are people of diverse class and social standing; they too love their families and kin and friends.[47] If, as scholars contend, the villagers of lower Galilee resisted Roman political interference and yearned for freedom from occupation and expropriation, then the enslaved people and their descendants would be encouraged. They too loved and continue to love freedom, to stand poised in its defense, to resist transgressions of liberty and life.[48] The Galilee of this historical reconstruction resonates with the Galilee of the spirituals.

"Meet me in Galilee" suggests that Mary or the singer must travel to see Jesus. Those who strike out on this journey walk by faith, not by sight. Those who follow Jesus know that to be his disciple means to walk in the "way" he lived and taught. Perhaps the stone to be rolled away connotes doubt or moral failure and sin, or perhaps the stone insinuates surrender to paths of indifference and least resistance, to complicity with the evils of slavery.

But heading out for Galilee also suggests that something or someone is left behind. Certainly many of the enslaved people recognized how pernicious slavery was—nesting in the heart and mind and destroying potential for personhood. The spirituals sang of running away:

Run, Mary, run / Run, Mary, run I say / You got a right to the
   tree of life.
You got a right, you got a right / You got a right to the tree
   of life.
Little Mary you got a right / Hebrew children got a right
Weeping Mary, you got a right / You got a right to the tree
   of life.
Cross is heavy, but you got a right / Children gone, but you got
   a right
You got a right to the tree of life.[49]

Run; run to Galilee. Run away; run to safety, run for life, run to life. Run after the North Star. Spirituals throw out a holy lifeline that "strengthens, blesses, and animates being."[50] Run to Jesus, he is freedom; he is the tree of life.

Freedom was the preeminent theme of black religion, and the enslaved people prayed sincerely for freedom. Alice Sewell recalled that the people in the area where she lived "prayed for [this day] of freedom. We [traveled] four and five miles to pray together to God that if we don't live to see it, to please let our [children] live to see a better day and be free."[51] Mrs. Sewell offers an astonishing testimony to the transcendent dimension of human beings. Enslaved women and men prayed for a different future for their children. The unselfishness of such prayer shines as a witness to hope, since the vast majority of the millions Africans enslaved in the Americas died in the bondage in which they had lived. The freedom for which enslaved people prayed proved impatient of political *or* social *or* spiritual *or* religious distinctions; rather, the freedom for which the people longed, struggled, fought, and died was holistic—at once political *and* social, psychic *and* spiritual, metaphysical *and* ontological, this-worldly *and* other-worldly.[52]

The enslaved people understood Jesus Christ as the Bringer of Freedom. Thus, long before the seminal theological studies of Ernst Käsemann or James Cone or Gustavo Gutiérrez, oppressed black people in the United States knew in mind and heart that Jesus *meant* freedom, Jesus *was* freedom.[53] They formulated this christological affirmation on the basis of their critical grasp of the Bible (oral text) and the qualities of skill and wisdom; spiritedness, courage, and love for the weak expressed in their culture.[54] But, as Howard Thurman observed, "It was dangerous to let the slave understand that the life and teachings of Jesus meant freedom for the captive and release for those held in economic, social, and political bondage."[55] A fearless and dangerous Jesus, unlike the "model servant," would break the crippling spell cast by the dominative culture. A fearless and dangerous Jesus would set the Spirit working free in the midst of those yearning to be free. A fearless and dangerous Jesus would be waiting for God's black people in Galilee.

Conclusion

African American culture reverberates with religious signification. While Christianity does not exhaust that signification, it has provided African Americans with a remarkable "orientation" toward ultimate meaning, that is, with a way for them to negotiate or come to terms with the world, and with a language for interpreting and expressing the meanings of that orientation.[56] Yet, that orientation or the appropriation of Christian faith that resulted was costly purchase. Any adequate understanding of black religion must account for (1) the religious, cultural, and social (i.e., political, economic, and technological) situation of the United States, (2) the multiple intercultural encounters of captive and enslaved Africans with one another, (3) the "distinctive culture" created in the United States from this forced intercultural contact, and (4) the perverse, pervasive, and persistent "situation of oppression and duress" to which the enslaved people were subordinated as they dealt with those realities.[57]

This essay assumes that the cultures of Africans in the Americas emerge from intercultural contact among themselves as well as with the cultures of Europeans and North Americans.[58] This process of intercultural contact began in duress; damage and destruction may not have been premeditated, but soon became predictable. Retrieval of the multiple distinct cultural contributions to African American culture is not possible, yet hints and fragments of ancient peoples surface in unintentional bodily phrasing, gestures, and comportment; in rhythms, vernacular expressions, and style. Diasporic Africans in the United States incarnate and signify interculturality. The profound encounter of our Ancestors with Jesus of Nazareth calls us to align ourselves with his preaching and his goal of a human order free of oppression and domination. If we would see him in Galilee, we must first meet him in excluded, despised, and poor children, women, and men of our time.

Notes

1. See Marcus Rediker, *The Slave Ship: A Human History* (New York: Viking Press, 2007).

2. Philip Curtin, *The Atlantic Slave Trade: A Census* (Madison: University of Wisconsin Press, 1969), 275. This rate varies in relation to the nation operating or backing the merchant slave ship. For example, Curtin notes that in the earliest years of the trade, the casualty rate suffered by Africans on Portuguese vessels was about 15 percent, but after "nineteenth-century abolitionist pressure forced the slave-traders to take chances, the casualty rate rose to 25 to 30 percent" (276).

3. Rachel Elizabeth Harding, "You Got a Right to the Tree of Life: African American Spirituals and Religions of the Diaspora," *CrossCurrents* 57, 2 (Summer 2007): 268–69.

4. See Page du Bois, *Slaves and Other Objects* (Chicago and London: University of Chicago Press, 2003).

5. Harding, "You Got a Right to the Tree of Life," 269.

6. For a timely, thorough, and demanding study of black religion, see Anthony B. Pinn, *Terror and Triumph: The Nature of Black Religion* (Minneapolis: Fortress Press, 2003).

7. Harding, "You Got a Right to the Tree of Life," 268–69.

8. Clarence Joseph Rivers, *The Spirit in Worship* (Cincinnati: Stimuli, Inc., 1978), 199.

9. Sterling Stuckey, *Slave Culture: Nationalist Theory and the Foundations of Black America* (New York: Oxford University Press, 1987), 27.

10. See John S. Mbiti, *African Religions and Philosophy*, 2nd ed. (Oxford: Heinemann, 1989) for an excellent discussion of African religion or *Nzambisme*; see Bienvenu Mayemba, SJ, "Christian Liberation and Postcolonial Consciousness: Jean-Marc Ela's Reappropriation of African Subjectivity and Christian Promise" (Ph. D. diss., Boston College, 2010).

11. Dale Massiasta, "Basic Concepts and Practices" in *Indigenous African Religion*, available at http://www.hypertextile.net/BLAKHUD/ind-reli/index.htm (accessed July 4, 2010).

12. Rediker, *The Slave Ship*, 17.

13. Ibid., 50–53.

14. Albert J. Raboteau, *Slave Religion: The "Invisible Institution" in the Antebellum South* (1978; Oxford: Oxford University Press, 2004); Mechal Sobel, *Trabelin' On: The Slave Journey to an Afro-Baptist Faith* (Princeton: Princeton University Press, 1979); and John W. Blassingame, *The Slave Community: Plantation Life in the Antebellum South* (1972; New York: Oxford University Press, 1979).

15. Raboteau, *Slave Religion*, 213.

16. See Joseph E. Holloway, ed., *Africanisms in American Culture* (Bloomington: Indiana University Press, 1990).

17. See Charles H. Long, "Structural Similarities and Dissimilarities in Black and African Theologies," *The Journal of Religious Thought* 32, 2 (Fall/Winter 1975): 14, 21.

18. Victor W. Turner, *Dramas, Fields, and Metaphors: Symbolic Action in Human Society* (Ithaca, NY: Cornell University Press, 1975), 67, 163.

19. Jan Assmann, *Religion and Cultural Memory*, trans. Rodney Livingstone (Stanford: Stanford University Press, 2006), 37.

20. Katie Geneva Cannon, "Slave Ideology and Biblical Interpretation," *Semeia*, 49 (1989): 9–24.

21. Riggins R. Earl, *Dark Symbols, Obscure Signs: God, Self, and Community in the Slave Mind* (Maryknoll, NY: Orbis Books, 1993), 33.

22. This point is also made by Arthur C. Jones, *Wade in the Water: The Wisdom of the Spirituals* (Maryknoll, NY: Orbis Books, 1993), 69–70, and John Lovell, *Black Song: The Forge and the Flame: How the Afro-American Spiritual Was Hammered Out* (New York: Macmillan, 1972), 191–92. This work is the classic and comprehensive treatment of the spiritual.

23. Martha Washington Creel, "Community Regulation and Cultural Specialization in Gullah Folk Religion," in *Africanisms in American Culture*, ed. Joseph E. Holloway (Bloomington: Indiana University Press, 1990), 51.

24. See Allen D. Callahan, *The Talking Book: African Americans and the Bible* (New Haven: Yale University Press, 2006).

25. See Lovell, *Black Song*, 257; also Janet Duitsman Cornelius, *When I Can Read My Title Clear: Literacy, Slavery, and Religion in the Antebellum South* (Columbia: University of South Carolina Press, 1991).

26. James Weldon Johnson, ed., *The Book of American Negro Spirituals* (New York: Viking Press, 1925), 20.

27. Renita J. Weems, "African American Women and the Bible," 61, in *Stony the Road We Trod: African American Biblical Interpretation*, ed. Cain Hope Felder (Minneapolis: Fortress Press, 1991).

28. Cheryl Townsend Gilkes, "Colonialism and the Biblical Revolution in Africa," *The Journal of Religious Thought* 41, 2 (Fall–Winter 1984–1985): 62.

29. Long, "Structural Similarities and Dissimilarities in Black and African Theologies," 12, 13.

30. Of course, the Bible was/is not such a *topos* for *all* black people, as womanists Weems and Delores Williams, among others, argue. Black women were also subjected to repressive treatment in church and society by biblical sanction and interpretation; see Delores S. Williams, *Sister in the Wilderness: The Challenge of Womanist God-Talk* (Maryknoll, NY: Orbis Books, 1993).

31. Zora Neale Hurston, *The Sanctified Church* (Berkeley, CA: Turtle Island, 1983), 80.

32. M. V. Bales, "Some Negro Folk Songs of Texas," 85, in *Follow De Drinkin' Gou'd*, ed. James Dobie (Austin: Texas Folklore Society, 1928): "De Lord jes' put hit en our mouf. We is ignorant, and de Lord puts ebry word we says en our mouf."

33. "Us ole head use ter make 'em on de spurn of de moment, after we wressle wid de Spirit and come thoo. But the tunes was brung from Africa by

our grandaddies. Dey was jis 'miliar song...dey calls 'em spirituals, case de Holy Spirit done revealed 'em to 'em. Some say Moss Jesus taught 'em, and I's seed 'em start in meetin'. We'd all be at the 'prayer house' de Lord's Day and de white preacher he'd splain de word and read whar Ezekiel done say, "Dry bones gwine ter lib again." And, honey, de Lord would come a-shining thoo dem pages and revive dis ole [woman's] heart, and I'd jump up dar and den and holler and shout and sing and pat, and dey would all cotch de words...dey's all take it up and keep at it, and keep a-addin to it and den it would be a spiritual" (cited in Raboteau, *Slave Religion*, 244–45).

34. Mark Fisher, *Negro Slave Songs in the United States* (New York: Citadel Press, Inc., 1953), 176.

35. Portia K. Maultsby, "Africanisms in African-American Music," in *Africanisms in American Culture*, ed. Joseph E. Holloway (Bloomington: Indiana University Press, 1990), 193.

36. Charles H. Long, *Significations: Signs, Symbols, and Images in the Interpretation of Religion* (Philadelphia: Fortress, 1986), 7.

37. Hurston, *The Sanctified Church*, 80. LeRoi Jones points out that the "rhythmic syncopation, polyphony, and shifted accents, as well as the altered timbral qualities and diverse vibrato effects of African music were all used by the Negro to transform most of the 'white hymns' into Negro spirituals" (*Blues People: Negro Music in White America* [New York: William Morrow Publishers, 1963], 47).

38. Hurston, *The Sanctified Church*, 70–71. The ring-shout persists in the worship of Africans in the Americas—those living in the small islands off the coasts of Georgia and the Carolinas and in Brazil in the rituals of *Candomblé*, the traditional religion of the West African Yoruba. New York-based folk artist Reginald Wilson directs the Reginald Wilson/Fist and Heel Performance Group, which preserves this and other African-derived ritual performances. In 1993, Wilson was invited to conduct a seminar at the Institute for Black Catholic Studies, Xavier University, on the ring-shout. After a lecture and breathing and body exercises, Wilson led a group of students and faculty in prayerful engagement with this centuries-old holy dance.

39. Long, *Significations*, 179.

40. I agree with Long that the enslaved people drew on Christian language to express their grasp and understanding of their religious experience and to re-configure their religious sensibilities. Long refers to the Trinity from the perspective of personal religious experience or "modalities of experience of the Trinity" (180). At the same time, neither Long nor I are making a formal modalist argument regarding the Trinity. I do not wish to be misunderstood: I do not endorse or adhere to any modalist understanding of the Trinity.

41. Esau Jenkins, *Been in the Storm So Long: A Collection of Spirituals, Folk Tales and Children's Games from Johns Island, South Carolina*, Folkways Smithsonian, (1966–67; Audio CD January 1990).

42. Long, *Significations*, 184, n. 15.

43. Clifton H. Johnson, ed., *God Struck Me Dead: Voices of Ex-Slaves* (Cleveland: The Pilgrim Press, 1969), 19.

44. *Been in the Storm So Long,* transcription from *Sing Out,* vol. 14, no. 2 (1965), 2.

45. Lovell, *Black Song,* 258, 260–61.

46. Richard Horsley, *Galilee: History, Politics, People* (Valley Forge, PA: Trinity Press International, 1995), and *Archaeology, History and Society in Galilee: The Social Context of Jesus and the Rabbis* (Valley Forge, PA: Trinity Press International, 1996).

47. John Dominic Crossan, *God and Empire: Jesus against Rome, Then and Now* (New York: HarperCollins Publishers, 2008).

48. Richard Horsley, *Jesus and Empire: The Kingdom of God and the New World Disorder* (Minneapolis: Fortress Press, 2003).

49. "Run Mary Run" transcribed in Bernice Johnson Reagon, *If You Don't Go, Don't Hinder Me: The African American Sacred Song Tradition* (Lincoln: University of Nebraska Press, 2001), 62–63.

50. Harding, "You Got a Right to the Tree of Life," 267.

51. Norman R. Yetman, ed., *Voices from Slavery* (New York: Holt, Rinehart and Winston, 1970), 263.

52. See, Henry Mitchell, *Black Belief* (San Francisco: Harper & Row, 1975), 120; Gayraud S. Wilmore, *Black Religion and Black Radicalism* (Maryknoll, NY: Orbis Books, 1983), 217.

53. Ernst Käsemann, *Jesus Means Freedom* (Philadelphia: Fortress Press, 1977); James Cone, *A Black Theology of Liberation* (1971; Maryknoll, NY: Orbis Books, 1990), and Gustavo Gutiérrez, *A Theology of Liberation: History, Politics, and Salvation,* trans. Sister Caridad Inda and John Eagleson (1973; Maryknoll, NY: Orbis Books, 1988).

54. See Roger D. Abrahams, *Afro-American Folktales, Stories from Black Traditions in the New World* (New York: Pantheon Fairy Tale and Folklore Library, 1985).

55. Howard Thurman, *Deep River and the Negro Spiritual Speaks of Life and Death* (Richmond, IN: Friends United Press, 1975), 16; and *Jesus and the Disinherited* (1949; Richmond, IN: Friends United Press, 1981).

56. Long, *Significations,* 7.

57. Ibid.

58. The notion was raised in English by Walter Hollenweger, "Intercultural Theology," *Theology Today* 43, 1 (April 1986): 28–35; see also María Pilar Aquino and María José Rosado Nunes, eds., *Feminist Intercultural Theology: Latina Explorations for a Just World* (Maryknoll, NY: Orbis Books, 2007).

5

JESUS' APPROACH AS A PARADIGM FOR MISSION

NOVEMBER 2008, XIX ANNIVERSARY OF THE MARTYRS
OF THE UNIVERSITY OF CENTRAL AMERICA

Jon Sobrino

For practical purposes *mission* and *evangelization* are interchangeable terms among contemporary followers of Jesus. Conceptually, evangelization points toward the "what" of an ecclesial praxis: announcing and initiating the good news. Mission implies that evangelization originates in being sent. Both are interrelated, then, but I believe it is logically and mystagogically important to begin with evangelization. This is especially true if we are to understand Jesus, whose "approach" (as suggested by the title of the theme I have been asked to address) should permeate the understanding of "mission" enunciated by the Latin American bishops at Aparecida, Brazil in May 2007.

Let us return for the purposes of this discussion to what is fundamental. Pope Paul VI writes in *Evangelii Nuntiandi* (On Evangelization in the Modern World, 1975), "Evangelization is...the grace and vocation proper to the Church, her deepest identity. She exists in order to evangelize" (14). Thus, everything that occurs in the Church *ad intra* achieves its full meaning only when it becomes a "proclamation of the Good News" (15). *Evangelii Nuntiandi* makes the fundamental claim that "Jesus was the very first...evangelizer" (7), and "it is above all his mission and his condition of being an evangelizer that [the Church] is called upon to continue" (15). We will focus on this, but without forgetting that Jesus, the Christ, mediator and Son of God, is the one who sends us on mission. To this I would like to add that the reality of the poor also calls us and sends us on mission. Matthew 25 is a symbol of the union of Christ and the poor, and, pastorally, I believe this is very important to take into account when thinking about mission. We must go to the poor. There is something in them that, analogically, moves us—sends us—to evangelize.

This essay includes some brief reflections about Jesus of Nazareth, the first "evangelizer" and "missionary," whose being and doing the church must continue. I will focus on two areas that are important both in their own right and for our "approach" to mission: the reign of God, and the cross. The first confers "gravity" on mission, and the second gives it an "edge." I believe these are very important today, given the lack of both in current discussions about mission. Finally, I will briefly mention two fundamental attitudes of "Jesus the missionary": Jesus' obedience "to God alone," and his way of acting with "liberty."

These days I think it is important that mission be carried out with "gravity," which goes beyond childishness and good intentions, with an "edge" that goes beyond simple pacifism and timidity; and with "liberty" that goes beyond paralyzing prudence and fear of authorities both outside and inside the church. This means we must carry out mission as an "ecclesial body" and as a "people of God" in which everyone has equal dignity. Certainly, to "send on mission" in this way is already itself a form of evangelization and good news.

The "Hard Edges" of Mission: Conflict and Cross

Bishop Demetrio Valentini has lucidly written, "We value [the bishops' meeting at] Aparecida as an experience of the profound dynamics of the Gospel."[1] The document produced by the bishops is part of this experience, and Bishop Demetrio recognizes that it has both value and limits. First, the precise way in which it relates mission to Christ is important: "We Christians need to begin again from Christ, from the contemplation of the one who has revealed in his ministry the plenitude of the fulfillment of the human vocation and its meaning" (#41). This is a very positive statement, even though speaking about the need to "begin again" raises the suspicion that something has been lost, the recognition of which I believe is quite positive. Certainly sections 129 through 135 are positive, where Jesus is presented as a man of great compassion toward all people who suffer and are marginated. This gives us the "imperative" of "creating a society in which no one is excluded" (#135).

But there are also gaps in the image of Jesus to the extent that José Comblin writes, "the weakest part of the document in my view is the Christology."[2] Indeed, the treatment of Jesus lacks historical context, and recovering it must be considered fundamental. In other words, we must understand the call of Aparecida to "begin again from Christ" as a call "to recover the historical Jesus." Juan Luis Segundo, Leonardo Boff, Carlos Bravo, and Ignacio Ellacuría worked on this decades ago.

And they did this not only along the line of Käsemann vs. Bultmann, accepting their basic parameters, but with an originality proper to Latin America: recovering a Jesus whom we can and should "follow" in announcing and building the reign of God. Also we must remember— in an up-to-date manner, of course—the impact that the historical Jesus had on believers and even nonbelievers long ago.[3] This is fundamental in generating a genuinely evangelical and Latin American approach to "mission."

It is often said that we must take into account the originality of the present and not insist so much on the past, in which there is some truth (perhaps even a lot), but also oversimplification and even danger. This occurs especially in Christology. There is no danger in recovering the past of the "historical Jesus," which is to say going back to the Jesus of Mark and Luke, to Jesus of Nazareth. Rather, this is fundamental in order to begin again with mission today. This is what we have learned in recent decades.

The Latin American church, known as the "church of the poor" and the "popular church"—a name that brought disfavor—went back to Jesus of Nazareth and how he announced the good news, initiated the reign of God, and struggled against the anti-reign. The Latin American church of this period was an evangelizing and prophetic church. I don't believe that it called itself a "discipleship" and "missionary" church, but that is what it was. It was like Jesus, and it suffered the fate of Jesus. Clearly we need to rethink many things. But I am convinced that this recent "past" is what continues giving life, without being recognized as such, to what Bishop Demetrio with good reason calls "an experience of the profound dynamic of the Gospel." This is what should finally motivate and guide mission.

Returning to our theme, then, there are two important lacunae in Aparecida's treatment of Jesus of Nazareth. What is missing is the synthesis, that which unites the sayings and the deeds we hear about from the life of Jesus. And the conflict in which Jesus lived as well as the cross to which he was sent by the great and powerful of his day are also missing.

Let us begin with the conflict. "Something fundamental for the Gospels does not appear: Jesus' conflict with the priests, the doctors of the law, the Pharisees, and the powerful people of his day. This conflict is a unifying thread running through the Gospels."[4] Also the text does not mention that this conflict becomes more or less acute depending on which of two moods is at work in the preaching of Jesus. To some he preaches good news, and to others bad news (Lk 6:20–26), to some he shows compassion, and to still others he shows anger.

This lacuna is not just a conceptual deficit for Christology, but rather shapes the historical process of mission *in actu*. Consciously or unconsciously it influences us to avoid conflicts with those who continue oppressing the poor today (section 65 of the Aparecida document admirably describes the faces of the poor), the successors to those who killed Jesus. It can also be seen in the treatment given to the innumerable martyrs of Latin America. When it uses the term "martyrs" Aparecida speaks of "martyrs for the faith" (#383), which presents no problem. And when the document alludes to the real martyrdom of our day—giving one's life—it sees its nobility as a participation in the cross of Jesus, which, once again, does not present a problem (#140). However, it does not mention that real conflicts with the powerful are the cause of the cross in our day. And this is a great problem.

The document praises the nobility and virtue of the martyrs and of Jesus on the cross, but not their denunciations of oppression and the conflicts that result. Consciously or unconsciously, it gives the impression that the participants at Aparecida—the majority—did not want to get to the bottom of the problem, so that they would not have to confront the powers of this world. Comblin writes, "It is a gospel to satisfy the bourgeoisie, a christology with a bourgeois inspiration. It does not express the feelings of the poor, or in any way understand the life and death of Jesus."[5]

There is no need to be surprised that there are things missing in the text—indeed, we could continue naming other examples, as Bishop Demetrio wants to do. But it does make one stop and think. It is surprising that such a central and obvious reality for the gospel and for the role of martyrs in the recent life of the church was apparently not central to the collective consciousness of the assembly. For whatever reason it did not come forward. But now, at this celebration of the martyrs of the University of Central America, and in an epoch of "mission," it is important to underline this lacuna, for our "approach" to "mission" will reflect whether or not we treat the conflicts of Jesus during his life, and his death on the cross, as central. It will either be an approach to mission without edges and at peace with the world, or an approach with edges and at peace with God.

We must return therefore to the historical cross of Jesus, not for masochistic reasons but in order to be honest about what is real about the reality of Jesus, and about the reality of our peoples. This is existentially decisive if we are to choose a mission like that of Jesus and to remain in it. I would offer the following reasons for this conclusion.

First, the present reality of Latin America demands it. Obviously there is a longing for life and, even more, for a "liberation from all forms of slavery," as the bishops said in Medellín at a time when the faith was filled with great hope. But it continues to be even truer today that Latin America is a continent of "crucified peoples" before whom the most important exigency for the church—call it a "mission" or a "command" from God—is "to take them down from the cross." Given the immense number of poor persons on the continent, when we do not make the cross central we lose a fundamental sense of perspective. And we lose theological, pastoral, and liturgical creativity in our theory and praxis, in ordinary life and in mission.

Second, the gospel story of Jesus is diluted without the centrality of the cross. The words of Martin Kähler are well known: "The gospels are the history of the passion with a long introduction."[6] And Jesus' conflict unto death with the powerful emerges right away in this "long introduction." In Mark 3:1–6 Jesus cures the man with the withered hand in the synagogue on Saturday. When he leaves, Mark says, "The Pharisees went out and immediately conspired with the Herodians against him, how to destroy him."

Third, the historical cross has been central to the most important Christologies: in Paul, Mark, and John; in Luther, Bonhoeffer, and Moltmann. At the present time I do not think this is still the case, although it is true of the most lucid authors. José Ignacio González Faus insists, speaking in the context of religious pluralism, on "the exclusivity of the crucifixion as inescapably Christian."[7] Here in El Salvador Archbishop Romero made it central in pastoral practice, and Ellacuría in theology. It is the one non-negotiable.

Fourth, Easter is the resurrection of one who was crucified. The risen one appears with his wounds, which are mentioned, I believe, not only for apologetical reasons, but so that we will not be mistaken about his identity.

Finally, without the cross the "approach of Jesus" during his life is seriously misunderstood, while on the other hand the reign of God, mercy, and hope are all better understood through the lens of the cross. Without the cross and the historical conflicts the "approach" of Jesus loses its "edge." We all know about the whirl of "christs" produced by devotions like the "niños dios" [God children] and "divina misericordia" [divine mercy]; we are familiar with a Christ like the all powerful *Kyrios*, *Pantocrator*; and we know about Christ as a conceptual abstraction, "a divine person who subsists in two natures." And we can legitimately make space for these in theology and piety. But in real life, with everything that happens, Jesus of Nazareth can—and usually does—disappear, or what remains is a Jesus without an edge. And as a result the mission loses its voice in the world.

Something similar occurs with Mary, wrapped in traditions of every type that sometimes obscure her reality. Frequently she ceases to be from Nazareth, the Jewish girl who asked God to give life to the lowly and to bring down the powerful, two elements that must be taken into account in the approach to mission. She is also the one who stayed with her assassinated son. Thus we can rightly call her, "Mother of crucified peoples."

From my point of view, when thinking about mission, evangelization, and the pastoral work of the church—to say nothing of liturgy—we no longer speak much anymore about either the conflicts or the historical cross of Jesus. Yet it doesn't seem like people are suspicious of why this occurs, or of why theology continues speaking about the "mystery of the cross," but not much about "the cross of history." Ignacio Ellacuría spoke about these things, however. In one fundamental article he asked the following two apparently innocent questions: "Why does Jesus die and why do they kill him?"[8] He asked the first in order to be faithful to the mystery of the God who was on the cross. And he asked the second to avoid being irresponsible regarding the world's cruelty, and so as not to avoid the conflict incarnated there. Nobody in the church should forget this; without it the mission becomes romanticized. It loses its edge.

The "Weight" of Mission: The Reign of God

Years ago a Copernican change occurred in my thinking when I realized that the reign of God was at the center of Jesus' life—both the "reign" and "God." I wrote at that time that "Jesus did not preach about himself, or just about God, but rather he preached about the reign of God." The point is that his reality was ex-centric (or other-centered), and that this is fundamental to the approach of Jesus. The church must take this into account in "speaking about Jesus," and it should reproduce this ex-centricity in its "sending on mission." To negate this *in actu* by putting itself at the center of its own preaching is to vitiate its essence at the roots. This is a recurring temptation into which the church repeatedly falls. And it makes it difficult—outside of miracles of grace—for the mission to be efficacious.

The Reign Must Be Announced and Initiated

First, then, let us examine how Jesus understood the reign of God. He believed that when God reigns the world is "a world in which peace with justice and universal solidarity reigns."[9] Today this has been formulated in a variety of ways. Here in El Salvador Rutilio Grande—who pioneered organizing "missions" among farm workers with great creativity and as the foundation for his entire pastoral project—said it in a way that everyone understood. I will quote him at some length in order to recall what was also said by Bishop Hélder Camara, Bishop Leonidas Proaño, and Bishop Sergio Méndez Arceo, who with good reason are called the "Fathers of the Latin American church." They are the ones who created the "Latin American approach" to being church and to "being on mission." Rutilio said,

> Jesus was a pilgrim walking among the people, going through the towns and villages. He taught the Good News of the Reign of God in every campesino home. And what markers do we use for the Reign of God?
>
> Every person has the same Father, and we are all his children. So, clearly, we are all brothers and sisters. All are equal, one to another! But Cain is a miscarriage in the plan of God, and there are groups of Cains. This is a denial of the Reign of God. Here in the country there are groups of Cains who invoke God for their cause, which is even worse.
>
> The Lord God gave us a material world in his plan for us, just like the material bread and the material cup with which we celebrate this material Mass. So the material world is for everybody, like this Eucharist, a shared table with long tablecloths to accommodate everyone. Each with his or her own stool, placemat, and place setting, so that all might find a place at the table.[10]

This is what the reign of God was like for Jesus. After his resurrection people understood him in different ways: the celestial beyond, the church, and the person of Jesus himself, the *autobasileia tou Theou* about which Origen wrote. There is an important exegetical and theological discussion about all of this today into which we are not going to enter at this moment.[11] But I believe that its echoes are somehow heard in Aparecida. On the one hand, the document says that "the Reign of God is present in Jesus" (which is commonly accepted, though this "presence" is interpreted in many ways). More emphatically it states, "Jesus Christ is the Reign of God, which endeavors to spread all its transformative force throughout the Church and society" (#382).

On the other hand, in what I consider its best passages, the document develops the idea of the reign of God by describing how human beings should live in accord with the Beatitudes (#385), and what tasks must be done—gestures of mercy and the creation of more just structures. This is what it means to follow Jesus, and that is what God desires. Without trying to be conceptually precise, the reign of God refers to a new way of being and acting as human beings, building a world in conformity with God's heartfelt desires for us.

Ellacuría stated it memorably in a congress on the three Abrahamic religions: "What Jesus came to announce and to realize, which is the Reign of God, is what should constitute the unifying object of all Christian theology... And true followers of Jesus should pursue the greatest realization possible of the Reign of God in history."[12] That is what the church should make real through word and deed in the everyday, and in the context of mission, treating it as fundamental.

It is the ultimate and the absolute, and it has two dimensions: the poor and God, God and the poor. "The Reign belongs *solely* to the poor," wrote Joachim Jeremias,[13] and Archbishop Romero said, "the glory of *God* is the poor person who lives."[14] Don Pedro Casaldáliga formulated it with absolute clarity in reference to an issue some people want to deny: "everything is relative except God and hunger."[15] What God has united must not be separated: God himself and the poor. The conclusion is that the reign of God must be central to mission. It was central for Jesus, and it continues to be the longed-for utopia for immense majorities of the poor.

In order to pursue mission following the approach of Jesus, the church must put itself clearly at the service of the reign, overcoming the temptation to put itself at the center. It should incarnate itself in history in what makes the reign grow or diminish, where it should *promote grace* and work to *eradicate sin*. It should do this with *solidarity*, making its own "the joys and hopes, the sorrows and the sufferings of all, especially the poor and those who suffer." And it must do this *seriously*: for sin is *trivialized* and salvation *vanishes* when the reign of God is not taken seriously.

Additionally, like Jesus, we must remember the reality of the anti-reign when speaking about mission. We should take responsibility for it, combat it, and be ready to suffer the consequences. We must get in tune with the God of the reign and above all with his *mercy* toward the oppressed, but also with his *anger*, which is most often forgotten: "Woe to those who sell the needy for a pair of sandals!" said Amos (Amos 2:6c) and "Woe to you who tie up heavy burdens, and who kill the prophets," said Jesus (Mt 23: 4, 30–31).

This prophetic approach is essential for mission. The church's social teaching and ethics are good, but as good as they are, they are not sufficient. A thunderous prophecy is needed. And the final reason for the church is that it must denounce *idolatry*, not in the form of the sterile tautology—"nothing created should be absolutized"—a denunciation that doesn't bother anybody, but rather as denunciation of what idolatry truly is: a cult of idols, realities that are very real. That is how Archbishop Romero expressed it, which he explained very well in his fourth pastoral letter in 1979. Idols are historical existential realities, they promise salvation, they demand orthodoxy and a cult, and they require victims in order to survive, like the god Moloch. Archbishop Romero denounced the absolutization of capital and national security as idols, as the bishops at Puebla also did (#393–397, #498–506), and he denounced the absolutization of popular organizations, which are good in themselves, but which become idols when they demand endless victims.

On our continent these idols who demand victims continue to exist. Yet there is a shortage of condemnations from the church about such an important matter. The reason is understandable: because confronting the idols automatically brings conflict, it is avoided. Additionally, we create ideologies legitimating a false peace and being on good terms with everybody, sometimes even those who favor the anti-reign, so that we can do all this with a clean conscience. But a mission following the approach of Jesus must take the idols into account, analyzing them deeply and combating them without deceiving ourselves. Short of this, we are lacking something fundamental from the approach of Jesus. Building the reign and struggling against the anti-reign is an essential task, and it is what gives "weight" to the mission of the church. Without it, mission is simply carried away by the wind.

"He went about doing good" (Acts 10:38)

The Aparecida document states beautifully that Jesus invites all those with him "to place their steps in his footprints" (Final Message). That is, we must pass through this world as he did, doing good in deeds and words, in mercy and truth. It is well known that "mercy"—others like Metz prefer to use the term "compassion"—was central for Jesus. Indeed, it lies at the heart of his "approach." In order to gain his support, the poor, sick, and marginalized had only to say, "Lord, have mercy on us." For his part, Jesus speaks and theorizes about mercy above all in the parable of the Good Samaritan (Lk 10:29–37). In telling this story he describes himself and the core of the mission of the church.

Mercy is not just a feeling, but rather an action; more exactly, it is a re-action against what the victimizers have done. It does not consist in fulfilling a commandment, even though Jesus tells the parable to demonstrate the meaning of the great command to love one's neighbor. It does not belong to the realm of the religious (though it can and should be present there), since neither God nor the synagogue—the churches, we would say today—seem necessary to require its fulfill ment. And it certainly does not appear that a special predisposition for its exercise exists in the religious realm, since the priests and the Le vites do not respond with mercy. In fact, it is the Samaritan, the one who is not well situated religiously, who reacts with mercy.

This means that for Jesus there is ultimacy in mercy. One cannot go beyond it. Tending the victim on the road touches the deepest fiber of what it means to be human: *splachnon*, entrails, heart. And mercy also restores what is ultimate to the victims, their life and dignity. This is important to emphasize. When Jesus acts with mercy, it is not only the persons in need who are helped. The division between *merciful benefac tors* on the one hand and *recipients of assistance* on the other is annulled. To those who are healed he says, "Your faith has healed you" (Mk 10:52; Mt 9:28; Lk 18:42), which is to say, "You have healed yourself." And to the woman in sin he says, "Your faith has saved you" (Lk 7:50).

Mercy takes specific forms according to the context. That of Fr. Kolbe, who takes the place of someone condemned to death in a con centration camp, is distinct from that of Mother Teresa, who does everything she can for the most abandoned, or that of Ignacio Ellacuría, who supported negotiations to end a cruel war in which he would lose his life. In Latin America mercy has taken many forms: assisting those fleeing oppression, helping community organizations, and more and more defending the human rights of women, the indigenous, African Americans, and youth, and even burying the dead. The horizon of this mercy has been *liberation*, and its fundamental tool has been *justice*. Mercy and justice can be distinguished conceptually, but not really exis tentially. Mercy-justice is essentially dialectical, and therefore conflict ual: it is a matter of defending the victims against those who victimize them. Mercy draws one into the struggle against the oppressor.

The connection between mercy and truth, which I have not dis cussed for lack of space, won for Jesus the love of the victims and the hate of the victimizers. This is why he was crucified, which continues happening to the present moment, though the forms of crucifixion vary. In the life of Jesus, just as in the third world, the cross brings new light to mercy. On the occasion of the assassination of one of the six priests that preceded his own, Archbishop Romero memorably stated, "Anybody who gets in the way is killed." Getting in the way consisted of stating the truth, and exposing and condemning the oppressors.

Most importantly, however, those who got in the way did not do this for personal gain, or to defend the church, but rather "to defend the defenseless, oppressed, tortured, kidnapped, and assassinated poor." So they ended up on a cross. The cross, then, is a consequence of a specific type of mercy: a mercy expressed in the struggle for justice and the defense of the victims. So it is from the perspective of this type of mercy, and none other, that we must understand the new and massive phenomenon of the martyrs.[16]

"Martyrdom" is a historical reality that is expressed through a historical concept. We can discuss ad infinitum the *analogatum princeps* (principal analog) for the martyrdom of Jesus in each historical epoch, and which is the most relevant. But in the third world today martyrs are those who give their life for the cause of justice so that the poor might live, and this is how believers give testimony about the Christ who was Jesus. Martyrs, then, are inevitably merciful. They die for helping the victims and for defending them from the victimizers. They are like Jesus, both in life and in death. That is why I call them "Jesus-like" martyrs.

This mercy-defense of the poor illumines the meaning of the statement that God is a God of mercy even more powerfully than the beautiful words of the psalms. The Puebla document does the same thing when it speaks about the option for the poor in a solemn *theologal* statement with two essential elements. One is that God's option for the poor is *gratuitous*, "whatever the moral situation in which it is found." The other is that God's option is *merciful*, not just generically, but rather in the sense we have just explained: "God *comes to their defense* and loves them" (#1142). And even though it does not say so explicitly, *mercy* also entails confronting the victimizers, not just for the sake of condemning their actions, but so that they will stop producing victims. Finally, in the mystery of faith, God suffers the consequences of mercy on the cross of his Son. This is the "God of mercy" of whom we speak.

It is essential to keep mercy and martyrdom alive in the mission of the church. They give it "weight." The importance of mercy is self-evident. We must practice what we preach: mission must be put into action through theologal Jesus-like martyrial mercy, not just helping the victims, but defending them against their victimizers. This is also true of martyrdom for it is essential to remember the martyrs when thinking about mission. Martyrdom is an exercise of gratitude, an essential Christian and human virtue. But it also means allowing oneself to be both shaken and moved by the martyrs even today, and accepting that, properly historicized, their example continues to be fruitful.

Indeed, nothing better has been found to raise hope. This is true in many places on the continent, certainly in Guatemala and El Salvador.

Passing through the world in this way, speaking with authority but without dogmatism, teaching with clarity but without being doctrinaire, making fundamental demands without giving in, resisting to the end, and dealing with the ups and downs of fear and hope, should all accompany mission. And we must not forget that Jesus, crushed at night and betrayed, accused with lies, insulted, tortured, and abandoned, had the immense kindness to say goodbye to his friends before dying on the cross. The Eucharist can and should be very present in a mission that reflects the approach of Jesus.

"Availability" and "Liberty" in Mission

Jesus the evangelizer and missioner was "available" to his Father God, and was "free" before humanity. He did not carry out his mission as a member of a synagogue or a church, nor, evidently, with their mandate. There is an obvious difference from us in this regard, those of us who live and are missioned within a church that is, moreover, structurally hierarchical. But this does not negate all similarity to Jesus. When we are missioned within the church we must continue being available to the God who cannot be controlled, and who is the ultimate origin of that mission. We continue to be human beings with a conscience that we must finally follow. And we continue being Christians through our obedience, but properly understood. The primary meaning of ob-audire is availability for an encounter with the word of God and for putting it into practice; this is the meaning of availability. Then we must take into account the various ecclesial authorities without losing our liberty and conscience, acting out of our liberty as children of God in a way that can be seen in mission.

Paul exemplifies this very well. He is both a member of the community and a believer in liberty; he is available to collaborate with Peter in a brotherly manner, and to do so with freedom, to the point of even reprimanding him.

Today liberty is not plentiful in the church, either in everyday life or in mission. We are reminded more often than we should be of the church's hierarchical nature. As a result, prudence and silence increase, and liberty and parresía (outspokenness) decrease. However, when this happens, only with difficulty is the church able to communicate that it acts in mission as a "people of God," a people of equal dignity. If only the bishops at Aparecida had pushed the theme of "a people of God in mission"! To carry out mission in this way as a people is, in itself, an act of evangelization.

Let me conclude with a few words about two important themes I have not been able to develop. First, clearly the church should announce "the Good News of Jesus Christ" (#380–381), since "its proper and specific mission is to communicate the life of Jesus Christ" (#386). And we have offered Jesus, before anything else, as the model for the missioner who motivates us to preach as missionaries. But this, of course, does not annul the task of announcing Jesus as the Christ; indeed in my opinion it can facilitate that task. The church, being and acting as Jesus, is able to present him not only through word, but also mystagogically and efficaciously as the Christ. And it can do this with credibility. Without "Jesus," the "Christ" is in danger of being manipulated. The historical Jesus is the best safeguard, and the best road for reaching the Christ of faith.

Second, what I have said may seem excessively utopian and prophetic, given that there should be at least a minimum of realism in our preaching about mission, as Pedro Trigo always insists in speaking about the Christianity of the majorities. And it may be that I have spoken too much about the cross, undoing the balance of cross and resurrection in the Pascal Mystery by not stressing the resurrection as Don Pedro Casaldáliga does so enthusiastically. Yet, if I have sinned through excess, perhaps it will serve to counteract the lack of emphasis on these things elsewhere in the church.

(Translated by Robert Lassalle-Klein)

Notes

1. Demetrio Valentini, "Aparecida: Valores y límites," in *Aparecida. Laicos, mujeres y jóvenes* (San Salvador: Cuadernos Centro Monseñor Romero, 2008), 22.

2. José Comblin, "El proyecto de Aparecida," *Revista Latinoamericana de Teología* 72 (2007): 278.

3. Something similar has occurred with the publication of the book by José Antonio Pagola, *Jesús: Aproximación histórica* (Madrid: PPC, 2007). This book exemplifies the impact of the "historical Jesus" in wealthy societies entranced by secularization.

4. Ibid., 280.

5. Comblin, "El proyecto de Aparecida," 281.

6. Martin Kähler, *The So-Called Historical Jesus and the Historic, Biblical Christ*, ed. and trans. Carl Braaten (Philadelphia: Fortress Press, 1964), 80.

7. José Ignacio González Faus, *El rostro humano de Dios* (Santander: Sal Terrae, 2007), 203.

8. Ignacio Ellacuría, "Por qué muere Jesús y por qué lo matan?" *Diakonía* 8 (1978): 65–75.

9. Jon Sobrino, "La resurrección de Jesús, esperanza para los pueblos cru-cificados. Aproximación desde la Biblia y la teología contemporánea," *Revista Latinoamericana de Teología* 75 (2008).

10. Rutilio Grande, "Homilia con motivo de la expulsión del P. Mario Bernal," Estudios Centroamericanos 347–348 (1977): 859.

11. See Andrés Torres Queiruga and María Clara Bingemer, "Jesús, como el Cristo en la nueva encrucijada cultural," *Concilium* 326 (June 2008).

12. Ignacio Ellacuría, "Aporte de la teología de la liberación a las reli-giones abrahámicas en la supercion del individualismo y del positivismo," *Revista Latinoamericana de Teología* 10 (1987): 9.

13. Joachim Jeremias, *Teología del Nuevo Testamento*, vol. 1 (Salamanca: Sal Terrae, 1974), 142; my emphasis.

14. This statement was made by Archbishop Romero on February, 2, 1980, in a speech accepting an honorary doctorate at the University of Louvain, Bel-gium (Archbishop Oscar Romero, "Una experiencia ecclesial en El Salvador, Centro America," *La voz de los sin voz: La palabra viva de Monsenor Oscar Ar-nulfo Romero* [San Salvador: UCA Editores, 1980], 52).

15. Don Pedro Casaldáliga, "Todo es relativo, menos Dios y el hambre," Friday, April 20, 2007, at RadioEvangelización, http://www.radioevangeliza-cion.org/spip.php?article375 (accessed September 1, 2010). Also cited in "Carta circular," January 2008.

16. Though well known, in order to illustrate the "added" significance that martyrdom brings to mercy, it is helpful to remember that Archbishop Romero and Mother Teresa were distinguished in mercy and that both were nominated in 1979 for the Nobel Peace Prize. Archbishop Romero died a martyr. Mother Teresa did not. And she has been beatified.

6

MARINA'S STORY AND
THE HISTORICAL REALITY OF JESUS

Robert Lassalle-Klein

"Statistics don't bleed," said a colleague upon learning that 40 percent of humanity survives on less than $2 a day and over 27,000 children die, mostly of poverty and malnutrition.[1] That afternoon my friend Marina Zavala left her job cooking for a local community of priests to visit the emergency room with chest pains from anxiety over the imminent loss of their home to a predatory mortgage. As Marina told her story, I was reminded of how our families and our lives had become inextricably intertwined through the global reach of U.S. foreign policy and the church. This is Marina's story in which my wife, Lynn, and I have a minor role. It begins for us about 5:00 in the afternoon of March 17, 1981, in the rural village of Santa Marta, El Salvador. The deafening sound of exploding bombs and bullets filled the streets as Marina (24), her future husband, José Antonio (28), and thousands of terrorized men, women, and children grabbed whatever they could and fled.

The situation in the countryside was desperate. The 1993 Report of the United Nations Commission on the Truth for El Salvador tells the story. "During the years 1980, 1981 and 1982 [the U.S. backed Salvadoran government carried out] ... mass executions ... in which members of the armed forces, in the course of anti-guerilla operations, executed peasants—men, women and children who had offered no resistance—simply because they considered them to be guerrilla collaborators." An adaptation of Vietnam War counterinsurgency tactics, it was part of "a deliberate strategy of eliminating or terrifying the peasant population in [order] ... to deprive the guerrilla forces of ... supplies and information and of the possibility of hiding...."[2]

But what could justify such a brutal strategy by a U.S. ally less than a thousand miles from Brownsville, Texas? A 1991 Rand Corporation study done for the Pentagon explains that Salvadoran forces pressing for reform or rebellion had reached critical mass by the beginning of 1980, driven by the fact that "over 70 percent of the land was owned by only 1 percent of the population, while over 40 percent of the rural population owned no land at all and worked as sharecroppers on absentee owners' land or as laborers on large estates."[3] The stubborn refusal of successive repressive civilian-military regimes to make even moderate changes in the status quo further fueled the push for land reform and a change in government, whether through elections, coup, or revolution. Norberto, a peasant farm worker, remembers, "We would go to the coffee plantations...to the cotton plantations and...the sugar cane fields," but "the wages were unfair...and our children were naked."[4] Eventually, "the people got organized and said, 'Now we are going to protest,'...but they answered us with death, and a great repression."

By 1981 peasants like Marina and her family knew exactly what this meant. Thus, she recalls that on March 17, 1981, "The Salvadoran army invaded Santa Marta, so we fled with most of the village on foot."[5] Their plan was to sneak, with thousands of terrified neighbors, through the deadly cordon encircling and bombarding the town, and to flee north with whatever they could carry in hopes of crossing the Lempa River and finding refuge in Honduras. Normally a two and a half hour walk, Marina says that it took hours and hours because of "pregnant women with swollen stomachs, small children, old people, and people who were injured or sick on stretchers." To avoid being heard, mothers squeezed crying children so tightly to their chests that some were asphyxiated. Thousands of peasants joined the march from other villages similarly under attack so that, "When we reached the Lempa River we were about 11,000 people."

José Antonio describes what happened next. "We got to the river at about 11:00 that night. Most of the people did not know how to swim, so we looked for tires, boards, or whatever could serve as a raft." Since he knew "a little bit" how to swim, José Antonio grabbed a branch and began swimming back and forth, ferrying frantic riders across the river. "By 3:00 in the morning I couldn't take it anymore," he recalls, but thousands more continued their desperate attempts to cross.

> A rope had been stretched across the river so that the people could grab it and try to make it over. Many people entered the river carrying children on their shoulders, using their hands to hold the few things they had brought. This worked fine until they got to the middle where it was too deep to stand and the weight made them drown, including the children. Sometimes we were able to save one or two who could swim a bit, but

many disappeared. At about 6:00 in the morning when the Salvadoran and Honduran armies woke up they came to the high ground on either side of the river and began throwing grenades and firing machine guns at the people crossing in the water. A terrible cry filled the air. The bullets fell on the water like rain.

Everyone ran for cover, dragging bloody and dying relatives under rocks and whatever cover they could find. José Antonio has a vivid memory of when the firing started: "I carried Marina's little brother, Adán, on my last trip across the river. When we reached the middle a mortar fell on the river bank we had just left, and we saw a mother and her child blown to pieces. Adán panicked and tried to break free, but I wouldn't let go until we got to the other shore and were able to hide in the underbrush." Rosario, an eighteen-year-old mother, was not so lucky.

It was a massacre . . . They shot my baby in my arms and wanted me to fall into the river and be swept away in the current just like those five hundred who were swept away at the Sumpul River massacre. I carried my baby through the long hike to Los Hernández [about two miles away]. All the while I was think-ing, "I can't bear this." The women had to forcibly take her out of my arms that night and I watched them bury her just as she was, wrapped in a cloth.[6]

Remembering their near escape, José Antonio concluded, "Maybe God helped me." Marina reflected, "I prayed to the Virgin, I believed she would save us. They were firing bullets that just missed our heads. It was a miracle. We should have died that day. I felt that the Virgin was protecting me with a covering. I could feel the bullets flying on ei-ther side of my head."

Marina and José Antonio survived, and were eventually forced to move to the Mesa Grande United Nations refugee camp, where they lived in very poor conditions for most of seven years as refugees. They were married there by Archbishop Rivera y Damas of El Salvador, who succeeded Archbishop Romero after his assassination on March 24, 1980. Marina and José Antonio had four children in the camp, Oscar, Elmer, Elsi, and Wil, and finally returned to their village in El Salvador in December 1987 with thousands of other refugees over protests from the military. But the U.S.–backed war was raging, and *campesinos* living in areas controlled by the rebels were still considered enemy collabora-tors. Marina recalls, "The army was executing many of the people who had returned from Honduras. Also the civilian paramilitary groups would kill people, cut off the head, and bring it to [the] military where they would receive extra points. They did this to Danielito Rivera, the husband of my cousin, Carmela Zavala."

Knowing they were certainly next, José Antonio and his cousin Chepe, a church worker who had been captured and tortured, found a *coyote* and immigrated illegally to the United States. Both were captured by the border patrol on January 31, 1987, and signed claims for political asylum, which were eventually granted nine years later. The moment of decision arrived for Marina and the children in mid-1988. "The area commander came to my mother's house and told her he was going to kill all of us. He said we had come from Honduras and that we were all guerrillas." Marina immediately wrote to José Antonio, who recalls, "I was really concerned when I heard what had happened, and realized that the only way I would ever see Marina and the children alive was if they fled to the U.S."

José Antonio was living in Oakland, California, where he was working in the Sanctuary Movement as a house coordinator at the Oakland Catholic Worker. I had co-founded the Oakland Catholic Worker Sanctuary Project in 1986 with a group of U.S. and Salvadoran friends and co-workers, and was serving as general coordinator in 1988 while juggling classes as a new doctoral student at the Graduate Theological Union (GTU) in Berkeley. José Antonio and I had become good friends while living and working side by side at the Catholic Worker and traveling to churches all over northern California to speak about human rights violations by the U.S.–funded government of El Salvador. In August 1988, Lynn Klein, a New Yorker studying at the GTU for a master's in spirituality and ethics, moved into the Catholic Worker community. In mid-October Lynn shared with the community that she was planning to participate in an upcoming December 1988 delegation to visit Salvadoran refugees living in the U.N. Refugee Camp at Colomancagua, Honduras. About a week later, José Antonio approached me at the weekly staff meeting. Since Lynn was going to Honduras, was there any way that we could arrange for her to safely accompany his wife and children to the U.S.?

Though she was new to the community and the Sanctuary Movement, we invited Lynn into the meeting and explained the request. After asking a few questions of José Antonio and me, she agreed. When I recently asked (after twenty years of marriage) why she was willing to take this risk, she replied, "It was the personal connection, not the big issue. I trusted you, I trusted José Antonio, our country was paying for the bullets, and the lives of his family were at stake."[7]

In a few weeks, we had our plan. Lynn would fly with our friend, Tim Iglesias, to San Salvador and accompany Marina and the children to Mexico City. From there they would fly to Tijuana, Mexico, where I would meet them. The Sanctuary Movement people would bring Marina and the children across the border, and we would bring them to a church in Los Angeles, where José Antonio would join us for the drive to Oakland.

The distressed father explained everything in a letter to Marina, who recalls, "I felt so happy when José Antonio asked if I would like to come. It was difficult there with four little children, and it was dangerous for me. The *comandante* had said he was going to kill all of us, so I was going to come with the children. Lynn would come to San Salvador, and Fr. Dick Howard would keep us safe."

Marina continued, "My brother, Adrian, took me to the house of the Jesuits in San Salvador. When Lynn arrived it was really beautiful, the encounter. She told me she had come for me." Relishing the memory of her first trip to a restaurant, Marina recalls, "They accompanied me to the airport where we had coffee," but in a sign of things to come, "the children spilled the coffee all over my dress." Several hours later I met Marina, Lynn, Tim, and the children at the Tijuana International Airport and drove to the *Casa del Migrante* run by the Scalabrini Fathers, where the family would stay until the Sanctuary people could arrange the crossing. We were surprised to learn it would be at least five days. The woman who would bring them across was very sick with cancer, and there were two other families with similar cases who had arrived first. The Scalabrinis explained that the shelter would provide meals for the children, showers, a clean, safe room, and hospitality. But Marina would have to buy her own food, and there was no room for Lynn and me. So we gave Marina money for food, visited the neighborhood store together, bid goodbye to Tim who returned home, and left to stay with friends in the next town.

Little did we realize that Marina and the children suffered while we rested. Marina recalls,

> They put me in a room with the children. They fed them breakfast, but not the adults. I was terrified to go outside the building to buy food, so I just ate a little from their plates. Being from the countryside, I had never seen hot water from a tap, and couldn't understand how the other people were able to bathe with such cold water. So we just slept all day in the room. It was freezing, and the children became sick. Wil, who was three, had diarrhea, but I couldn't bathe him.

To this day, I am ashamed when our dear friend Marina recounts how she suffered in the confusion that followed. "I felt sad, and was crying the whole time. Then we got to know a Guatemalan family who was also waiting to cross, but the mother told me you were going to steal the children and sell them." Sadly, that family broke apart, with the men moving onward, and the terrified woman left alone to manage the dangerous journey home. Fortunately, Marina put her faith in the same thread of trust that had moved Lynn. "I asked myself, why would my husband send me people like that? I'll just have to do what they say. So I prayed to God, and trusted that things would not turn out they way those people said."

When Lynn and I returned three days later we were told that there was only one Sanctuary person available, and that while she would help, we would have to cross Marina and the children ourselves. This was an unexpected and frightening development! The next day Marina kissed the children and turned them over to Lynn and the Sanctuary angel, who bought them clothes, filled them with Kahlúa liquor so they would sleep (and not talk) through the crossing, and drove them through the border as Lynn's children. I took Marina to a dry drainage canal known as the *bordo*, where we picked a *coyote* to accompany her across the border and through a field to the K-Mart on the other side, where we would meet. Unfortunately, she soon realized that he had red eyes, which the Guatemalans had told her was typical of drug addicts.

Marina remembers, "I crossed with a lot of panic, and was praying to the Virgin. The *coyote* with the red eyes took my hand. He said his eyes were like that because of the wind and the fires to keep warm. We had to climb the side of the canal, and he helped me do it by putting his foot on the wall and letting me stand on it, step by step, all the way up the side." A frantic dash into the U.S. followed. "When the *migra* didn't come, we ran from the canal into the field. But I couldn't keep up. So we walked for about twenty minutes. The red K glowed in the dark, and is branded in my mind to this day. That is where you said you would meet us, when we would finally be safe."

The red K is surely an appropriate replacement for the World Trade Towers in symbolizing the consumer society that Marina and her children were about to enter. And the irony of the fact that their family now stands on the brink of losing their home to a predatory mortgage deal is lost on none of us. But Marina has a larger view. "Honestly, what I feel is a deep sense of thanks to God for having brought me safely into this country, and that José Antonio was able to gain political asylum, which saved our lives, and made it possible for me and the children to get our papers. I have to give thanks to God for this." José Antonio adds, "If I had to do it again, I don't think I would survive. I give thanks to God that I was able to come into this country and that so many people helped me at the Catholic Worker and the Central American Refugee Committee." When I asked Marina if the possible loss of their home and life savings left her feeling that her prayers had been denied, she replied,

> No, I'm so happy that I came! I prayed to God that I would be able to survive and have a grandchild from each of the children. And look, we already have two, I'm so happy! I'm not going to say that I go to church a lot, but when I've prayed to the Virgin for my children or in times of trouble, she has always helped us. I'm praying to her now about the house.

Marina's story of hope and courage in the face of suffering and evil gives flesh and (sadly) blood to the bare bones with which we began: 40 percent of humanity struggles through resourcefulness and faith to survive on less than $2 a day. In a report ambivalently entitled, "*The Developing World Is Poorer Than We Thought, But No Less Successful in the Fight against Poverty*," the World Bank tells us that the level of poverty decreased in the developing world from almost 70 percent in 1981 to 47.6 percent in 2005.[8] But when half of humanity lives in poverty, ambivalence seems wildly self-congratulatory.

The real story here, in the words of Peruvian theologian Fr. Gustavo Gutiérrez, is the "irruption" of Marina and her family as actors into the history and civil societies of El Salvador and the United States. Some examples serve to make the point. First, when the birth of the first Salvadoran farm worker union led to the assassination in 1977 of the local pastor, Fr. Rutilio Grande, SJ, the stakes for organizing the *campesinos* were clear. Yet Norberto, one of the peasant workers, told how the peasant farm workers of Cabanas "got organized" a few years later and began "to protest" for better wages for picking coffee and cotton and harvesting sugar cane, well aware that "death and a great repression" might follow.

Second, the Pentagon report cited earlier concludes that the Salvadoran government, the Salvadoran military, and the right-wing landowners knew that they "had America trapped" in a Cold War "pact with the devil." As we have seen, massacres by the Salvadoran military like the one recounted here would be tolerated and covered up so that "El Salvador [would] not fall to the FMLN [insurgency]."[9] Yet Marina and her family survived to tell the whole world their story at the U.N. Mesa Grande Refugee Camp.[10] And U.S. support for the government of El Salvador would eventually collapse in 1991 under the cumulative weight of mounting evidence of U.S. tolerance for gross violations of human rights.

Finally, in the late 1980s the U.S. State Department systematically opposed political asylum claims by Salvadoran refugees fleeing persecution by U.S. trained and supported military forces. Yet on January 31, 1990, federal immigration judge Bernard J. Hornbach of the Ninth Circuit Court of Appeals granted political asylum to José Antonio Zavala and seven other family members, declaring that in the early 1980s the Salvadoran government had created an enormous group of victims of persecution forced to flee to refugee camps in Honduras. This same case also led the U.S. Ninth District Court to throw out several years of denials of claims for political asylum by Salvadoran refugees based on prejudicial negative recommendations by the State Department under President Ronald Reagan. Literally thousands of claims were reconsidered under this decision, and the lives of countless families were affected. There can be no doubt, then, that Marina and her family "irrupted" as actors into both U.S. and Salvadoran civil society and history! Yet Marina and José Antonio do not speak of their journey as a triumph of personal agency or will. Rather, they emphasize their gratitude to God for inspiring so many people to support them in their struggles, and for protecting them in their perilous journey. In the next section, we will look at Jesus of Galilee as seen through the eyes of Marina and her community, especially her pastor, Archbishop Oscar Romero of El Salvador.

Jesus of Galilee, and His Followers Today

Countless women and men like those in Marina's story meet the demands of Christian discipleship today in Africa, Asia, Latin America, Oceania, Antarctica, North America, and Europe by asking, "Who was Jesus of Galilee, and what does it mean to be his follower today?" Biblical scholars have mounted three quests since the nineteenth century trying to recover the "historical Jesus" behind the gospels, and their portraits have influenced the faith of countless believers, theologians, and skeptics who reflect on that faith. Yet people like Marina and José Antonio and their pastor Archbishop Oscar Romero have always been less interested in the "historical Jesus" reconstructed by biblical scholars than in what Romero's martyred friend and adopted countryman, Fr. Ignacio Ellacuría, SJ, called the "historical reality of Jesus."

Three questions come to mind about this approach. First, what is the *historical reality* of Jesus, and what is its relationship to the story of

Marina and José Antonio?[11] Second, how is the *historical reality* of Jesus different from the object of the three scholarly quests for the *historical Jesus*? And third, how do the faith, hope, and love manifested in Marina's story help us to understand the "historical reality of Jesus?"

What Is the "Historical Reality of Jesus?"

Vatican II, the twenty-first ecumenical council of the Christian church, ended on December 8, 1965, sending the bishops home to every continent with a mandate "of reading the signs of the times and of interpreting them in light of the Gospel" (*Gaudium et Spes*, 4). The Latin America bishops were the first to answer this call at Medellín, Colombia in May 1968 when they made a "a clear and prophetic option" to embrace "the need for conversion on the part of the whole Church to a preferential option for the poor...aimed at their integral liberation" (Puebla, 1134).

Marina's pastor, Archbishop Oscar Romero of El Salvador, was assassinated on March 24, 1980 for his commitment to this principle, now a central pillar of Catholic social teaching. Many date his political conversion to the government's persecution of people like Marina and José Antonio. Just three weeks after Romero was consecrated archbishop, his old friend, Fr. Rutilio Grande, SJ, was pulled from his jeep and brutally executed by the national police. Fr. Grande's executioners were government allies of reactionary landowners intent on suppressing the first Salvadoran farm worker union (FECCAS) founded a few years earlier by seminarians affiliated with his parish in Aguilares, El Salvador.[12] A brutal military repression of the area followed, and three months later Romero traveled at great risk to celebrate Mass for the now traumatized and isolated peasants of Aguilares, telling them, "You are the image of the pierced savior."[13]

The following year Fr. Ignacio Ellacuría, SJ, president of the University of Central America and an occasional theological advisor to Archbishop Romero, gave a theological response to the implicit question behind Romero's homily: What does it mean to say that the crucified peasants of Aguilares are "the image" of the crucified Jesus? Ellacuría responds with the claim that they are part of the "crucified people," that "vast portion of humankind, which is literally and actually crucified by natural, ...historical, and personal oppressions."[14] He asserts that the crucified people are the "principal" sign of the times "by whose light the others should be discerned and interpreted." And he argues that the confrontation of the Latin American church with the historical reality of its crucified people demands a "new historical logos...which takes into account the historical reality of Jesus."[15] Stated from the perspective of Marina and Archbishop Romero, if the crucified peasants of Aguilares are "the image" of the crucified Jesus, then what does the historical reality of his persecution and death have to do with their deaths at the Rio Lempa massacre, and Aguilares?

Ellacuría responds that the historical reality of Jesus of Galilee is defined by his basic stance on the world he encounters: his relationship to the Father as beloved Son (*ho huios mou ho agapaetos*; Mk 1:11b, Mt 3:17b, Lk 3:22c, par. Jn 1:34c), his commitment to the people of Israel as prophet and Christos (Mk 1:10, Mt 3:16, Lk 3:22a, Jn 1:32), and his mission to initiate the reign of God as good news to the poor. Ellacuría asserts that it is Jesus' actions in announcing the kingdom of God as good news to the poor that explains why he is persecuted and killed.

How Is the *Historical Reality* of Jesus Different from the *Historical Jesus*

The authors of the gospels, like Marina, Archbishop Romero, and Christian disciples everywhere, are focused on the basic commitments to Israel, the Father, and the reign of God that guided the life of Jesus and provoked others to put him to death. But readers may be surprised to learn that the three quests for the historical Jesus are largely focused on positivistic claims about words and deeds that can be linked to Jesus, rather than the defining commitments mediated through them. In this section I argue that the *historical reality* of Jesus is a different object from the various versions of the *historical Jesus* that have been the object of each of the three quests.

The first "quest" for the historical Jesus began with the work of Hermann Samuel Reimarus (1694–1768). A lifetime proponent of English deism and the religion of reason, the goal of Reimarus was to "pull ...back the curtain" concealing the real history behind the gospels, so that he could "expose the poverty of Christian origins."[16] Asserting (ahead of his time) that Jesus was a Jewish prophet and an apocalyptic figure, Reimarus argued that the apostles faked his resurrection and proclaimed him the Christ, thereby permanently detaching Christianity and Jesus from Judaism and creating a new religion. His lasting methodological contribution, according to Gerd Theissen, is that Reimarus "distinguishes the preaching of Jesus from the apostles' faith in Christ."[17] Despite the hostility of Reimarus to Christianity, N. T. Wright argues that "the invitation to look more closely [at the history of Jesus], once issued, could not be withdrawn," and that "within the unpromising historical specificity of the story of Jesus we can now...discern...the buried treasure of the gospel."[18]

Later Christian proponents of the first quest added important literary-critical tools to the study of the historical Jesus, establishing the historical priority of Matthew, Mark, and Luke over the Gospel of John (F. C. Baur), gaining acceptance for the two-source hypothesis (Mark and the sayings source known as "Q"), and promoting the historical priority of Mark and Q (Heinrich Julius Holtzmann, 1832–1910). While followers of the first quest were generally united in their conviction that gospel faith and history (the history of Jesus) could not be reconciled, Wright argues instead that "rigorous history (i.e., open-ended investigation of actual events in first-century Palestine) and rigorous theology (i.e. open-ended investigation of what the word 'god,' and hence the adjective 'divine,' might actually refer to) belong together, and never more so than in discussion of Jesus." While a truly Jewish Jesus might lead us to question the use of certain Greek philosophical categories in formulating aspects of Christian doctrine about Jesus, Wright says, "It would be pleasant if, for once, the historians and the theologians could set the agenda for the philosophers, instead of vice versa."[19]

I would argue that a historically oriented metaphysics is exactly what is provided by the concept of "historical reality" developed by Ignacio Ellacuría. It provides a way of thinking about the transcendence of Jesus as a "transcendence within" the history of Israel and El Salvador, overcoming the Greek philosophical tendency to conceptualize transcendence as moving away from, or outside of history. This move also undermines the general presupposition of the first quest that gospel faith and history cannot be reconciled by dealing with the gospels as interpretations of the historical reality of Jesus, rather than as collections of allegedly historical words and deeds.

In 1906 Albert Schweitzer destroyed scholarly confidence in the first quest with his book, *The Quest for the Historical Jesus*, which argued that the nineteenth-century liberal lives of Jesus had uncritically projected the authors' biases onto their object. Schweitzer's skepticism produced a fifty-year hiatus in serious attempts to reconstruct the historical Jesus, punctuated by the startling claim of Rudolf Bultmann that the life and message of the historical Jesus was just a "presupposition" to the preaching of Paul and the first generation of disciples, and was therefore not essential to "the theology of the New Testament ...itself."[20]

Echoes of this skepticism in relation to the historical Jesus are heard today, in my opinion, in the idealist claim of a variety of biblical experts that the "real Jesus" is an unknowable object, much like the "thing in itself" that Kant argued is not directly accessible to the understanding. This is how I would characterize the minimalist claim of Fr. John Meier, a leading Catholic biblical authority on Jesus, who argues that "the 'historical Jesus' is...a theoretical abstraction of modern scholars" based on what we can "reconstruct by using the scientific tools of modern historical research," and who must never be confused with "the real Jesus of Nazareth."[21] Such warnings against naïve realism are fine and good, but Christians like Oscar Romero and Marina are looking for more than scholarly abstractions.

Eventually, on October 23, 1953, Ernst Käsemann, a former student of Bultmann, announced a "new quest for the historical Jesus."[22] Käsemann proposed to limit his investigation to whether the disciples' preaching of the exaltation of Jesus as the Christ after his death and resurrection (sometimes called the *kerygmatic* Christ) finds historical support in the pre-Easter proclamation of Jesus. To their credit, Käsemann, Gunther Bornkamm, and others tried to develop precise "criteria for historical judgments." In the end, however, Wright argues that their efforts "did not represent a turning to history in the fullest sense" and produced limited results due in part to their narrow focus on the tools of form and tradition criticism, while tending to diminish the Jewishness of Jesus.[23]

By contrast, Sean Freyne, a leading Catholic expert on the first-century Galilee of Jesus, asserts that Ellacuría's concept of the "historical reality of Jesus" leaves ample room for conventional historical methods and generally tries to place Jesus *in continuity with both his Jewish inheritance and early Christian reception.*[24] Like Marina and Archbishop Romero, and unlike the scholars of the second quest, Ellacuría's approach is interested in Jesus as a historical figure in his own right, which takes us beyond Jesus' role as the object of New Testament preaching or *kerygma.*

Finally, the third quest has been described in the following terms by Wright, who coined the term.

> The pursuit of truth—historical truth—is what the Third Quest is all about...[,] serious historical method as opposed to the pseudo-historical use of home-made "criteria...The much vaunted "normal critical tools" [of the second quest], particularly form-criticism, are being tacitly bypassed in the search for Jesus; enquiry is proceeding by means of a proper, and often clearly articulated, method of hypothesis and verification.[25]

The task, therefore, "is not...conceived as the reconstruction of traditions about Jesus, according to their place within the history of the early church, but [rather] the advancement of serious historical hypotheses—that is, the telling of large-scale narratives—about Jesus himself, and the examination of the...relevant data to show how they fit." Thus, he concludes, "I am, after all, suggesting no more than that Jesus be studied like any other figure of the ancient past."

There can be no doubt that these elements, tempered by an awareness of the provisional nature of any historical hypothesis about Jesus, advance the reconstruction of what Ellacuría means by the *historical reality* of Jesus. However, Ellacuría's concern is more specific, and it is driven by his awareness of the faith of people like Archbishop Romero and Marina. Ellacuría is interested in the historical reality defined or historicized through the words, actions, and other details of the actual life of Jesus, many of which are lost, but some of which can be plausibly reconstructed utilizing ancient texts like the gospels in combination with historical and archeological research on ancient Israel and Rome.

While the gospels do not claim to know everything Jesus said and did, they do claim to understand the *basic stance* embodied in his words and deeds. This leads Ellacuría to state that "only a *logos* which takes into account the historical reality of Jesus can open the way for a total Christology," one that, like the gospels, "must start from the fact, indisputable to the eye of faith, that the historical life of Jesus is the fullest revelation of the Christian God."[26] Freed from narrow positivistic approaches to the words and deeds of Jesus recounted by the evangelists, we can legitimately ask whether the claims of the gospels about the historical reality of Jesus are validated by the evidence. We can investigate what we might learn today about the meaning of his words and deeds recounted there. And, finally, perhaps more to the point, we can see why the interest of Ignacio Ellacuría in the stories of Marina, Rutilio Grande, and Archbishop Oscar Romero would lead him to ask, why was Jesus killed, and what it was about the historical reality of Jesus that led to his death?

How Does Marina's Story Help Us Understand the Historical Reality of Jesus?

We have seen, then, that Marina's faith, hope, and loving struggle to keep her family alive have "irrupted" into civil societies on two continents that have no place for her. And now that she has been noticed she dares to "interrupt" important scholarly quests for the historical

Jesus with "naïve" questions and concerns that have been ruled out of order. Still, no less a figure than Archbishop Oscar Romero, whom many consider the most important episcopal martyr of the twentieth century, can be said to have posed a similar question: What does it mean to say that the crucified peasants of Aguilares are "the image" of the crucified Jesus?

Fr. Jon Sobrino, SJ, was perhaps Archbishop Romero's closest theological advisor during his three years as shepherd of El Salvador. Thus, in what follows, I will briefly examine Sobrino's answer to the question, "Why was Jesus killed?" and explore what the answer reveals about the historical reality of Jesus. I will then conclude with a few words about what that reality has to do with Marina, her family, and her friends.

Sobrino asserts that the crucifixion should be seen as the reaction of the Temple leadership (and indirectly of Pilate) to the implications for them of Jesus' *basic stance* toward the history and people of Israel, his relationship to the Father, and his mission to initiate the kingdom of God as good news to the poor. Sobrino insists that Jesus' belief that his Father sent him to bring the kingdom of God as good news for the poor is what led to his crucifixion, the defining moment of his life and person.[27]

Biblical scholar Daniel Harrington praises this dimension of Sobrino's work, arguing that his "'historical-theological' reading of Jesus of Nazareth offers important methodological contributions to the historical and theological study of Jesus and his death."[28] Harrington is glad that Sobrino is not constrained by the "narrow version of historical criticism" practiced by many biblical critics and asserts that Sobrino has developed a "more adequate and fruitful way of treating ancient sources," which "involves taking seriously the historical data about Jesus and trying to do theology on the basis of and in light of these data."[29] This allows Sobrino to develop "strong analogies between first-century Palestine and late-twentieth-century El Salvador" that open up new insights "that other interpreters in other circumstances may miss."[30]

Sobrino is modest about his own contribution, asserting, "I have nothing to add" to the scholarly discussion regarding "exegetical and historical-critical methods in presenting the reality of Galilee and Jesus."[31] Rather, his focus is more pastoral. Sobrino wants to reflect, in light of the gospel, on "the path I have tread in El Salvador" with the likes of Marina, Rutilio Grande, and Archbishop Romero.[32] The reader should not miss the echo in these words of the 1965 Vatican II mandate of reading the signs of the times in light of the gospel. Nor should we be surprised that Sobrino can say that "being consciously and actively immersed in the reality of El Salvador during the 1970s and 1980s has greatly enhanced my understanding of Jesus of Galilee."[33]

Harrington endorses this approach, and agrees with Sobrino on historical-exegetical grounds that "Jesus' death was not a mistake, tragic or otherwise," and that "what got Jesus killed...was the fact that he was a radical threat to the religious and political powers of his time."[34] The problem was that Jesus "got in the way" of powerful actors by defending the victims of their policies in the name of the kingdom of God.[35] As evidence, Harrington cites the fact that "the four Gospels are united in presenting Jesus as the victim of persecution and in suggesting that his death was...the logical consequence of who Jesus was and the circumstances in which he lived and worked."[36]

But, Harrington asks, if Jesus was killed for his defense of the poor and persecuted by the powers of his day (particularly those associated with the Temple), "Did Jesus know beforehand that he was going to suffer and die in Jerusalem?"[37] And, we may add, what was the significance of that death? Putting aside the three passion predictions as later insertions (Mk 8:31, 9:31, 10:33–34), Harrington says that Sobrino "wisely points to the fate of John the Baptist" in order to argue that Jesus went to Jerusalem ready to accept death "out of fidelity to the cause of the kingdom of God, out of confidence in the one whom he called 'Father,' and out of loyalty to his prophetic calling."[38] In this way, he says, Sobrino correctly locates "the link between the historical Jesus and the Christ of faith" precisely at "the root of Jesus' resolve to go to Jerusalem...[and] his understanding of his life as service on behalf of others, even to the point of sacrificial service." This, then, is a critical clue to the possible meaning of Jesus' death, and it is captured in what the gospels portray as a defining moment of the historical reality of Jesus: his decision to accept suffering and death in order to fulfill his messianic, prophetic, and priestly mission from the Father to bring the kingdom of God as good news for the poor.

But what is it about Jesus' ministry of announcing and enacting the kingdom of God as good news for the poor that was so provocative as to bring about his crucifixion? Sobrino argues persuasively that in the synoptic gospels, Jesus announces the kingdom as "good and liberative"[39] news for the poor, a "hoped-for utopia in the midst of the sufferings of history."[40] Sobrino also asserts that Jesus is driven by a spirit of ethical responsibility for the kingdom. He enacts this sense of responsibility through miracles that promote hope and overcome fatalism among the common people, through challenges to the powerful to stop oppressing the weak, and in the form of inclusive meals that serve as joyful "signs of the coming of the Kingdom."[41]

Sobrino argues that Jesus also enacts a "prophetic praxis" by means of controversies, unmaskings, and denunciations that call for reforms among "the scribes, the Pharisees, the rich, the priests, the rulers"; that expose abuses of institutional power; and that "show that the anti-Kingdom seeks to justify itself in God's name."[42] All of this demonstrates, in Sobrino's view, "that Jesus, objectively, faced up to...society as a whole —including its structural dimension—and sought to change it."[43]

This, then, brings us to the role of the Temple incident (Mk 11:15–19) and Jesus' prophecy that the Temple would be destroyed (Mk 13:2) in the chain of events that bring about his death. Citing the Temple incident, Harrington says:

> It is reasonable to conclude that at the "religious trial" [before the Sanhedrin] Jesus was accused of wanting to destroy the Temple, not only because he criticized certain aspects of it, but also because he offered an alternative (the kingdom of God), which implied that the Temple would no longer be the core of the political, social, and economic life of the Jewish people.[44]

Harrington also endorses Sobrino's position that Luke's charges in the "political trial" before the Roman governor, Pontius Pilate (Lk 23:2), can be defended as historical: "We found this man perverting our nation, forbidding them to pay taxes to the emperor, and saying that he himself is the Messiah, a king."[45] Harrington adds that "the charge that Jesus made himself 'the Messiah, a king,' would have been especially incendiary in this context." He says the evangelist's description of the inscription on the cross, "The King of the Jews" (Mk 15:26), not to mention the public torture of the crucifixion, would have served as brutal public warnings to other "would-be Messiahs... tempted to lead an uprising against the Roman occupiers."[46] Thus, Harrington agrees with Sobrino that Jesus' confrontation with the merchants at the Temple and his prophetic words there likely played a role in provoking the Jewish leadership to demand his trial and crucifixion on charges of blasphemy (before the Sanhedrin) and sedition (before Pilate) in Jerusalem.

What, then, does all of this tell us about the historical reality of Jesus? While Sobrino insists that Jesus' zeal to reform the Temple demonstrates that it is incorrect to argue "that Jesus was against the Temple as such," he argues instead that in the Temple incident "Jesus distances himself from and criticizes [its] alienating and oppressive worship."[47] So the Temple incident emerges as the action of a Jewish

prophet who seeks to reform the Temple to authentic worship, to expose its financial exploitation of the poor as "an expression of the
anti-Kingdom," and to "show that the anti-Kingdom seeks to justify
itself in God's name."[48] He interprets Jesus' prediction that the Temple will be destroyed (Mt 24:1–2, Mk 13:1–2, Lk 21:5–6) as "a symbolic expression denouncing the...false god and the oppressive
structure" of Roman rule, "upheld by religious power and justified in
the name of [Jewish] religion."[49] This leads Sobrino to conclude that
"in this praxis, Jesus can be seen to be in the line of the classic prophets
of Israel, of Amos, Hosea, Isaiah, Jeremiah, Micah..., and in that of
the modern prophets, Archbishop Oscar Romero,...[and] Martin
Luther King Jr."[50]

This, then, is how Jesus fulfills his mission from the Father to announce the kingdom of God as good news to the poor and salvation to
the nations. But as in the case of so many prophets before and after
him, Jesus' reward is persecution and death for speaking the word of
God to those who persecute the poor. In this way Jesus also shares the
"fate" of the prophets when "the anti-Kingdom reacts and puts him to
death." Sobrino's argument, then, is that Jesus historicizes what he believes is his mission from the Father to initiate the kingdom of God as
good news for the poor through a culturally Jewish practice that is both
liberating and prophetic. Sobrino argues that this commitment to his
Father, his mission to Israel, and his preaching of the kingdom of God
as good news for the poor are the defining elements of the historical reality of Jesus, and that they are enacted in a form that leads the Temple
leadership to persecute Jesus and to orchestrate his faith-filled death on
the cross.

Conclusion

What, then, does the historical reality of Jesus of Galilee and his persecution and death have to do with Marina, her family, and her friends?
First, we have seen that Marina and José Antonio do not speak of their
journey as a triumph of personal agency or will (though it certainly is),
but rather emphasize their gratitude to God for inspiring so many
people to support them in their struggles and for protecting them in
their perilous journey. Second, we saw that the suffering of other
peasants like Marina led Archbishop Romero to ask, in what sense
are the crucified peasants of the Rio Lempa massacre and Aguilares
"the image" of the persecution and crucifixion of Jesus? Third,
Romero's question led Ignacio Ellacuría to argue that the historical

reality of Jesus was defined by his commitment to his mission from the Father to initiate the kingdom of God as good news for the poor and that he was killed by those who rejected this message. But what does all this have to do with Marina, her family, and her friends?

For Marina, Jesus of Galilee speaks of his Father as a God of compassion, a God who longs to give life to his beloved children, and a God who raises up disciples as living signs of the kingdom of God and good news for the poor. On the one hand, it is true that Jesus, like the prophets before him, is persecuted and killed by those who reject the changes implied by God's message, just as the children of privilege today crucify the poor to protect their interests. On the other hand, God raises up new disciples, not to be crucified yet again, but so that, moved by their faith in the resurrection of Jesus, they might help to break the endless cycle of oppression and crucifixion by taking today's crucified peoples down from the cross and supporting their struggles to live and to make a life for their children and grandchildren.

This is a core of Marina's faith, and a sign of the redemptive outcome of the persecution and death of Jesus for her, her family, and those of us who are her friends. The life of Jesus was built around his commitment to realize God's will for Israel and the nations by initiating the kingdom of God as good news for the poor. Marina's faith reminds us that the message of Jesus awakens hope and love that empowers the struggles of families to survive and thrive in a world of both oppression and hope. Marina believes that God raises up communities of solidarity and friendship to help people like her on their way, allowing their demands for justice and a better life to irrupt into civil society on two continents. In response, I can only say that Lynn and I have come to share Marina's hope, and the faith that supports it. This is the gospel of Marina, the gospel of Archbishop Romero, the gospel of Jesus. Like her namesake, the peasant girl, Mary of Nazareth, Marina proclaims, "My soul magnifies the Lord, and my spirit rejoices in God my Savior...For the Mighty One has done great things for me, and holy is his name" (Lk 1:46b–47, 49).

Notes

1. *United Nations Human Development Report, 2007–2008, Fighting Climate Change: Human Solidarity in a Divided World,* (New York: United Nations Human Development Program, 2007), 25, and Shaohua Chen and Martin Ravallion, *The Developing World Is Poorer Than We Thought, But No Less Successful in the Fight against Poverty* (Washington, DC: World Bank, August 2008), 4.

2. United Nations, Report of the Commission on the Truth for El Salvador, *From Madness to Hope: The 12-year War in El Salvador* (New York: United Nations, March 15, 1993), 126.

3. Benjamin C. Schwarz, *American Counterinsurgency Doctrine and El Salvador: The Frustrations of Reform and the Illusions of Nation Building* (Santa Monica: RAND, 1991), 44.

4. "Norberto, Mesa Grande," in *Forced to Move: Salvadorean Refugees in Honduras*, ed. Renato Camarda, with an introduction by Congressman Ronald V. Dellums (San Francisco: Solidarity Publications, 1985), 8.

5. All quotes from José Antonio Zavala and Rosa Marina Zavala, interview by the author, June 24, 2010, Pittsburg, California, transcript, files of author; or José Antonio Zavala and Rosa Marina Zavala, interview by Marybeth, 1990, Oakland Catholic Worker, transcript, files of Robert Lassalle-Klein.

6. Yvonne Dilling, "Suffering Together at Valle Nuevo," Center for Christian Ethics at Baylor University (copyright © 2005), http://www.baylor.edu/christianethics/SufferingarticleDilling.pdf.

7. Lynn Lassalle-Klein, interview by the author, August 27, 2010.

8. *The Developing World Is Poorer Than We Thought*, 33.

9. Schwarz, *American Counterinsurgency Doctrine and El Salvador*, 82.

10. See United Nations, *Report of the Commission on the Truth for El Salvador*, 1993; and Camarda, *Forced to Move*, 1985.

11. For a fuller development of the following points, see Robert Lassalle-Klein, "Jesus of Galilee and the Crucified People: The Contextual Christology of Jon Sobrino and Ignacio Ellacuría," in *The Galilean Jesus, Theological Studies*, ed. Robert Lassalle-Klein, 70, 2 (Spring 2009): 347–76.

12. Rudolfo Cardenal, *Historia de Una Esperanza, Vida de Rutilio Grande* (San Salvador: UCA Editores, 1985), 434–43, at 436.

13. "Homilia en Aguilares [June 19, 1977]," *La voz de los sin voz: La palabra viva de Monseñor Oscar Arnulfo Romero* (San Salvador: UCA Editores, 1980), 207–12, at 208.

14. The term "crucified people" first appeared in Ignacio Ellacuría, "El pueblo crucificado, ensayo de soteriología histórica," in *Cruz y resurrección: anuncio de una Iglesia nueva*, ed. Ignacio Ellacuría et al. (Mexico City: CTR, 1978), 49–82; translated as "The Crucified People," in *Mysterium Liberationis* (Maryknoll, NY: Orbis Books, 1993), 580–604, at 580.

15. Ignacio Ellacuría, *Freedom Made Flesh: The Mission of Christ and His Church* (Maryknoll, NY: Orbis Books, 1976), 27.

16. N. T. Wright, *Jesus and the Victory of God*, vol. 2, *Christian Origins and the Question of God* (Minneapolis: Fortress Press, 1996), 18.

17. Gerd Theissen and Annette Merz, *The Historical Jesus, A Comprehensive Guide* (London: SCM Press, 1998), 3.

18. Wright, *Jesus and the Victory of God*, 18.

19. Ibid., 8.

20. Rudolf Bultmann, *Theology of the New Testament*, vol. 1 (New York: Charles Scribners Sons, 1951, 1955), 3.

21. John P. Meier, *A Marginal Jew: Rethinking the Historical Jesus*, vol. 2, *Mentor, Message, and Miracles* (New York: Doubleday, 1994), 4.

22. Ernst Käsemann, *Essays on New Testament Themes* (London: SCM, 1964), 15–47, cited in Wright, *Jesus and the Victory of God*, 23.

23. Wright, *Jesus and the Victory of God*, 23.

24. Sean Freyne, e-mail message to author, June 4, 2010. Also see Sean Freyne, "Jesus, Prayer, and Politics: 'Contemplative Action for Justice,'" in *Studies of Religion and Politics in the Early Christian Centuries*, ed. David Luckensmeyer and Paul Allen (Strathfield, Australia: St. Paul Publications, 2010), esp. 3–7.

25. Ibid., 87.

25. Ellacuría, *Freedom Made Flesh*, 27.

26. Ibid., 52–54.

27. Daniel J. Harrington, SJ, "What Got Jesus Killed? Sobrino's Historical-Theological Reading of Scripture," in *Hope and Solidarity: Sobrino's Challenge to Christian Theology*, ed. Stephen J. Pope (Maryknoll, NY: Orbis Books, 2008), 79–89, at 81.

28. Ibid.

30. Ibid., 85.

31. Jon Sobrino, S.J., "Jesus of Galilee from the Salvadoran Context: Compassion, Hope, and Following the Light of the Cross," in *Theological Studies* 70, 2 (Spring 2009): 438.

32. Ibid., 460.

33. Ibid., 438.

34. Harrington, "What Got Jesus Killed?" 81.

35. Ibid., 82.

36. Ibid.

37. Ibid.

38. Ibid., 82–83.

39. Jon Sobrino, *Jesus the Liberator: A Historical-Theological View* (Maryknoll, NY: Orbis Books, 1993), 75.

40. Ibid., 70.

41. Ibid., 103.

42. Ibid., 161.

43. Ibid.

44. Harrington, "What Got Jesus Killed?" 83.

45. Ibid.

46. Ibid., 84.

47. Sobrino, *Jesus the Liberator*, 177.

48. Ibid., 161.

49. Ibid., 178.

50. Ibid., 179.

PART II

THE BIBLE

7

THE WOMAN WHO CHANGED JESUS

TEXT AND CONTEXT

Pablo Alonso

The intercultural encounter between Jesus the Jew and a Syrophoenician woman in the territory of the pagan city of Tyre northwest of
Galilee (Mk 7:24–30) is a puzzling story that has prompted many different interpretations over the centuries.[1] Four specific features make
this encounter unique in the Gospel of Mark. First, the stress on the
woman's identity, "Greek, Syrophoenician by race," is important. Nobody else in Mark is identified in such a precise way, nor so clearly as
pagan. Second, Jesus' initial refusal to help the woman stands in sharp
contrast with what the gospel has hitherto presented as Jesus' responsive attitude and mission toward people in need, including non-Jews
like the Gerasene. Third, this is the only case in Mark when a woman
directly speaks to Jesus. And fourth, in the end the girl is healed, but it
is not clear why. Jesus neither does nor says anything to expel the
demon. Instead, he praises the woman's word and announces that the
exorcism has already occurred.

In the following pages I will re-examine this interesting intercultural story, paying special attention to its literary setting in a section of
Mark (chapters 6 through 8) characterized by the two feeding narratives. My ultimate goal is twofold: to better understand the meaning of
this narrative for its original audience, and to explore its relevance for
readers in our own time of globalization and migration.

Why Does Jesus Refuse the Woman's Plea?

When the story begins, Jesus has just challenged the Pharisees and the
scribes about tradition (7:1–13). He has revoked Jewish dietary laws
(7:15) and confronted the disciples' lack of understanding (7:17–19).
He clearly states that it is what comes out of a person that defiles

(7:20–23). Mark says that Jesus then leaves Galilee and goes "away to the region of Tyre" (7:24), a wealthy Phoenician town on the Mediterranean Sea. The narrator points out that Jesus has no apparent intention to proclaim the good news in this Gentile territory, saying, "He entered a house and did not want anyone to know he was there." But his presence is discovered by a woman, "Greek, Syrophoenician by race," who Mark says "bowed down at his feet," and "begged him to cast the demon out of her daughter" (7:25–26). Jesus then replies, "Let the children be fed first, for it is not fair to take the children's bread and throw it to the dogs" (7:27). This surprising retort propels us out of the world of exorcism and into the sphere of domestic life. Jesus is now talking about children, dogs, and bread![2]

If we look at the Hebrew Scriptures, we find a self-definition of the Jews as "children of God" (for example, Is 30:1; 63:8; Jer 3:19). On the other hand, dogs are despised in the New Testament (Lk 16:21; 2 Pet 2:22), and the word is offensive when ascribed to people (Mt 7:6; Phil 3:2; Rev 22:15). Dogs, especially stray dogs, are considered to be unclean animals, for they feed on corpses (for example, Ex 22:31 and 1 Kings 14:11).

Without doubt, then, this is an insult, though some commentators try to soften the blow by noting that Jesus uses the diminutive (*tois kunariois*). To speak of "little dogs" instead of "dogs" does not change the point, however, in view of the great difference in status between children and dogs. Jesus' saying is to be taken as offensive to the woman, keeping in mind the Jewish context, the plural form, and the fact that she is the child's mother (in other words, it refers to both of them). The woman and her daughter are firmly situated as outsiders by this response.[3]

Others have suggested that Jesus might be quoting a proverb similar to one documented by Erasmus in his *Adagia*, in which he collects 4,151 adages of antiquity.[4] The meaning of the proverb in question seems different, however, and a further examination of the work of Erasmus bears no special fruit. There are several proverbs related to dogs, even two that link dogs with bread, but none expresses the same idea articulated by Jesus. If we want to go this route, then, we will have to content ourselves with the conclusion that Jesus is echoing local domestic wisdom about children and dogs.[5]

But why the reference to bread? Tyre was important for the number and the size of its colonies spread around the Mediterranean, reaching even the Atlantic. The Hebrew Scriptures mention Tyre's commercial ties with Judah and Israel, its need for wheat and oil (1 Kings 5:15–26; Ezek 27:17), and the existence of a rural territory (Ezek 26:6, 8). Although conflicts happened from time to time, political and commercial contacts continued through the reconstruction of the Temple (Ezra 3:7) into the Greco-Roman period (see 2 Macc 4:18–20, 8:11; *Jewish Antiquities* 14.197–198; *Jewish War* 1.231–238, and elsewhere). Due to its lack of cultivable land, Tyre needed to buy agricultural products from the Galilean hinterlands (see Acts 12:20), which created food shortages and caused suffering among the rural Jewish population. Thus Jesus' words turn a well known hierarchy on its head, with the rich Gentiles of the cities cast in the role of hungry dogs, and priority given to the poor rural Jews.[6]

We must also take into account that the woman is presented as Greek (7:26), which suggests she is a member of the upper class, the first people to be Hellenized. Two other signs that the woman is afflu-ent include the note that her child sleeps in a bed (7:30), and the image employed to answer Jesus, "the dogs eating under the table" (7:28). Both refer to pieces of furniture (the bed and the table) and not to the usual pallet or mat.[7]

In summary, Jesus was a Galilean Jew, and the socio-economic and religious context of mid-first century CE Galilee sheds light on his reply. Galilean Jews maintained a complex and often controversial re-lationship with Tyrians (whom they regarded as pagans) in this period, especially in the border regions, and against this background the re-sponse of Jesus to the Syrophoenician woman makes sense. Theissen speaks of "aggressive prejudices, supported by economic dependency and legitimated by religious traditions."[8] For the contemporaries of Jesus, the world exists as a zero-sum game: bread is limited, and thus the gain of the dogs implies a loss for the children.[9] Behind Jesus' words we see an assumption that Gentiles are excluded from his mission. Jesus dedicates himself to the "children of God," and yet he is speaking with a foreigner, one of those who deprive his people of bread. The gap that separates Jesus and the woman is emphasized by a variety of identity factors: male and female, Galilean and Syrophoenician, Jew and pagan, itinerant preacher and upper-class woman, man of God and mother of a possessed girl. All of these provide cultural, religious, social, and eco-nomic reasons for distance.

Why Does Jesus Change His Mind?

The woman does not accept Jesus' brusque reply, however, and answers, "Lord, also the dogs under the table eat the little children's crumbs" (7:28). Jesus responds, "For this word go, the demon has left your daughter" (29). The story concludes with the narrator's comment, "So she went home, found the child lying on the bed, and the demon gone" (30).

In briefly analyzing this exchange, we can see that Jesus acknowledges the major role that the woman's word—her *logos* in Greek (29)—plays in it. In her rejoinder she does not dispute that she is a "dog," a pagan, and a "taker of bread," even picking up the metaphor and developing it further. But she changes the word for children from *tekna* to *paidia*. This is significant, for the latter focuses more on age rather than social status. And the nuance is telling. Though the Jews continue to be called children, the emphasis is no longer on having been begotten by God, but on their dependence on God, a characteristic that is not exclusive to Jews.

Further, the woman shifts the effect of the metaphor by introducing the idea of simultaneity: the spatial distinction remains, but the temporal one disappears. The dogs are under the table, but they eat at the same time as the children, being fed on the crumbs during the meal. Whereas in 7:27 the type of dogs to which Jesus is referring is not clear, the woman is clearly talking about house dogs, most likely pups. She has interpreted Jesus' words in the best possible way, in terms of closeness. While the woman treats Jesus as a superior by falling at his feet, begging, and calling him Lord, she is arguing her position. She cleverly employs the dynamics of honor and shame so as to get her request granted.[10] And her capacity to hear and to speak honestly and directly with Jesus contrasts significantly with the disciples who listen but do not understand (7:14, 18; 8:18), and with the Pharisees who refuse to eat bread without having performed their ritual purifications. She is happy with the crumbs.

Many authors hold that Jesus recognizes the woman's faith in her words (7:29), a faith in him that goes beyond his power to heal, which is evident in her request. Others stress only the force of her argument, full of intelligence and wit. David Rhoads argues that "in Mark, faith is embodied in action." An implicit trust that the healing will take place is embedded in her actions of coming, kneeling, asking, and persisting. Rhoads asserts that Markan faith has little to do with beliefs about Jesus; its focus is "trust that a request will be granted."[11] Undermining this position, however, we observe that by this point in the gospel narrative Jesus has already performed two exorcisms and one healing (1:21–28; 3:1–6; 5:1–20) in which there has been neither mention of faith nor display of "faith in action."

The key characteristics of our pericope, then, are: (1) faith is not mentioned; (2) faith shown in action is not sufficient for Jesus to perform an exorcism; and (3) Jesus explicitly acknowledges the significance of the woman's words. If it is true that faith is not mentioned in other miracles in Mark, the last two elements are specific to this one. Rhoads finds faith in the intelligence of the woman's reply,[12] but Mark does not note this. Although unique, this encounter joins other episodes in the Gospel of Mark in which faith is not the reason why a miracle takes place.

Mark 7:29 emphasizes the word or *logos* spoken by the woman, though it would appear to be up to the reader to clarify exactly why Jesus appreciates what she says. In the parallel text, Matthew 15:21–28, Jesus' recognition of the woman's faith provides an explanation absent in Mark. In Mark, however, it is not only that the woman accepts the priority of Israel. Mark also stresses her argument in favor of the little dogs, her wit, her intelligence, and her resilient attitude, all manifestations of her dignity as human being, a *logos* that flows from her God-given humanity. Suprisingly, then, it is the woman who brings Jesus the word of God through her ability to see beyond divisions that separate them, providing a glimpse of a messianic feast where there is abundant food for everyone. Her words point toward a new creation, reminding Jesus and the hearers of Mark's gospel of the power of speech at the creation of the world in Genesis.[13] This *logos*, which Jesus heeds, echoes the "voice" he hears both at his baptism and at the transfiguration (Mk 1:11, 9:7).

Mark's narrative seems to suggest, then, that the reason for the exorcism lies in the interpersonal interaction and the mirroring changes that draw the woman and Jesus to one another. But it is the woman who takes the initiative, and the healing comes about because of the relationship established between them. From the woman's side, we may call it "trust" that the healing will take place, rather than "faith" in Jesus. But both the woman and Jesus count as actors in this little drama, and the answer to our question (why does Jesus change his mind?) emerges from their conversation, or (more precisely) *dia-logos* in Greek.

For his part, Jesus modifies his initial stance toward the woman and her daughter. His perception of the girl changes from "dog" to "daughter." He undergoes a change of mentality, that is to say, a *meta-noia* or "conversion," which leads him to acknowledge her human dignity. Just as Jesus' Jewishness plays a role in his refusal, it now plays a role in his decision to heed the truth of her words and his subsequent recognition of the woman as a child (*paidion*) of God. Jesus' relationship with the Father leads him to accept both the woman's word (or *logos*) and the woman herself, simultaneously restoring right relationship with a Gentile and deepening his own Jewishness.[14] Thus we see that love for God and love for the neighbor cannot be separated (Deut 6:4–5; Lev 19:18;

see Mk 12:28–34). If Jesus is "bested" by the woman, the woman has already been "bested" when she takes recourse to Jesus. She has already acknowledged her powerlessness, limitation, and need for assistance when she decides to go to him. God, Father, and the Spirit of God as Mother have heard that word and granted the healing.

Feminist exegesis has highlighted the role of the Syrophoenician woman as a dramatic subject who changes the mind of Jesus and is not just the object of his mercy.[15] And it must be emphasized that the woman is an outsider. She shares very little with Jesus, yet nevertheless becomes the agent of change. She is a minor character in the gospel, anonymous, yet essential. In this way she joins two other Markan characters who are also anonymous but vital as they change Jesus: the leper (1:40–45), and the woman with a hemorrhage (5:25–34). None of the three belong to the core of Israel or the traditional "children of God," but to the margins. But all three coincide in taking initiative and prompting Jesus to cross boundaries where legal, ritual, and social issues intersect. In this way, each one elicits something new in Jesus.

With regard to its historicity, the episode is understandable in the context of the border regions of Tyre and Galilee.[16] To those who maintain that the episode was created by first-generation Christians[17] one may ask, why create a story in which the point of view voiced by Jesus is refuted?[18] The fact that the story violates cultural norms for both purity codes and gender roles, together with its critical view of Jesus, serves as a warrant to reconsider the authenticity of the story.[19] Thus, I would agree that "the historicity of this encounter is plausible, if unprovable,"[20] which differs from the claim that it includes Jesus' authentic words.

In my view, then, the aim of the story is not to justify the mission to the Gentiles by tracing its origins back to Jesus, because by the time of the writing of the Gospel of Mark this is already an established fact. Rather, I would argue that the evangelist seeks to help the readers of his narrative tackle problems of inclusion arising in the early Christian community through reminders of the historical attitude of Jesus. Mark challenges Christians to change their minds just as Jesus did and attacks narrow assumptions about "who may share in God's salvation."[21]

The Outcome of This Encounter for the Rest of the Gospel

As the story ends, the narrator tells us that Jesus then "returned from the region of Tyre, and went by way of Sidon toward the Sea of Galilee, in the region of the Decapolis" (7:31). The route described is awkward on three grounds. Sidon is north of Tyre, while Galilee and the lake (or sea) are to the south, so a long detour would be required. Then the lake is not located in the Decapolis, and in addition Tyre and Sidon are on the opposite side of the lake (northwest) from the Decapolis (southeast). If Jesus were returning to the Sea of Galilee from Tyre and Sidon, he would not normally cross the Decapolis. We are not dealing here with Mark's ignorance of the geography of Palestine, however, but with an itinerary constructed for a theological purpose: it demonstrates the impact of the change that Jesus has just experienced, the newfound openness just acquired with regard to his mission. Even if no missionary activity is depicted, Jesus' return to Galilee touches all the surrounding Gentile regions.

Jesus immediately heals a deaf-mute man in the Decapolis (7:31–37). Word spreads, "a great crowd" gathers, and Jesus feeds the multitudes with "seven loaves" and "a few small fish" (8:1–9). A prior feeding (6:31–44) has already taken place on the western shore of the lake where Jesus has been portrayed as the good shepherd teaching his sheep. In that story the hour has grown late and, responding to the concerns of his disciples, Jesus feeds the crowd of "five thousand men" with five loaves of bread and twelve baskets left over. The figures, five and twelve, evoke Israel, the five books of the Torah and the twelve tribes of Israel.[22] Now on pagan soil following his interaction with the Syrophoenician woman, Jesus takes the initiative in the second feeding narrative. Some of those who are fed have come from a great distance, an expression associated with Gentiles,[23] and this time the crowd numbers four thousand, a figure that calls to mind the four ends of the earth, which comes up in Mark 13:27.[24] The number of loaves, seven, is a symbol of totality, the sacred number of fulfilment.[25]

Scholars are divided over the identity of the beneficiaries of the second feeding, whether Gentiles or a mixed group. The location does not imply that the crowd is pagan only. The disciples who are Jewish are certainly present, and only "some" have come from a great distance. Further, the distinction between first feeding five thousand Jews and then feeding four thousand Gentiles does not work with the metaphor of simultaneous feedings for children and dogs argued by the Syrophoenician woman after the first feeding. Thus, I would suggest instead that Mark wants the reader to see a progression from the first to the second feeding. The first one is for the Jews, while in the second we reach the common meal, open to everybody. In between, the Syrophoenician woman has changed the mind of Jesus through her metaphor of simultaneous, though still unequal, feedings. In my opinion, then, the symbolism of the numbers four and seven does not point toward the pagan, but to the whole of humanity. The presence of the disciples confirms that Gentiles and Jews alike partake in the second feeding, and that Jewish people are included.[26] Further, while those who have eaten in the first feeding are described as "men" (6:44), the gender of the crowd in the second feeding is not identified (8:9).

This parallels the historical development of the early Christian community.[27] The access of the Gentiles to salvation was in question, as was their welcome to table fellowship (Gal 2:1–14; Acts 10–11). I would assert, then, that Mark's doublet of the feeding narratives serves to emphasize this two-step movement from the feeding of Jews to the feeding of all peoples. The pericope of the Syrophoenician woman provides the hermeneutical key: strict boundaries between Jews and Gentiles are to be removed.[28] The section shows the growing inclusiveness of the project of Jesus, which ultimately comes to embrace every human being.

This reading is confirmed in Jesus' challenge to his disciples, who have taken only one loaf of bread in the boat (8:14), regarding their lack of understanding of the two feedings (8:18–21). This is part of a pericope (8:14–21) that may be considered the climax of the section (6:31–8:26). The section is framed by discussions about Jesus' identity, whether Jesus is John the Baptist raised from the dead, or Elijah (6:14–15 and 8:28), and by two occurrences of Jesus' name (6:30 and 8:27) which, however, is absent from the middle section.

In my opinion, these two verses form an *inclusio* indicating the message of the section: Jesus is to be identified with the "bread." The bread that is multiplied, that feeds and satiates, that is sought by the pagans and finally offered to all, is Jesus himself. He gives the bread, he is the bread. Furthermore, he is the one loaf in the boat (8:14),[29] the sole source needed to feed everybody at the common table of the Eucharist.[30] There is one bread, one table and Jesus' role as unifier is highlighted.[31] Mark's point is that the Eucharist is Jesus, who gives his life, and empowers the commitment of his followers to build an inclusive community. The bread is also a symbol of the benefits of the kingdom: we are called to struggle for justice for those who are marginated or excluded.

Text and Life

Real interpretation terminates in actualization—the mutual transformation of text and reader. The story of the Syrophoenician woman has long spoken to readers who are marginalized or impoverished, and to those who listen to their voices, searching to foster liberation and inclusion. This includes feminist and postcolonial interpreters, minority groups, those immersed in interreligious or intercultural dialogue, and even critics of oppressive international relations.[32]

In facing the ethical and political consequences of this reading of Mark's story about Jesus and the Syrophoenician woman,[33] I look to my own social context of southwestern Europe, and specifically Spain, where I was born, and where as a citizen and a Christian I join others in a common effort to build an inclusive society. This encounter, with all its complexity, reminds me of the situation of refugees and undocumented migrants[34] who, after surviving a dreadful trip in small boats, arrive at the Spanish coasts, whether in Andalusia or the Canary Islands, or at other countries of the European Union such as Italy and Malta.[35] The first reality they meet is very often exclusion: asylum seekers, including children, are detained and confined in what are effectively jails; assistance to undocumented migrants, including health care, is criminalized in some countries. Indeed, their mere existence is ignored, as seen in the fact that undocumented migrants are excluded from the Social Inclusion Strategy of the European Union.[36] Our countries do not want more people. Migrants stand in front of us in line at the emergency room and the unemployment office, and their children pack the primary schools. Social workers and ecclesial ministers are exhausted by the tremendous need, or tired that some are taking advantage of them. We feel that difference divides us, and we want someone else to pay for it. We feel we must protect our wealth and our rights, and only when those are secure will we care for the refugees. In some ways, we are like Jesus at the beginning of the story. He understands us, for he has shared some aspects of our situation.

Yet the story illustrates that we are missing a deeper reality, we are missing the presence of God when we do not listen to the suffering of these women, children, and men. Jesus shows us the way. Indeed, he is the way. We need to learn from those we label as outsiders, the refugees we want to exclude, for they show us what we do not see about ourselves, our communities, and our society.[37] When we ignore their word, we ignore God's own word. The daily challenge we face is whether or not to listen. Gender, origin, culture, and religion separated Jesus and the Syrophoenician woman. Mark tells us that he did not want to be disturbed, and that he initially refused to accept the appeal of an other in need. With humility, intelligence, and courage, however, the woman taught Jesus to bridge those differences. We can still hope. Jesus shows us that, by accepting difference and engaging in dialogue, we can be transformed and enabled to share with others what we have received. Vimal Tirimanna writes, "In this sense, our frontier-crossing can be a moment of grace when we encounter one another... For no one, not even a religion, is an independent, self-sufficient island. God uses each of us to speak to the other, especially in and through our frontier cross-ings and the ensuing encounters."[38]

How might this story, then, nurture our spirituality and action? First, we can look to Jesus as a model of someone who evolves and is open to the influence of others (see also Mk 1:40–45 and 5:25–34). The divinity of Jesus does not diminish his humanity. He gains no ma-terial advantage by being the son of God. He must learn and suffer as he comes to terms with his identity, like any of us. Looking at Christ, the perfect human being, we learn that we all have prejudices, but they need not have the last word. Conflict may give way to dialogue. Thus we should ask for this gift: internal knowledge of Christ, who allows others to transform him. He accompanies us in our struggles to accept the other, he invites us to follow him in his openness.

Second, it is the Syrophoenician woman, an outsider for Jesus, who prompts his change. She reminds the reader that we have much to learn from people who seem invisible to us, people we have placed out-side of our circle of relationships, whom we may despise or exclude, whose initiatives we tend to reject. They are "children of God," and may become a source of new life.

Third, the text casts light on what it means to be a follower of Jesus in a multicultural society. The absence of any reference to faith in Mark's story reminds us that action on behalf of human dignity and jus-tice is grounded first in an appreciation of the other's need regardless of whether they have faith or not. It is linked to our faith, not theirs. At the end of this intercultural conflict, we discover that there is an ab-solute respect of who the woman is. We learn that we must not try to make others like us, but rather learn to respect God's action and pres-ence in each person, in her options, beliefs, and culture.

Fourth and last, but not least, Mark places the story of the Sy-rophoenician woman who changed Jesus in a section that deals with the Eucharist. The origin of the Eucharist lies not only in the Last Sup-per but in the whole of Jesus' life and praxis, including his habit of eat-ing with tax collectors and sinners and his feedings of the multitudes. His followers celebrate the Eucharist in order to commemorate Jesus' life and death for all. Thus the Eucharist is about inclusion, and should be linked to building and developing inclusive social relations and struc-tures in which each one may have equal access to resources and oppor-tunity. We share in Christ, the bread of life, and become one body, which means that we are called to join with him in giving life to the whole body.

For me, the most surprising aspect of this story is that it keeps silence on why Jesus goes to the region of Tyre. In the light of the Christian tradition I tend to interpret this narrative gap by evoking the spiritual experience called *xeniteia*, that is, voluntary exile or expatriation. In the words of Michel de Certeau, "this movement consists in setting out, as Abraham did, for an unknown destination (Heb 11:8), in order to hear the human word of God in a new land, or perhaps in receiving from elsewhere his human face, in what remains a constantly unpredictable story."[39] The comparison with Abraham is not precise, however, as God does not command Jesus to set out. Still, Jesus leaves his land for unknown territory, and the woman's arrival, which seems an interruption, turns out to be the way God chooses to communicate his word (Mk 7:28–29). As A.-J. Levine suggests, Jesus goes to the periphery, and on the periphery he is challenged. This is the challenge of the *basileia*, or reign of God.[40]

Thus, the interaction of the Syrophoenician woman with Jesus reminds us that his followers in Christian communities around the globe are called to take the lead in accepting foreigners, in working with migrants and refugees, and in intercultural and interreligious dialogue. We live in a time when some speak of a clash of civilizations, and the wealthy societies of Europe and the United States protect themselves from accelerating globalization by excluding outsiders and by hardening migration laws. Followers of Jesus have always drawn inspiration from the epic of Israel's journeys into exile and return narrated in the Hebrew Scriptures. I have tried to point to another resource in Mark's account of Jesus' journey into "voluntary exile" and his story about the Syrophoenician woman who changed Jesus. It is a story that leads his disciples to remember him by welcoming the exile, and by accepting those who have been rejected into the one body of Christ.

Notes

1. See Pablo Alonso, "La mujer sirofenicia en la interpretación patrística," *Estudios Eclesiásticos* 80 (2005): 455–83, and for a fuller discussion of the questions raised here see Pablo Alonso, *The Woman Who Changed Jesus: Crossing Boundaries in Mark 7:24–30*, Biblical Tools and Studies, 11 (Leuven: Peeters Publishers, forthcoming).

2. Camille Focant, *L'évangile selon Marc* (Paris: Cerf, 2004), 283.

3. Glenna S. Jackson, *"Have Mercy on Me": The Story of the Canaanite Woman in Matthew 15:21–28* (New York, Sheffield, 2002), 57.

4. David Smith, "Our Lord's Saying to the Syro-Phoenician Woman," *Expository Times* 12 (1900–1901): 319–21, at 320. The proverb is no. II v. 88 of Erasmus: "Who has no more bread than needs must not keep a dog" (see

Desiderius Erasmus, *Adages II I 1 to II vi 100*, in Roger A. B. Mynors, trans. & annotation, *Collected Works of Erasmus*, 33 [Toronto: University of Toronto Press, 1991], 281, 436).

5. The proverbs are no. III x 86, "a dog dreaming of bread," meaning that everybody dreams about the things they desire eagerly, and no. IV i 23, "a dog living on breadcrumb," used of parasites and those who live on food provided by others (M. M. Engels, *Concordantie op Erasmus' Adagia* [Leeuwarden: Bibliotheek, 1996], 9). Also Gerd Theissen, *The Gospels in Context: Social and Political History in the Synoptic Tradition* (Minneapolis: Fortress Press, 1991), 75; and Focant, *Marc*, 283–84.

6. Theissen, *The Gospels in Context*, 73–75. On the trade relationships between Tyre and Galilee, see Sean Freyne, "Galileans, Phoenicians, and Itureans," in John J. Collins & Gregory E. Sterling, eds., *Hellenism in the Land of Israel* (Notre Dame: University of Notre Dame Press, 2001), 182–215, 200–205.

7. See Theissen, *The Gospels in Context*, 69–72; Joachim Gnilka, *Das Evangelium nach Markus: 1. Teilband: Markus 1–8*, 26 (Zürich: Benziger, 1978), 292; and Bas M. F. van Iersel, *Mark: A Reader-Response Commentary* (Sheffield: Sheffield Academic Press, 1998), 249–50.

8. Theissen, *The Gospels in Context*, 78-79.

9. Jerome Neyrey and Richard Rohrbaugh, "'He must increase, I must decrease' (John 3:30): A Cultural and Social Interpretation," *Catholic Biblical Quarterly* 63 (2001): 464–83, at 465–67, 474.

10. David Rhoads, "Jesus and the Syrophoenician Woman in Mark: A Narrative-Critical Study," *Journal of the American Academy of Religion* 62 (1994): 343–75, at 358–59.

11. Ibid., 359–60.

12. Ibid., 360–61.

13. Susan Miller, *Women in Mark's Gospel* (London: T and T Clark International, 2004), 110–11. See Dolores Aleixandre, "Jesus and the Syrophoenician Woman. A Tale from the Margins (Mark 7:24–30)," in *Concilium* 280 (1999): 73–79, at 77.

14. The idea of God "correcting" the one He has sent is present both in Judaism and Islam. For Abraham and Judaism see "Der Alte aus der Wüste," in M. J. Ben Gorion (Micah Joseph Berdichevsky), *Die Sagen der Juden* (Frankfurt: Insel-Verlag, 1972), 270–72; for Islam see the Qur'an, Surat 'Abasa 80, 1–11.

15. Sonja A. Strube, "Wegen dieses Wortes...," in *Feministische und nicht-feministische Exegese im Vergleich am Beispiel der Auslegungen zu Markus 7,24–30, Theologische Frauenforschung in Europa* 3 (Münster, 2000), 167 and passim, with bibliography.

16. Theissen, *The Gospels in Context*, 79, and Mark Chancey, *The Myth of a Gentile Galilee* (Cambridge: Cambridge University Press, 2002), 176–77.

17. John P. Meier, *A Marginal Jew: Rethinking the Historical Jesus*, vol. 2, *Mentor, Message and Miracles* (New York: Doubleday, 1994), 660–61. Meier's position depends entirely on the interpretation of 7:27b for which, in my view,

Mark seems to bear responsibility. It would seem that Meier fails to make the distinction between tradition and redaction.

18. Joel Marcus, *Mark 1–8: A New Translation with Introduction and Commentary* (New York: Doubleday, 2000), 466.

19. Joanna Dewey, "Jesus' Healings of Women: Conformity and Non-Conformity to Dominant Cultural Values as Clues for Historical Reconstruction," *Biblical Theology Bulletin* 24 (1994): 123–31, 128–29.

20. Chancey, *The Myth of a Gentile Jew*, 176.

21. Robert C. Tannehill, "Types and Functions of Apophthegms in the Synoptic Gospels," *Aufstieg und Niedergang der römischen Welt* II.25.2 (1984): 1792–1829, at 1812–13.

22. Werner H. Kelber, *The Kingdom in Mark: A New Place and a New Time* (Philadelphia: Fortress Press, 1974), 57. This is the majority position.

23. Jean-François Baudoz, *Les miettes de la table: Étude synoptique et socio-religieuse de Mt 15,21–28 et de Mc 7,24–30* (Paris: Gabalda, 1995), 268.

24. This interpretation of the number four thousand is already found in Hilary of Poitiers (*In Matt.* 15:10).

25. John Drury, "Understanding the Bread: Disruption and Aggregation, Secrecy and Revelation in Mark's Gospel," in Jason P. Rosenblatt and Joseph C. Sitterson, eds., *"Not in Heaven": Coherence and Complexity in Biblical Narrative* (Bloomington: Indiana University Press, 1991), 98–119, at 111.

26. Strube, *"Wegen dieses Wortes . . . ,"* 259.

27. Theissen, *The Gospels in Context*, 64–65.

28. John Donahue and Daniel J. Harrington, *The Gospel of Mark*, Sacra Pagina Series, 2 (Collegeville, MN: Liturgical Press, 2002), 238.

29. Drury, "Understanding the Bread," 113–14, and Andreas Käser, "Den Juden zuerst, aber auch den Heiden: 'Mission' im Markusevangelium. Beobachtungen einer kompositionellen Lesung von Markus 4,35–8,26," *Theologische Beiträge* 35 (2004): 69–80, at 69.

30. Note the verbal connections between the feeding narratives and Jesus' words at the Last Supper (6:41, 8:6, 14:22).

31. See Kelber, *The Kingdom in Mark*, 58.

32. For a survey, see chapter 5 of Alonso, *The Woman Who Changed Jesus*.

33. Elisabeth Schüssler Fiorenza, "The Ethics of Biblical Interpretation: Decentering Biblical Scholarship," *Journal of Biblical Literature* 107 (1988): 3–17.

34. Catholic social teaching applies the expression "de facto refugees" not only to all persons persecuted because of race, religion, or membership in social or political groups, but also to victims of armed conflicts, misguided economic policies, or natural disasters (Pontifical Council *Cor Unum*, and Pontifical Council for the Pastoral Care of Migrants and Itinerant People, *Refugees: A Challenge to Solidarity* [Rome: Vatican, 1992], nn. 3–5).

35. According to official statistics in 2006, more than 39,100 undocumented people arrived in Spain from the coasts of Africa, 18,000 in 2007, 13,425 in 2008, and 7,285 in 2009. There is no reliable data about those who died in the attempt. On the other hand, repatriations reached 46,731 in 2008,

and 38,129 in 2009. See www.mir.es/DGRIS/Balances/Balance_ _2009 and www.frontex.europa.eu/ newsroom/news_releases. Also Albert Bastenier, "Immigrants and Asylum Seekers. Signs of Globalization and a Question for Theology," *Concilium* 280 (1999): 18–27.

36. For more on these matters, see www.jrseurope.org and www.picum.org.

37. Let us recall Bakhtin's notion of "outsider": "in order to reveal the hidden potential meanings in a text, it is crucial to have an outside voice to show us what we ourselves do not see" (L. Juliana Claassens, "Biblical Theology as Dialogue. Continuing the Conversation on Mikhail Bakhtin and Biblical Theology," *Journal of Biblical Literature* 122 [2003]: 127–44, 132).

38. Vimal Tirimanna, "The Church and the Crossing of Frontiers," *Concilium* 280 (1999): 80–89, at 89. Also Pablo Alonso et al., eds., *God in Exile: Towards a Shared Spirituality with Refugees* (Rome: Jesuit Refugee Service, 2005).

39. Michel de Certeau, *L'Étranger ou l'union dans la différence*, ed. Luce Giard (Paris: Seuil, 1991), 16.

40. Amy-Jill Levine, *The Social and Ethnic Dimensions of Matthean Salvation History: Go Nowhere among the Gentiles*, Studies in the Bible and Early Christianity, 14 (Lewiston, NY: Edwin Mellen, 1988), 134–35.

8

DRAWN FROM THE SHADOWS

THE SIGNIFICANCE OF THE GALILEAN MARY FOR WOMEN IN IGBO SOCIETY

Caroline N. Mbonu

Among the Igbo of Nigeria one cannot claim to truly know another without knowing that person's family, particularly the mother. It is understood that more often than not the character of a child will reflect that of the mother. So too from an Igbo perspective, the story of the Galilean Jesus cannot be fully appreciated without understanding his mother, the Galilean Mary, whom Luke characterizes as the *doulē kyriou*.

Christian traditions have variously characterized the Galilean Mary as a virgin, handmaiden, or mother, and such descriptions continue to enrich our understanding of Mary today. However, the self-understanding of this female character tends to escape the attention and imagination of exegetes. Thus, when the Galilean Mary who appears in Luke 1:2–38 presents herself as *doulē kyriou*, a "servant of the Lord," it leads the reader to ask how and why she comes to describe herself in these terms. Here *doulē*, servant, is a self-designated identity. In what follows I will suggest that Luke's account, and the questions it raises about the self-perception of this icon of Christianity, have the potential to both enrich and challenge the faith of women, especially the women of Igbo society.

The translation, "handmaid," understood in formal English as a person who has a part in supporting or helping another, downplays the role of this valiant woman in salvation history. This rendering tends to minimize Mary's agency. The term handmaid both trivializes and marginalizes her role. The freight carried by the designation of handmaid situates its bearer in a subordinate position. But a reading that interprets *doulē* as servant and leader reverberates with redemptive significance. Interestingly enough, the more authoritative New Revised Standard Version of the Bible uses "servant," while the New American Bible still uses "handmaid."

Awareness and recovery of the historical traditions influencing the construction of important characters in scripture play a key role in my understanding of the Galilean Mary. When a traditional text is re-read in light of the other texts that form its original context,[1] a number of voices emerge that provide important resources for constructing theologies of positive self-identification among new interpreters. In an earlier work I plumb a variety of biblical traditions representing a plurality of voices that speak of the *doulē*.[2] The investigation examines the Hebrew Scriptures, the Greek Septuagint,[3] and Deuterocanonical sources in order to retrieve *doulas* characters (for example, Ruth, Abigail, Esther, Judith, and the woman of Shunem[4]) that constitute the literary context for the image of the Lukan *doulē kyriou*, understood both as servant and leader. Canadian scripture scholar Lawrence Frizzell notes that, since the fourfold gospel offers only limited material on Mary the mother of Jesus, the great doctors of the early church and the theologians of the Middle Ages turned to the Hebrew Scriptures and non-canonical literature, where they found abundant resources for their meditations on Mary.[5]

Vatican II's Dogmatic Constitution on Divine Revelation, *Dei Verbum*, also emphasizes the broader use of scripture and tradition in bringing the role of Mary "into a gradually clearer light."[6] But here it is worth noting that the council's recognition of the need to bring Mary into the light is suggestive of a previously shadowy existence, which I would assert indicates the need to re-read the story of Mary in the context of a broader and more adequate selection of scriptural templates than has been customary. This is what I will do in the four short sections that follow.

First, I will offer a linguistic analysis of the term "handmaid" as a translation of the term *doulē* that Mary applies to herself in Luke 1:26–38. Second, I will provide a rhetorical analysis of the text, showing how her character functions as a sign of salvation in Luke. Third, I will read and interpret the text from an Igbo perspective, focusing on the importance of Mary's Galilean hearth as an interpretive tool. And fourth, I will offer a more complete linguistic analysis and ideological reading of the text from an Igbo perspective.

Revisting the Translation of Doulē from a Contextual Perspective

Luke's ascription of the word *doulē* to Mary remains problematic for many. *Doul*-stem words denote slave in first-century Greek. However, the Septuagint uses the *doul*-stem to translate the Hebrew word, `*ebed*,[7] which describes prophets, rulers, and holy persons as servants or slaves of God. Several sources support both uses of *doul*-stem words. Ancient writers such as Josephus and Philo of Alexandria suggest that *doul*-stem words and `*ebed* can be roughly synonymous.[8] The two ancient authors also employ *doul*-stem words metaphorically in their writings. As in the case of Josephus, Philo's use of other Greek synonyms for "slave" crowds out this meaning for *doul*-stem words.

Biblical literature of the period provides assistance in this regard. Literature from the Second Temple period tends to favor translating the Hebrew `*ebed* as *doulos*.[9] Scripture scholar Raymond Brown echoes a similar idea, tracing the Lukan use of the *doul*-stem word back to its Septuagint use. Brown insists that because Luke sets most of the adult figures of his infancy narrative against the background of the Hebrew Scriptures, it would be surprising if he did not develop Mary's character against the same backdrop.[10] Moreover, the author of Luke believes that the direction of history flows from the Jewish past recounted in Hebrew scripture into the Christian future. Thus, he begins his narrative with archetypal figures from the past: the barren childless parents of Jesus' herald, John the Baptist. John Drury writes, "His characters are revivals of old Jewish types. Elizabeth and Zacharias are 'righteous before God' like Noah, childless like Abraham and Sarah. Mary greets Elizabeth with an 'occasional poem' very closely modeled on Hannah's (Lk 1:46–55; 1 Sam 2:1–11)."[11] Positioning Mary alongside figures from the past, the author of Luke casts her in the tradition of Israel's heroines: faithful, wise, and courageous women, savior figures who were servants of God's work in Israel. Thus Mary of Galilee is ranked alongside Israel's *doulas* (cf. Mt 1:5–6), an arrangement that befits her role as the mother of the Savior, the one who brings the fullness of life. One can claim that the Galilean pair, mother and son, encapsulate the good news (Lk 4:18–19).

In the Lukan passage, the author paints in bold strokes a portrait of the lowly village maiden drawn gradually from the shadows into the light. The humble beginnings of the young woman from Nazareth are crucial to the story's liberative potential, which I understand to include words, actions, or events that unburden, lift up, or promote the humanity of persons, individuals, and collective groups in the face of oppression. The liberative resonances of the Galilean Mary are intricately woven into the tapestry of Roman Catholic religious imagination. Those who find themselves in the shadows of life, particularly women who are shut off from participation in the public sphere, can identify with the liberative motif that the Galilean maiden portends. God's choice of a Galilean village, a place to which the Hebrew scriptures assign no role in the drama of salvation, functions as a sign of the total newness of what God is about to accomplish.[12]

Though many exegetes move quickly through these elements in the text to Mary's role as mother, I would suggest that motherhood does not represent the central theme of the pericope. This story is about God raising up Mary. Luke's good news is intertwined with this lifting up; it consists of the opportunity for the disenfranchised to be seen and to speak (Lk 4:18–19). The 1993 document of the Pontifical Biblical Commission, *The Interpretation of the Bible in the Church*, challenges women to read and interpret scripture from their own perspective, that is to say, to seek out the good news for women in scripture. In this spirit, then, I will claim the authority to reread this passage from the perspective of a woman, an Igbo, and a religious for more than thirty years, highlighting the fact that Luke's presentation of the birth narrative of Jesus is intertwined with the liberative call of Mary. The Biblical Commission states:

> Women have played a more active part in exegetical research. They have succeeded, often better than men, in detecting the presence, the significance, and the role of women in the Bible, in Christian origins, and in the Church. The world view of today, because of its greater attention to the dignity of women and to their role in society and in church, ensures that new questions are put to the biblical text, which in turn occasions new discovery. Femininity helps to unmask and correct commonly accepted interpretations that were tendentious and sought to justify the male domination of women.[13]

The critical study of scripture by women is imperative, particularly in Africa today. Such readings interrogate and challenge centuries of androcentric scholarship that have shaped biblical interpretation. In what follows, therefore, I will offer a close reading of Luke 1:26–38 in an attempt to extract what the good news has to say about women's fuller participation in God's plan for society.

The Development of Mary's Character as a Sign of Salvation in Luke (1:26–38)

Scripture provides few details regarding Mary's social position. The reader, however, is able to add texture to the portrait through synchronic and diachronic readings of the gospel. Evidently Mary was what might be called a small-town girl, unsophisticated in many ways, but profoundly knowledgeable in others. In Luke's narrative, however, this small-town maiden is invited into the presence of Adonai, the

Lord God. In the world of a first-century Jew, where God's messenger is present, there is God. Gabriel represents God as the salvific event begins to unfold in the backwaters of a Galilean village. It is typical of Luke that Nazareth, a place of no particular interest and inhabited by the absentees of history, should light up with marvelous significance. Emmaus will play a similar role at the end of the gospel (24:13–35). Here then, the unimaginable occurs; God comes to a village to speak with a young unmarried female.

The author wastes no time in reminding the reader that the young woman is bound to a staunchly patriarchal system. Mary first appears as an unnamed figure defined by her relationship with a man and his tribe: "a virgin engaged to a man whose name was Joseph, of the house of David" (1:27a). This introduction reflects a worldview that does not recognize the female character in her own right. Mary's identity is grounded in her relationship to a man, Joseph, and his family.

Ivoni Richter Reimer describes the situation of women in first-century Palestine:

> In the Greco-Roman and Jewish society in the first century … Judaism emphasized that both men and women were made in the image of God, thus establishing equality between the sexes. But practically, and in daily life, a woman was for the most part only valued when she lived in a condition of patriarchal dependency on a man, either her father or her husband.[14]

Accordingly, although Mary and Gabriel are the principal characters in this section of Luke's drama, the narrator introduces Mary as the betrothed of Joseph. In this way the author subtly renders the young woman partially invisible, seen only through the lens of her future husband, Joseph. It is interesting to note that by locating the narrative of Mary's call in this patriarchal structure, Luke sets the stage for the reversal that the Galilean maiden portends.

In verse 1:34 Mary challenges the angel's proclamation that she will conceive and bear a son. With her protest, the author subtly enhances the portrait as that of a young woman able to see, to hear, and to face contradictions, possessed with the ability to analyze, question, and ultimately make a life-defining decision. The young woman speaks out! Here, at the beginning of Luke's narrative, the reader hears a woman's voice: "How can this be, since I am a virgin?" Surprisingly, perhaps, I would suggest that this constitutes the turning point of our little drama. By giving voice to her deepest reservations, Mary sets the stage to take a life-defining stance only moments later, accepting God's miraculous self-offer and thereby reversing the status quo and reshaping her identity from one of patriarchal "servitude" to servant of the living God. While we should not minimize the content of Mary's reservation, we must also recognize that Mary's question to this commanding authority figure is a groundbreaking event.

Mary's power to question and to take a stance on the answer contradicts assertions of some feminist/womanist theologians who claim that the Virgin Mary cannot be a model of a liberated human being.[15] Twice in this short pericope the voice of Mary comes alive. In the first instance she questions the angel's life-altering message (1:34). Second, in her self-defining response to God's offer she articulates her self-understanding as the servant of the Lord, boldly cast in the mold of the prophets (v.38), "Behold, I am the servant of the Lord. May it be done to me according to your word."[16] Mary offers a self-gift, as well as her explicit acceptance of a defining role in God's plan for her people. Only a person with dignity can make such a self-gift. Rather than turning inward toward self-seeking ambitions and desires, the voice we hear comes from an other-centered self. It is not the voice of self-immolation, but the voice of a self that is freely turned toward the Other who is drawing Mary out from the shadows of life into the light (cf. Lk 46–55).

The angel immediately takes leave of Mary, but not without fulfilling its promise that the transformative presence of "[t]he Holy Spirit will come upon you" (v. 35). Thus empowered by the Spirit, Mary breaks the socially imposed silence of her early life. The verse that follows attests to a new transformation. She leaves "with haste" on her own initiative, traveling "to a Judean town in the hill country" (v. 39) where she meets Elizabeth, who, upon the mere event of the traveler's arrival, is also "filled with the Holy Spirit." In the verses that follow (39–55) Mary brings glad tidings, announcing the good news that God liberates the voiceless and invisible of Judea. In Mary's Magnificat, this formerly shadowy figure becomes luminous, occupying the role of a prophet with her ageless proclamation, "My soul magnifies the Lord, and my spirit rejoices in God my Savior, for he has looked with favor on the lowliness of his servant" (1:47–48). In this story, God is a God of reversals.

The voice we hear in Luke's text has little of the mute character we associate with a submissive handmaid. As noted, some exegetes who move too quickly to Mary's *fiat* miss the groundbreaking significance of Mary's question to God's messenger. They leave us with an inaccurate picture of Luke's Mary as a mute, invisible object, acted upon by God for a higher purpose. This unfortunate distortion misses the freely self-defining nature of Mary's proclamation as "the servant of the Lord."

Mary's inquiry undermines interpretations that would cast her in the role of a human slave. Slaves in first-century Roman-dominated Palestine could be expected to remain mute before great authority figures. Similarly, female slaves were given no voice in engendering offspring for their owners.[17] And slaves lacked the legal standing to enter into bonds. But Mary does enter into a new bond, implying that she cannot be a slave in the sense of the *doul*-stem word used in the New Testament.

Contextually, the role played by Mary in Luke's account of the incarnation is not consistent with that of a servant in first-century Palestine. Rather, her character remains consonant with that of Israel's *doulas*, or savior figures. Given Luke's attention to the role of Mary in the Galilean origins of Jesus, it is no coincidence that Jesus' first words in Luke are a response to a question from Mary (cf. 2:48, 49). Luke's narrative highlights a deep sense of intimacy between mother and son that has been nurtured at their Galilean hearth. This picture lends itself to appropriation by women in Igbo society for whom the hearth is the locus and core of their engagement with life.

The Importance of Luke's Galilean Hearth for Igbo Women

The encounter of Igbo women with life, particularly the act of mothering, generally takes place in the ordinary circumstance of the hearth. Yet very few writings situate Mary in the mundane ordinariness of the Galilean hearth. Nonetheless, Luke's gospel implies that Mary's life as wife, mother, and widow takes place at her Nazareth hearth, or *mgbala* in Igbo. The hearth is not merely a fireplace, but rather represents the soul of the household, the female domain. Within this humble space, the passion, compassion, and imagination of Igbo women coalesce in the art of sustaining and preserving the community's life. It is at the hearth that life is born, nurtured, and celebrated. In this locus, the head of the *mgbala* conscientiously teaches her offspring the critical tools they will need to participate in life's processes. At the hearth, a child learns the quintessential human qualities with which to engage the world. Mary's capacity to maintain and sustain her hearth is critical to the upbringing of the Galilean Jesus.

During one of Jesus' encounters, an unnamed woman in the crowd commends his upbringing (Lk 11:27). She praises the womb that carried him and the breasts that nursed him, in effect honoring the hearth at which Jesus was raised. In her admiration, the woman makes an explicit association between Jesus' profound relationship with God and experiences acquired at the hearth. The assumption here is that this character speaks as a mother. The reader may assume she has been affected by

Jesus' profound teaching on prayer with which Luke begins the chapter (11:1–13), or that she has witnessed the subsequent casting out of Beelzebul in the verses that follow (11:14–26). When seen as a mother, her character embodies the belief that such richness of spirit, character, and conduct as was manifest in Jesus could only be the product of a mother whose hearth was suffused with the presence of the Lord.

This kind of outburst of praise for a mother is not uncommon in Igbo society. The Igbo might say, "*Nne gi muru gi*," or "*inghujuru mmiri anrha afo*," which, loosely translated, means that one was raised by a very good mother! The expression, "the breast at which you nursed," translated as *inghujuru mmiri anrha afo*, resonates with the Igbo experience. It connotes the profound teaching and learning that goes on between a suckling child and its mother. The Igbo reinforce the importance of this experience when they berate the *mgbala*, or hearth, of the child who does not measure up to the community's expectations. Similarly, the unknown woman who praises the mother of Jesus indicates the importance that the community places on the intimacy between mother and son in Luke's rendering of the Galilean hearth.

For thirty years Luke's Jesus lives and matures at the hearth of a Jewish village maiden (3:23). The human-God encounter that defines the life of Jesus begins in this hearth, where Mary, who "kept all these things in her heart" (2:19), teaches him the language of the heart. Jesus is called the Nazarene, which identifies him as the child of his mother. The son's sense of servanthood is surely developed in part from lessons learned at his mother's hearth. Interestingly enough, the prayer of Jesus at the Mount of Olives in Luke 22:42, "Thy will be done," echoes his mother's *fiat*, "let it be with me according to your word" (1:38). Mary's response portrays her as responsible and responsive to God's initiative in her life. She demonstrates a grounding in the story of her people, as Frizzell notes, "acutely aware of her bond to the people of Israel in her own generation and back to Abraham and Sara (1:37, 54–55)."[18]

Taken out of context, the idea of Mary's servanthood has been used to legitimate the submission of women to the representatives of patriarchy. Such interpretations idealize a passive image of Mary. But the Mary of Luke is not passive, as we have seen, and she raises a son who shows sufficient independence to leave his parents to go teach in the Temple at the tender age of twelve.

Regardless of the evidence, however, New Testament interpreters rarely apply the term "servant of God" to Mary. In my opinion, these exegetes fail to recognize the significance of Mary's role in Luke's narrative, including the claim that Jesus lived at his mother's hearth for thirty years, where he "increased in wisdom and in years" before God and man (2:52). My point is that the servanthood of Jesus emerges in the context of lessons learned at his mother's hearth. Thus, the Light of the World emerges from the hearth of an obscure Galilean maiden located in an unimportant town, of which his first followers would ask in John, "Can anything good come out of Nazareth?" (Jn 1:46).

Curiously, the image of Mary as an active participant in Luke's birth narrative of Jesus does not resonate with some African women scholars who can see Mary only as one still caught in the shadows of life. The Nigerian Igbo scholar, Becky Iwuchukwu, holds this opinion. Iwuchukwu writes, "Mary showed deep faith in God, and complete obedience to the divine will. The African woman will also learn from Mary how and when to be silent, obedient to her husband and always very ready to make the sacrifices demanded by one that has answered God's call."[19] However, Iwuchukwu's reading of the Mary of Luke's gospel altogether misses the significance of her role in the narrative, leading her to reinforce the ideology of subordination. Such interpretations deny Luke's interest in Mary's character and ability, which fit her for the role of the Mother of the Redeemer.

Iwuchukwu's insistence on the subordination of wives and the value of uncritical sacrifice is typical of efforts throughout the ages to silence Christian women, and of efforts to silence women in Igbo society today. A synchronic reading of the text reframes Mary's self-designation as "the servant of the Lord" (1:38) as the prototype for the disciples' freely chosen listening obedience to God's call. It is a choice grounded in her faith that a future explanation will be forthcoming, and that God's plan for her people will be fulfilled. As Turid Karlsen Seim suggests, "Mary's obedience is not portrayed merely in passive terms: she expresses active acceptance and positive response (1:38), and further she proclaims God's wondrous acts with prophetic authority (1:46–55)."[20]

Mary's response and her prophetic and timeless Magnificat that follows (1:46–55) summon images of the prophets from the Hebrew Scriptures: servant of God, leader, bridge-builder, advocate, and, most significantly, voice for the people. By dressing Mary in the prophet's robe and placing her at the beginning of his gospel, Luke points to the liberative dimensions heralded by the gospel. In announcing the good news, Luke's Jesus simultaneously denounces injustice (cf. 1:42–55, 4:18–19). By means of her self-description as *doulē kyriou*, Mary voluntarily submits to God's plan for her people, embracing her role in the history of salvation.[21] This kind of voluntary submission and embrace of one's role is constitutive of all relationships of love and respect. It is important to note, however, that in Luke, Mary's submission to God's plan does not conform to the dehumanizing aspects of power, authority, or obedience imposed by first-century patriarchal society. Indeed, the divine messenger, Gabriel, does not force God's will on Mary. As women have always known, love does not do that.

Iwuchukwu's assertion that African women learn the art of submission and sacrifice from Mary demands analysis. Her notion of sacrifice is suggestive of self-immolation, a violation of human dignity. Voluntary sacrifice, however, remains redemptive in its foundation. Teresa Okure points to this redemptive aspect when she writes, "Through sacrifice, humans seek to encounter the divine, project themselves into the invisible world, penetrate into the divine presence and commune with the deity. Sacrifice creates a bridge between humans and God and serves to sustain the established relationship."[22] In this view, voluntary sacrifice is necessary in order to cooperate with the divine plan. The *doulē kyriou*, or "servant of the Lord," has a key role to play through her cooperation with God's plan of fostering salvation and redemption, communion, and reconciliation. She cooperates with God to restore dignity to her people and to humankind.

The African woman in Iwuchukwu's view remains utterly passive, an empty vessel waiting to be filled by her husband or by the representatives of patriarchy. An exploitative and oppressive reading of Mary's obedience to the divine furthers the oppressive hegemony explicitly challenged by Mary's Magnificat. Iwuchukwu's uncritical embrace of women's roles in patriarchal traditions has deeply negative implications for the experience of contemporary women in Igbo society. This type of religious socialization and its developmental counterparts have forced women to accept the subsidiary and complementary roles reserved for them in Igbo Westernized society and church life. Iwuchukwu's reading empties the Lukan text of the good news for such women. It denies the witness of the Galilean pair, Mary and her son Jesus, to an all-powerful liberating God, whose concern for the ultimate and holistic liberation of all humanity begins with a young woman in a Galilean village.

Rereading the Text from an Igbo Woman's Perspective

The translation of biblical texts poses special difficulties for biblical interpretation in Igboland in eastern Nigeria. The translation into Igbo (the people and the language are known as Igbo) of the *doul*-stem word provides a case in point. Of course Igbo exegetes and hermeneutists face the same challenge as other scholars in translating the *doul*-stem word. Like the Septuagint scribes, and not unlike Josephus and Philo, contemporary Igbo Bible translators face the challenge of translating the meaning of the `ebed-pais-doulos (slave-slave/son-servant) term in ways that retain the dignity of the word. These translators utilize two Igbo words, *ohù* and *odibo*, to translate the *doul*-stem word.

While both words connote various degrees of slavery, servitude, and stewardship, they differ markedly in the concrete. In common usage *ohù* represents slave or slavery in the absolute, while *odibo* stands for steward, or one in temporary service of another. Among Nigerian Igbo Christians, for example, the *doulē* in Luke 1:38 has been translated in two different versions. In the Igbo Catholic Bible, Mary is *odibo nwanyi*, a female servant. The Igbo Protestant Bible, however, translates the same text as *ohù nwanyi*, a slave woman. Socially, the terms *odibo* (servant) and *ohù* (slave) have completely different meanings. A temporary servant's status is redeemable, while that of a slave may not be. The proper use of the terms *odibo* and *ohù* in translating *doulē* can make a critical contribution to the efforts of those seeking to re-imagine the self-understanding of Christian women in Igbo society.

In addition, certain devotions to Mary in Igbo popular religiosity mirror the image of her as a shadowy figure. The designation, *nwa Nmeri* (*nwa* = a child; *Nmeri* = Mary), meaning a child of Mary, represents one such expression. *Nwa Nmeri* can be a favorable expression that designates a pious person, male or female. But the title can take on a different, less positive meaning as well. When a female is addressed as *nwa Nmeri*, it is usually pejorative, referring to an unsophisticated or innocently naïve person. In an Igbo context, this ascription does not capture the liberative dimensions of Luke's portrait of the Galilean Mary as the *doulē kyriou* ("servant of the Lord").

For first-century readers Luke's description of Mary's role in the Galilean pair suggests that the good news involves a fresh model for the roles that women can play at the hearth and in society. The newness of this message is embodied in Luke's narrative, which places a female's experience and subjectivity at the center of the birth narrative of Jesus. Thanks in part to this witness, women have a platform from which they can re-dream and re-imagine the world. Luke's gospel invites readers and hearers to another way of imagining social relations in the kingdom of God. Only under God's rule can a woman from a rural community that is staunchly patriarchal in form undergo the kind of transformation that Luke chronicles at the beginning of his gospel. Indeed, Luke's narrative represents good news for rural women the world over, even today. Most especially, this Lukan text awakens new hope, a hope that another world is possible for the disenfranchised.

Critical engagement with scripture enables women to enter into texts that can unburden and lift up their humanity. Certainly correlations between historical understandings of the Galilean handmaid and socio-cultural changes in the roles of women are complex and difficult to establish.[23] However, we can be certain that Mary's image is being constantly rewoven to meet the spiritual needs of the times. Indeed, it could be argued that the phenomenon of Our Lady of Guadalupe represents one such reweaving for Mexicans. However, the experience of the Galilean Mary in Africa has not undergone such reweaving or renewal. In African Christianity the images of Mary as Virgin and as Mother dominate the Marian landscape. Introduced by missionaries over a century ago, images of Mary have not advanced much beyond this type of devotion. Some forms of popular religiosity and spiritual practice subliminally reinforce submissive and passive stereotypes, thus sustaining women's subordination. Women who engage in such forms of spiritual practice often find themselves locked down by the patriarchal freight they carry, which tends to domesticate their best efforts to empower women.

African women can profit from the insights of Joel Green who offers a positive and provocative interpretation of the role of the *doulē kyriou* image in the Galilean household. Green states that Mary's claim to be the "servant of the Lord" gives her a place in God's household that relativizes and actually jeopardizes her status in the household of Joseph, for membership in the household of God, and partnership in God's plan for Israel, would seem to transcend the claims of family.[24] On the other hand, Green suggests that by situating Mary as the *doulē kyriou*, Luke subverts the competitive maneuvering for position and status that was prevalent in first-century Palestine. African biblical scholars could well bend their translations and interpretive work toward suggestions like Green's. My own suggestion would be that the 1993 document of the Pontifical Biblical Commission encouraging accurate biblical interpretation sensitive to the needs of the church can be understood to encourage precisely such readings.

Conclusion

I have argued, then, that Mary of Galilee as she appears in the Gospel of Luke represents good news for women. Working with a carefully crafted character situated at the beginning of his gospel, Luke draws Mary from the shadows into prominence. While she first appears as a marginal figure from an obscure village, incapable of standing on her own, Luke soon casts her in the tradition of Israel's heroines and in the role of a prophet. Her experience speaks to many women as well as men whose voices are silenced by the dominant culture, whose contributions are shut out by society, and who are denied access to the liberating dimensions of the good news. In addition, Mary illumines the circumscribed female space, the hearth, to the fullest, enabling her son, Jesus, to realize his own vocation. Such empowering evidence of what God accomplishes through the seemingly mundane life of this Galilean maiden encourages women in Igbo society, indeed, all women, to disallow depictions of themselves as naturally inferior, subordinate, eternal victims of male oppression. We are ready to engage the world as servants and leaders in our communities! Understood correctly, Luke's portrait of the Galilean Mary is an inspiration to Igbo women striving for abundant life in a society that continues to define us as the other.

Notes

1. Ogbu U. Kalu, "Daughters of Ethiopia: Constructing a Feminist Discourse in Ebony Strokes," in *African Women, Religion, and Health: Essays in Honor of Mercy Amba Ewudziwa Oduyoye*, ed. Isabel Apowo Phiri and Sarojini Nadar (Maryknoll, NY: Orbis Books, 2006), 274.

2. Caroline Mbonu, "A Redemptive Reading of the Doulē in Luke 1:26-38: Towards a Liberative Process for Women in Igbo Society" (Ph.D. dissertation, Graduate Theological Union, Berkeley, California, 2009).

3. The Septuagint is the Koine Greek translation of the Hebrew Bible, done between the third and second centuries BCE in Alexandria.

4. See the Book of Ruth; Abigail in 1 Samuel 25; the Book of Esther; the Book of Judith (Septuagint, Catholic, and Eastern Orthodox Bibles); and the woman of Shunem, 2 Kings 4:8–17.

5. Lawrence E. Frizzell, "Mary and the Biblical Heritage," in *Marian Studies: Marian Studies* 46 (1995): 26.

6. Second Vatican Council, Dogmatic Constitution on Divine Revelation (*Dei Verbum*), n. 11.

7. Alfons Weiser, "δουλεια, as η," in *Exegetical Dictionary of the New Testament*, vol. 1, ed. Horse Balz and Gerhard Schneider (Grand Rapids, MI: Eerdmans Publishing Company, 1990), 349–50.

8. Benjamin G. Wright, "'Ebed/Doulos: Terms and Social Status in the Meeting of Hebrew Biblical and Hellenistic Roman Culture," in *Semeia* 83–84 (1998): 98.

9. Ibid., 85.

10. Raymond E. Brown, Karl P. Donfried, Joseph A. Fitzmyer, and John Reumann, *Mary in the New Testament: A Collaborative Assessment by Protestant and Roman Catholic Scholars* (Philadelphia: Fortress Press, 1978), 34. Also R. Timothy McLay, *The Use of the Septuagint in New Testament Research* (Grand Rapids, MI: Eerdmans Publishing Company, 2003), 30.

11. John Drury, "Luke," in *The Literary Guide to the Bible*, ed. Robert Alter and Frank Kermode (Cambridge: Harvard University, 1987), 419.

12. Raymond E. Brown, *The Birth of the Messiah: A Commentary on the Infancy Narratives in Matthew and Luke* (New York: Doubleday, 1977), 314.

13. Dean P. Béchard, ed., "Pontifical Biblical Commission, Document on the Interpretation of the Bible in the Church, September 21, 1993," in *The Scripture Documents: An Anthology of Official Catholic Teaching* (Collegeville, MN: The Liturgical Press, 2001), 272.

14. Ivoni Richter Reimer, "Life Calls for Triumph and Celebration," in *Transgressors: Toward a Feminist Biblical Theology*, ed. Claudia Janssen, Ute Ochtendung, and Beate When, trans. Linda M. Maloney (Collegeville, MN: The Liturgical Press, 2002), 90.

15. Delores S. Williams, *Sisters in the Wilderness: The Challenge of Womanist God-Talk* (Maryknoll, NY: Orbis Books, 1993), 182.

16. Note that I have followed the translation of *doulē* used by the *New Standard Revised Version Bible* (Oxford: Oxford University Press, 1991), and substituted the word "servant" for "handmaid" in this translation from the New American Bible (2002).

17. Jennifer A. Glancy, *Slavery in Early Christianity* (New York: Oxford University, 2002), 17.

18. Lawrence E. Frizzell, "Mary and the Biblical Heritage," *Marian Studies* 46 (1995): 30.

19. Becky Iwuchukwu, "Women and Religion in Africa," in *Where God Reigns: Reflections on Women in God's World*, ed. Elizabeth Amoah (Accra: Sam-Woode, 1997), 47.

20. Turid K. Seim, *The Double Message: Patterns of Gender in Luke-Acts* (Nashville: Abingdon Press, 1994), 115.

21. Joel B. Green, *The Gospel of Luke: The New International Commentary on the New Testament* (Grand Rapids, MI: Eerdmans Publishing Company, 1997), 92.

22. Teresa Okure, "Hebrews: Sacrifice in an African Perspective," in *Global Bible Commentary*, ed. Daniel Patte (Nashville: Abingdon Press, 2004), 535.

23. Sarah Jane Boss, *Empress and Handmaid: On Nature and Gender in the Cult of the Virgin Mary* (London: Cassel, 2000), 12.

24. Green, *The Gospel of Luke*, 92.

9

JESUS OF *MINJUNG* ON THE ROAD TO EMMAUS (LUKE 24:13–32)

ENVISIONING A POST-*MINJUNG* THEOLOGY

Sophia Park

Minjung ("common people") theology, a powerful contextual theology, rose out of the suffering of the people of Korea during the struggle for the liberation of our country. As a member of the generation of Korean *minjung* theology, I was baptized by the *minjung* Jesus of the oppressed, poor, and marginalized. *Minjung* theology once provided for the Korean people a profound spirituality that emphasized the preferential option for the poor, sustained the people's struggle for freedom and human rights, and nurtured our minds and hearts for justice.

But now that Korea is an advanced and highly technical society, the *minjung* Jesus seems invisible, and the concept of *minjung* appears out of reach. Who, then, is the Jesus of this post-*minjung* period? Where can we again encounter the Jesus of *minjung*? This essay engages in a dialogue with the story of Emmaus (Lk 24:13–32)[1] as a way to envision the Jesus of *minjung* in the post-*minjung* era. Through this dialogue I hope to open a space for recollecting the past, while suggesting what seems to me a way of re-engaging with the Jesus of *minjung*.

Brief History of the Quest for the *Minjung* Jesus

As a liberation movement, the quest for the Jesus of *minjung* was very influential in shaping the faith lives of Korean Christians during the 1970s. This movement emerged from those who had experienced severe oppression—laborers, college students, and even intellectuals—and whose experiences were articulated and developed by an exploration of Jesus in the context of Korean society.

By its nature *minjung* theology is allied with Latin American liberation theologies that claim the liberating power of God for the oppressed and a preferential option for the poor. Just as Latin American liberation theologies use economic and political theories as tools to analyze the experiences of the oppressed, *minjung* theology pays attention to injustices in an economic system that thrives on the cheap labor of factory workers and farmers.

Additionally, *minjung* theology pays attention to biblical historical studies and to the theology of suffering. In the history of Korea, as this theology attests, the common people have undergone great suffering, poverty, and oppression at the hands of the colonial powers of China and Japan, and under successive military dictatorships.[2] During this period, thousands of people were incarcerated, tortured, and killed. *Minjung* theology reflects on resistance movements that developed during this time through the lens of Jesus of Galilee; it examines Jesus of Galilee through the lens of the lived experience of the *minjung*, or common people. In so doing, it claims that Jesus is with the *minjung*, that Jesus serves the *minjung*, and, in fact, that Jesus is the *minjung*.[3] In this spirituality, the oppressed are encouraged to find salvific power in the *minjung* Jesus who is always among the people.

Minjung theology examines Korean traditional cultures, particularly rituals or popular dance and drama, which have been practiced among the common people as an expression of frustration or resistance against oppression. This theology ingeniously reclaims indigenous religions, such as shamanism[4] and Donghak,[5] as unique Korean theological and spiritual resources. It has become a grounding contextual theology, paying close attention to the notion of the option for the poor.

This theology claims that the *minjung* have finally irrupted as subjects of history.[6] Yong Bok Kim explains that the *minjung* are a permanent reality of history. Kingdoms, dynasties, and states rise and fall, but the *minjung* remain as an ongoing reality in history. The *minjung*'s socio-political biography is the predicate of historical drama.[7]

Along with the quest for the Jesus of *minjung*, feminist *minjung* theologians have also drawn attention to women's experiences within this movement. Despite this theology's focus on the liberation of the oppressed, women theologians have generally believed that women's commitment to the *minjung* has been underestimated or ignored. Very often women's existence, especially in regard to the body and sexuality, has been objectified and described from a male perspective.[8] *Minjung* theology's approach pays attention to the experiences of women, listening to our narratives and providing the opportunity for oppressed women to tell their life stories.[9] *Minjung* feminist theologians have engaged critically with *minjung* theology as well as with Western feminism, often by utilizing postcolonial concepts.

The decades of the 1970s and 1980s were a time in which *minjung* theology irrupted and shaped mainstream theological thought. Since then, *minjung* theology has had to face a new reality. First, the term *minjung* has lost its collective power to unite the Korean people. Under military dictatorship most Koreans easily identified with the suffering *minjung*, putting aside distinctions based on complicated notions of economy, class, and education. However, after Korea achieved democracy, those with resources or education among the *minjung* became the middle class and, in this process, attained various socio-economic privileges. As a result, the essential definition of *minjung* as the oppressed is no longer viable.

Also, the term *minjung* is very elusive in today's globalized capitalistic society, in which national boundaries do not apply to multi-national corporations. *Minjung* theology is based on a critical analysis of the political and economic situations within which the Korean people were exploited and abused. However, in the current free-trade capitalistic environment, poor laborers are often undocumented foreign migrants whose experiences of oppression arise from global-scale immigration and dislocation. Thus, the old paradigm of *minjung* theology—in which the *minjung* are poor Koreans—does not neatly fit with the current Korean context. Second-generation of *minjung* theologians have struggled with the development of a new paradigm, calling this time the post-*minjung* period. This essay, then, will attempt to re-define the Jesus of *minjung* as he exists in today's spirituality.

The Story of the Road to Emmaus

The story of the road to Emmaus as a resurrection narrative is unique to the Gospel of Luke. The third gospel pays attention to the theme of a journey through which one can experience transformation of life, something the story clearly exemplifies. This section will examine the location of this story and its literary function, paying attention to its transformative application.

The pericope is located in a transitional space between the first resurrection narrative (24:1–12) and the third (24:36–49). The first narrative is about the women who visit Jesus' tomb and find it empty. They hear a message from the angel saying, "'Why do you look for the living among the dead? He is not here, but has risen. *Remember* how he told you, while he was in Galilee'…then they *remembered* his words, returning from the tomb and told all this to the eleven and the rest" (24:5–8; italics mine). In this episode, it is the memory of Jesus' words that helps the women to understand the resurrection.

Here, the reader is told that the door to the new (transformed) reality of resurrection is the memory of what Jesus taught and did. He talked about the passion and resurrection, which helps his followers deal with his crucifixion and death; so too must readers turn to his words in order to recognize and understand the reality of the resurrection. Unfortunately, the women fail to make the male disciples comprehend the reality of the resurrection, perhaps indicating that they do not fully grasp the reality themselves.

In the third narrative, Jesus appears directly to the disciples, teaching them about his resurrected reality. Here again, Jesus says, "These are my words that I spoke to you while I was still with you" (24:44). Jesus rebukes them for their suspicions and doubts, which are rooted in their failure to remember. The narrator reminds the reader that the disciples have enough memory to grasp the reality of the resurrection. With this in mind, the episode concludes with the mission narrative in which Jesus commissions the disciples to go out to the whole world.

The second narrative functions as a bridge between the first and the third, providing a way of understanding the spiritual journey of the two disciples from frustration and confusion to faith-filled acceptance of the mystery of the resurrection. With this structure, Luke moves the reader from the death of Jesus into the world of the resurrection. The narrator embraces the tension and confusion the reader feels with the crucified and the resurrected, the visible and invisible Galilean, Jesus Christ.[10] This story prepares the reader to enter into the world of the resurrection by challenging her to shift paradigms from the passion to the reality of the resurrection.

The pericope comprises three parts of a journey: on the way to Emmaus, at the inn, and back to the other disciples in Jerusalem. On the way to Emmaus the two disciples talk with sadness and frustration about Jesus who died on the cross, ignoring what they heard from the women about the resurrection. They engage in a dialogue with a "stranger" who takes the lead in the conversation by raising questions. The word *stranger*, in Greek *genophone*, means a person who does not share the mother tongue and thus causes uncomfortable and uneasy feelings. There is no familiarity, only oddness and strange feelings, yet the two disciples' openness in listening to the stranger is an expression of hospitality.

However, they do not recognize the resurrected Jesus on the road—something the reader cannot understand. Perhaps this is due to a difference in appearance on the part of Jesus, or it may be because of the disciples' emotional state. The narrator uses the passive tense, literally saying, "their eyes were held" (hoi de ophthalmoi moi autōn ekratounto; ὁι δε οφθαλμοι αυτων εκρατουντο) (24:16). By using the passive verb, the author stresses their lack of agency; something is being done to them. But the narrator cannot say at this time—or does not want to reveal—who is doing it.[11] However, the gospel describes a process through which the disciples come to see reality, implying that the resurrection is meant to be understood within this more extended context.[12]

The Lucan narrative pays attention to hospitality as one of its most essential themes, and in this pericope a scene of hospitality is paired with the scene of the journey. Earlier, in the story of Jesus and his disciples on the way to Jerusalem, the narrative introduces an episode about being a neighbor (10:29–37) in which Jesus tells the parable of the Good Samaritan. The narrative then continues with the story of Jesus at Martha's house, a story in which the two sisters, Mary and Martha, exemplify hospitality.[13] Later, in the story of Zacchaeus, Jesus reveals the reality of salvation with the exclamation, "I must stay at your house today" (19:5). In the Lucan narrative the house that provides hospitality is often the space where Jesus' messiahship is actualized and revealed.

Thus the scene of Jesus' stay at the inn is situated at the center of the periope, creating a space for the disciples to be transformed and transported into the world of the resurrection through various boundary-crossings. Jacques Derrida stresses that crossing is an essential element of hospitality. Anne Dufourmantelle explains that, according to Derrida, "the place of hospitality is the place originally belonging to neither host nor guest, but to the gesture by which one of them welcomes the other—even and above all if he is himself without a dwelling from which this welcome could be conceived."[14]

The two disciples, then, are determined to provide hospitality to the stranger. The narrative says, "Stay with us because it is almost evening and the day is now nearly over" (24:29). In Greek the phrase, "But they urged him strongly saying, 'Stay with us,'" (kai parebiasanto auton legontes meinon methhāmōn; και παρεβιασαντο αυτον λεγοντες μεινον μεθ ημων), literally means the disciples pressed or urged him to stay. Here the disciples are active in inviting the stranger, the guest, who had initiated their dialogue by asking questions and explaining the scriptures. Jesus then accepts their invitation to stay with them, though the narrative indicates he originally appeared to be going further (24:28b). The reader then hears that the stranger, who does not own the dwelling, takes the initiative to break the bread, bless it, and give it to them. In the words of Brendan Byrne, "He, who is receiving their hospitality, provides for them the 'hospitality of God.'"[15]

The sharing of the meal is one of the most crucial symbols in Luke's gospel. In a major boundary-crossing, the guest becomes the host by breaking the bread. In the Lucan community, breaking bread is a symbol of the Eucharist, which is "the cultic extension of the multi-plication of the loaves and of the Last Supper, the continuation of the fellowship meals Jesus had with his disciples during his earthly life, done as a memorial of Jesus the martyr in obedience to his command (22:19)."[16] At the moment of crossing the boundary, when the stranger breaks the bread, the narrative says that "their eyes were opened" (24:31). In the narrative of Luke, "to see"—here in the passive voice, to have their eyes opened—implies having faith and experiencing con-version.[17] As an example, Saul hears a voice on the way to Damascus and "though his eyes were open, he could see nothing" (Acts 9:8). Only after his conversion was his sight restored (Acts 9:4-18).

As soon as the disciples identify the stranger as the risen Jesus, he disappears, and their immediate reaction is recollection. They begin to remember and to reflect upon what occurred on the way to Emmaus, and in the conversation with Jesus on the street. They cry out, "Were not our hearts burning within us while he was talking to us on the road, while he was opening the scriptures to us?" (24:32). This echoes an earlier use of the word "remember." In the first narrative of the res-urrection, the angel exhorts the woman to remember what Jesus told her (24:6). Here, the two disciples remember not only what he just said to them, but also how they felt during the conversation; it is a deep-ened way of remembering. Although the narrative does not elaborate on their process of recollection and remembering, it is clear that they are ready to move into the next stage.

Here, the narrative prepares the reader for the realization that the risen Jesus will be invisible in their own faith journey as well. Byrne of-fers the following insight: "The sudden disappearance of the Lord they have just regained does not seem to dismay the disciples... The com-munity of faith that is to grow out of these experiences will not have the physical presence of Jesus. But that does not mean they will not have him as companion upon the journey."[18] Therefore, this experi-ence of not seeing him any longer is different from not recognizing him; they will recognize him in various unexpected ways.

In this way the story guides the reader to attend to the role of doing or acting in the process outlined above whereby the disciples complete a journey from the crucifixion into the reality of the resurrec-tion. Recognition of the resurrection of Jesus arises from their actions of hospitality and welcome to the stranger.[19] The opening of their eyes, or the regaining of faith that follows, leads the disciples to return to Jerusalem and share their experiences with the community.

When they explain their experiences to the other disciples and friends of Jesus, they summarize it by reporting that they saw him on the road and recognized him "in the breaking of the bread" (24:35b). Scholars agree that this episode reflects the way that the early Christian community sustained its faith—remembering what Jesus said, joining the community, breaking bread, and sharing their life experiences.[20] I believe this story invites Christians experiencing confusion and frustration today to follow a similar path from the shattered dreams of the crucifixion into the mystery of the resurrection. The journey into the reality of the resurrection entails crossing boundaries in order to create a space for hospitality and for recollection—for remembering in a contemplative way what has happened and continues to happen, for action, and for sharing what we experience.

Post-*Minjung* Jesus

Luke's story of the road to Emmaus provides light for those of us who seek the Jesus of *minjung*. *Minjung* theology still has the power to empower the poor, and the Jesus of *minjung* still invites people to join this living spirituality. However, we must redefine the search for the *minjung* Jesus, much like the disciples who walked on the road to Emmaus had to redefine their search for Jesus. When we talk about the post-*minjung* Jesus, *post* simultaneously implies both continuity and discontinuity. In this endeavor, the basic notion is that *minjung* does not designate a fixed concept, but rather a relational and fluid reality.[21]

Minjung theologians are frustrated and saddened by a certain failure to recognize the *minjung* Jesus in Korea today. As a Korean theologian and member of the generation of Korean *minjung* theology, I would suggest that, if we hope to find a new way toward the *minjung* Jesus, we follow the same process as the two disciples on the road to Emmaus. Movements in this direction are already well under way. First, in re-membering the *minjung* movement and the origins of its theology, current *minjung* theologians have refocused on the thoughts of earlier *minjung* theologians such as Ahn Byung Mu, Ham Sok Hon, and You Youngmo. Significantly, Ahn's theology has been re-invited into the *minjung* discourse, and his followers have tried to reclaim and further develop his theology. In this effort to continue Ahn's *Minjung* theology, second generation *minjung* theologian Yong Yeon Hwang claims *minjung* as *sosuza*, stressing the importance of the human experiences of alienation and exclusion.[22]

Second, *minjung* theology has entered into dialogue with *dalit* theology from India, as well as with other indigenous liberation theologies that prioritize the empowerment of the oppressed.[23] In this approach, *minjung* theologians collaborate with *dalit* theologians, enjoying mutual hospitality. Similarly, many feminist *minjung* theologians examine the "emerging spiritualities" that come from the *minjung* movement. In the pursuit of these spiritualities women's life stories are being voiced and analyzed from post-colonial and feminist perspectives, nurturing women-centered spiritualities and ways of doing theology. In this movement, women *minjung* theologians collaborate and share hospitality with other Asian women theologians.[24] *Minjung* theology has also developed into a path for interfaith dialogue. The *minjung* Jesus has been placed in dialogue with the Buddha and the Tao, creating interesting new possibilities for sharing religious experience. Paul S. Chung explains that this new avenue of Asian contextual *minjung* theology integrates the wisdom of world religions.[25] This approach should be understood as a development of Korean contextual theology.

Third, the paradigm of *minjung* theology has found fruitful application to the situation of immigrants. Andrew Sung Park in *The Wounded Heart of God* develops a theology of *han*, translated as "deep sadness" or "deep woundedness of the heart, caused by unfulfilled wish and bitterness of life experience," which emerges from *minjung* theology.[26] Park extends *han* to all Asian Americans, as well as to other minority groups who suffer from poverty and discrimination in the United States. He examines the Los Angeles riots of 1992, paying particular attention to the experience of *han* among African Americans and immigrant Koreans, including feelings of *han* they have harbored against each other. Furthermore, in *Heart of the Cross: A Postcolonial Christology*, Wonhee Anne Joh examines Jesus' suffering and salvation using the concept of *han* and *jeong* (affection of heart) from the prominent *minjung* theologian Ham Sok Hon.[27]

In speaking of post-*minjung* thought, one must include the continuity and discontinuity manifested among *minjung* theologians themselves. In this regard, continuity certainly includes an ongoing commitment to the option for the poor. Post-*minjung* theology will undoubtedly continue to take into account human oppression, including the sufferings of poverty that permeate our global society. Post-*minjung* theology exhibits an important discontinuity with its predecessors, however, in the move to include as *minjung* all who suffer from socio-economic, ethnic, and/or political forms of oppression. The virtue that is required in order to "see" and embrace the reality of the resurrection in this time of continuity and discontinuity in the development of *minjung* theology is the ability to recognize the *minjung* Jesus in the foreigner or stranger, which I have been calling the resurrection imagination.

As we have seen in Luke, the post-*minjung* Jesus will be invisible, appearing only when we share memory and break bread. In the story of Emmaus, the process of entering into the reality of the resurrection begins with the openness manifested by the disciples toward a stranger. The disciples choose to cross boundaries in order to provide the hospitality through which the guest becomes the host, leaving them to remember that they recognized him only in the breaking of the bread. The process ends with their return to Jerusalem, where the story leads the community to an ever more inclusive celebration of the Eucharistic meal.

Similarly, I would suggest that the most promising development of post-*minjung* theology is its new openness to dialogue with strangers, crossing over boundaries and stepping out of comfort zones to break bread with others. Post-*minjung* theology will continue to reflect from its own perspective on what is occurring now in our globalized society. But Koreans will grasp the post-*minjung* Jesus only through action to change and humanize the life of the *minjung*.

Following Luke, then, I would suggest that we will find the post-*minjung* Jesus through expressions of hospitality to the stranger, the undocumented migrant worker in Korea, the victim of a natural disaster in Haiti or New Orleans, or the genocide survivor in Rwanda. When the presence of the post-*minjung* Jesus among the victims of our globalized world is revealed by these experiences of mutual hospitality, Koreans and others become ready to go wherever the post-*minjung* Jesus continues to suffer. For it is there that the community that gathers in his name continues to exclaim, with the disciples at Emmaus after the breaking of the bread, "Were not our hearts burning within?" (24:32b).

Notes

1. All biblical references used in this essay are from the *NRSV* unless otherwise specified.

2. Kwang-Sun David Suh, *Theology, Ideology and Culture* (Hong Kong: World Student Christian Federation, Asia/Pacific Religion, 1983).

3. Ahn Byung Mu, *Jesus of Galilee* (Hong Kong: Christian Conference of Asia, 2004).

4. For example, Chung Hyun Kyung describes the traditional Korean shaman's ritual practice as a resource for Asian women doing theology, whose work is often related to *minjung* theology. See Chung Hyun Kyung, "'Han-pu-ri' Doing Theology from Korean Women's Perspective," in *We Dare to Dream: Doing Theology as Asian Women*, ed. Virginia Fabella and Sun Ai Lee-Park (Maryknoll, NY: Orbis Books, 1990), 135–46.

5. Donghak claims that *minjung* is heaven (人乃天).

6. Yong Bok Kim, *Messiah and* Minjung: *Christ's Solidarity with the People for New Life* (Hong Kong: Christian Conference of Asia, 1992), 36–37. See also Ahn Byung Mu, *Jesus of Galilee*, 125–26.

7. Ibid.

8. For a critique and evaluation of feminist *minjung* theology, see Sophia Park, "Doing Theology: Asian Women's Christian Spirituality," *Ewha Journal of Feminist Theology* 3 (2005): 151–73.

9. See Marion Kennedy Kim, ed., *"Once I Had a Dream . . .": Stories Told by Korean Women Minjung* (Hong Kong: Documentation for Action Groups in Asia, 1992).

10. Stanley P. Saunders, "Discernment on the Way to Emmaus: Resurrection Imagination and the Practices in Luke 24:13–35, *Journal for Preachers* (Easter 1997): 44.

11. Jan Wojcik, *The Road to Emmaus: Reading Luke's Gospel* (West Lafayette, IN: Purdue University Press, 1989), 2.

12. Brendan Byrne, *The Hospitality of God: A Reading of Luke's Gospel* (Collegeville, MN: Liturgical Press, 2000), 187.

13. The story of Mary and Martha has various interpretations. For example, traditionally Mary represents prayer, and Martha represents service. Feminist scholars have suggested Martha might be a female disciple, or that Martha and Mary were a missionary team. In this essay, I do not address this issue; rather I focus on the matching literary structure between the episode on the road and the episode at a household that provides hospitality.

14. Jacque Derrida and Anne Dufourmantelle, *Of Hospitality*, trans. Rachel Bowlby (Stanford, CA: Stanford University Press, 2000), 62.

15. Brendan Byrne, *The Hospitality of God*, 189.

16. Charles H. Talbert, *Reading Luke: A Literary and Theological Commentary*, rev. ed. (Macon, GA: Smyth & Helwys, 2002), 260.

17. Talbert, *Reading Luke*, 259.

18. Byrne, *The Hospitality of God*, 190.

19. Alan Culpepper, *The Gospel of Luke: The New Interpreter's Bible* (Nashville: Abingdon, 1995), 479.

20. Byrne, *The Hospitality of God*, 190.

21. Koo D. Yun, "Minjung and Asian Pentecostals," in *Asian Contextual Theology for the Third Millennium: Theology of Minjung in Fourth-Eye Formation*, ed. Paul S. Chung et al. (Eugene, OR: Pickwick Publications, 2007), 89.

22. *Sozusa* is a Korean term that literally means "the minority" and carries prejudicial connotations referring to people who are unacceptable in Korean society. Jin Ho Kim et al., *The Time of Dead Minjung: Re-examining Minjung Theologian An Byung Moo* (Seoul: Samin, 2006). These authors claim themselves as the second generation of *minjung* theologians and try to explore various ways to examine and develop *minjung* theology (see Yong Yeon Hwang, "*Sosuza*, Today's *Minjung*," in *The Time of Dead Minjung*, 163–204).

23. Samson Prabhakar and Jinkwan Kwon, eds., *Dalit and Minjung Theologies: A Dialogue* (Bangalore: Btessc/Sathri, 2006). See also Manohar Chandra

Prgsad, *The Book of Exodus and Dalit Liberation: With Reference to Minjung Theology* (Bangalore: Asian Trading Corp., 2005).

24. See Virginia Fabella and Sun Ai Lee Park, eds., *We Dare to Dream: Doing Theology as Asian Women* (Hong Kong: Asian Women's Resource Centre for Culture and Theology and the Asian Office of the Women's Commission of the Ecumenical Association of Third World Theologians, 1989).

25. Paul S. Chung, Beli-Matti Karkkainen, and Kyoung-Jae Kim, eds., *Asian Contextual Theology for the Third Millennium: Theology of Minjung in Fourth-Eye Formation* (Eugene, OR: Pickwick Publications, 2007).

26. Andrew Sung Park, *The Wounded Heart of God: The Asian Concept of Han and the Christian Doctrine of Sin* (Nashville: Abingdon Press, 1993); the *minjung* have been often characterized as "*han*-ridden" people.

27. Wonhee Anne Joh, *Heart of the Cross: A Postcolonial Christology* (Louisville: Westminster John Knox Press, 2006).

10

THE MYSTERIOUS YOUNG MAN
WHO RAN AWAY NAKED (MARK 14:51–52)

Giacomo Perego

The account of the passion, death, and resurrection of Jesus in the Gospel of Mark opens with a minor episode that has intrigued interpreters of the New Testament for centuries. Mark informs us that, at the moment when Jesus is arrested in Gethsemane, after all his disciples have fled, "a certain young man was following him, wearing nothing but a linen cloth. They caught hold of him, but he left the linen cloth and ran off naked" (Mk 14:51–52). Who is this "young man"? Why is there such an insistence on what the young man was wearing, and upon his nakedness?

Even though various studies treat the scene as a minor and insignificant episode without any bearing on the unfolding events of Jesus' arrest and trial and their interpretation, nonetheless, after nearly twenty centuries, the world of exegesis is still inquiring as to its significance.[1] If Mark wanted to push his readers to reflect on this passage and the depth of his account, who can say what fruit a study of it might bear?[2]

History of Interpretation: Proposed Names

Surveying the diverse authors who have attempted to resolve "the enigma" of the mysterious young man who ran away naked, one is amazed at the wide array represented. Authoritative fathers of the church such as Ambrose, Bede, John Chrysostom, Gregory the Great, and Peter Chrysologus thought that the young man was John, the beloved disciple.[3] At the moment of Jesus' arrest, the Fourth Gospel does indeed place "another disciple" in the scene, who, together with Peter, follows Jesus to the house of the high priest (Jn 18:15–16).

Eutyhymius and Theophylactus[4] offer a different solution: the young man could be James the lesser, the son of Alpheus. According to certain indications found in the New Testament,[5] this disciple did indeed have a residence in Jerusalem. In Mark 15:40 Mark himself, making mention of the mother of the disciple, uses these terms: "Mary, the mother of James the lesser and of Joses."

W. Schenk advances a third hypothesis: the young man could be Peter, deliberately left unnamed by the evangelist (as in Mk 14:47). Schenk suggests that after having been put to flight, Peter would not have given up, but would have continued to follow the events from afar (14:54).[6]

While interesting, such solutions do not explicitly address how strongly the evangelist maintains in 14:50 that *all the disciples* fled, abandoning Jesus. If the situation was such, the young man in question could not have been John, or James, or Peter. Following this line of reasoning, Olshausen proposed in 1837 that it might be an autobiographical sketch of Mark himself, recalling that Mary "the mother of John, also called Mark," lived in Jerusalem (see Acts 12:12–17).[7] Perhaps this was the house where Jesus gathered with his disciples for the paschal meal. Perhaps the family was in possession of a property in Gethsemane where the Master retired with his disciples. Perhaps Mark, awakened at the coming of Judas and the crowd, and having dressed quickly with a linen cloth, came to look for the Master in the place of the paschal banquet and then rushed to Gethsemane to warn Jesus. Olshausen's hypothesis, while criticized for advancing too many "ifs," attained a certain amount of acceptance.

Finally, two other possibilities occur. First, in 1998 a new study took up a hypothesis from the second century identifying the young man with Lazarus, the "friend" of Jesus, already "at risk" (12:10) and indebted to the Master.[8] And second, one can simply limit oneself to speaking of a generic "eyewitness" present at the moment of the arrest.

Suggested Biblical Passages

Among the diverse hypotheses proposed, there is no lack of critics who find echoes in this scene of a passage of the Old Testament: "Those who are stout of heart among the mighty shall flee away naked on that day" (Amos 2:16). Nor is there a lack of those who think of the following passage, which refers to the patriarch, Joseph. "One day, however, when he went into the house to do his work, and while no one else was in the house, she [the wife of Potiphar, his master] caught hold of his garment, saying, 'Lie with me!' But he left his garment in her hand, and fled and ran outside" (Gen 39:32). This refusal cost the patriarch dearly: the wife of Potiphar accused Joseph of making advances and he was cast into prison. Bede the Venerable is the first commentator to suggest the resemblance between these two passages.[9] However, for Joseph, his flight was an act of fidelity toward his God and toward Potiphar, while for the young man of Mark, it was an act of "betrayal."

Others refer to Genesis 3:9–10: "the Lord God called to the man, and said to him, 'Where are you?' He said, 'I heard the sound of you in the garden, and I was afraid, because I was naked; and I hid myself.'" The young man of Mark's gospel finds himself in the same situation as Adam: naked, full of fear, in search of a place where he can take shelter.

Hypotheses Based upon Symbolic Readings

In any case, the enigma remains unresolved at this point. There are promising suggestions that come from a symbolic reading, however, which I believe permit one to draw near to a solution. Up to this point, commentators have suggested three positions.

The first position proceeds from one of the given facts: in Mark, the disciples are never at the level of their Master! Their following of Jesus is full of superficiality and hesitation, which come to a head in our passage (14:51–52). Also, the issues and concerns plaguing the disciples are all found in the young man: a lot of good will, but a lot of inconsistency as well. Many promises are made (see 14:31), which the disciples end up abandoning at the crucial moment, revealing the nakedness of their fidelity. While such a reading is fascinating, however, it leaves much out.

The second position avers to the other side of the coin to which this brief episode is closely linked: the passion of Jesus. It is true that the young man's flight highlights the infidelity of the Twelve. And it is also true that, by contrast, the fidelity of Jesus stands in bold relief. Jesus is arrested and is faithful to the will of the Father to the end, which is death on the cross. Stripped of his clothing, the nakedness of Jesus is not the sign of a shameful flight, but the testimony of his fidelity to God and to man. Cardinal Vanhoye writes,

> The omen becomes even clearer at the time of the burial. In the burial, one finds Jesus wrapped in the same type of clothing with which the young man was clothed: a linen cloth. Jesus seems to be definitively trapped: death imprisons him. But like the young man, He will leave the linen cloth in the tomb and flee from the bite of death.[10]

In my opinion, these two perspectives should be united. The brief scene functions as a bridge between that which precedes (the following of the Master) and that which follows (his passion, death, and resurrection). A complete reading cannot favor one aspect to the detriment of the other.

The third position exploits the link between our episode and the announcement of the resurrection in Mark 16:1–8. Mark is the only evangelist in which the announcement of paschal joy comes not from an angel but from a young man dressed in white who sits at the entrance of the tomb. The young man does not have any supernatural features, which is all the more evident given that the women's fear is tied not to his presence, but to the good news with which he entrusts them. Authors such as B. Standaert see this as a probable reference to a baptismal liturgy. At Gethsemane the young man would represent the catechumen who strips himself of all his clothing in order to immerse himself in the baptismal font where he will experience the passion and death of Jesus. At the tomb the young man would represent the neophyte who, after baptism, receives the white tunic and becomes, in the fullest sense, a witness of the resurrection. The letters of Paul also suggest a baptismal liturgy associated with the rite of divestiture and re-investiture (see, for example, Rom 13:11–14; Gal 3:26–28; Col 2:11–12; and Eph 4, 5:22–24, 30).

Three Clarifications

Before proceeding, it is useful to clarify three terms used in 14:51–52. The term that identifies the "young man" is the substantive, *neaniskos*. In Greek, when one speaks of *neaniskos* one is referring to that age-bracket (between eighteen and thirty-five) that follows adolescence and precedes the age of maturity. It is the time frame during which one's capacity for judgment and personal choice reaches mature expression. The term does not indicate a chronological age, but a time-bracket related to the process of maturation and formation of a more solid personality.

The article of clothing also deserves attention. What we call a "shroud" in English is a *sindōn* in Greek, a term that evokes the cloth with which Jesus was wrapped before burial. The word designates an Egyptian or Syrian manufactured cloth of linen or, more rarely, of cotton. Rectangular and large, it was wrapped around the body and often used as a cloak or a coat. The type of garment found in our passage is distinguished from a coat by the quality of the cloth (whether it is of

linen rather than wool) and by its price. The *sindōn* was a cloth of nobility and valuable; thus, it is with good reason that Mark, when presenting Joseph of Arimathea, designates him as a man of social position
(15:43). Mark 15:46 is not describing a sheet taken from bed and
thrown over one as a night cloak. The fine and valuable garment found
in our passage was used as a "night-shirt" and a funeral shroud. What is
a young man doing in Gethsemane dressed in this manner, during a
season in which the temperature at night does not rise above 50 or 55
degrees Fahrenheit (10 to 13 degrees Celsius)?

Finally, there is the issue of nakedness. Our translations often
smooth over the roughness of Mark. Yet he does not write that the
young man was "wearing nothing but a linen cloth." Rather, he says
more precisely that the young man was "wearing nothing but a linen
cloth on his naked body." This was his only clothing, which the evangelist reaffirms when he notes, "he fled away naked." In biblical literature the condition of nakedness is the sign of a loss of identity; nakedness is the condition of prisoners, slaves, prostitutes, the insane, the
possessed, and the impious. We find in the classical world a similar understanding of the condition of nakedness:

> In the classical ancient world the contrast between a clothed
> human body and a naked one is used to express some of the
> fundamental contrasts present in human experience: God and
> man, human nature and animal nature, man and woman, the
> public and the private sphere, prosperity and poverty, admira-
> tion and compassion, the social state of the citizen and the so-
> cial state of the slave, the civil man and the barbarian, the
> spirit and the flesh, life and death, power and misery. The rep-
> resentation of a naked body has a significant magical power
> that the artist attentively uses and emphasizes. Its significance
> changes with the times, but its power does not change, its
> evocative force—even when man would annul it—reminding
> us of our nature of being animal and mortal.[11]

Obviously a positive use of the term also existed, but not only is
this usage not supported by the context, it is also rare in biblical literature. In a few words, then, the attempt of the young man to remain at
Jesus' side ends badly: his flight takes place under a sign of scandal and
public reprobation more shameful than one can imagine.[12]

Having established these clarifications, we are now ready to immerse ourselves in the rich message set forth in Mark 14:51-52.

One Possible Interpretation:
Three Announcements of the Paschal Mystery

During Jesus' journey toward Jerusalem, the three announcements of the paschal mystery (Mk 8:31, 9:31, 10:33–34) both disorient the disciples and serve to emphasize their difficulty in understanding the Master. What happens to Jesus unfolds in the following manner: he is handed over, he is tried and condemned, and he dies and rises after three days. The three announcements of these coming events are important because they distinguish the beginning and end-points of the paschal mystery, which extends from the handing over of the Son of Man to the high priests all the way to his resurrection. They cover the entirety of what is narrated between 14:53 and 16:8, from the moment of Jesus' being handed over to the high priest to the moment of the proclamation of Jesus' resurrection.

Another piece of evidence confirms the notion that Mark 14:53 opens another great chapter of the good news of Mark: the scene of the arrest (14:43–50) is presented as the concluding scene of Jesus' entire public ministry. If the public ministry of Jesus opens with the calling of the first disciples (1:16–20), it now closes with their flight (14:50). If the public ministry is characterized by the preaching and teaching of Jesus, in this scene the evangelist describes the last public words that the Master addresses to the crowd (14:49), which make reference to that ministry. What was initiated under the proclamation, "The time is fulfilled" (1:15), is now closed with the teaching, "let the Scriptures be fulfilled" (14:49).[13] In other words, the scene of the arrest constitutes the "final" word of his public ministry: Jesus' relationship with the disciples is broken. His word is suppressed. His movements are blocked. And it is into this delicate place of passage that the brief episode of the young man who fled naked is inserted.

A Guide to Reading

If Mark 14:51–52 constitutes a "lever" for the paschal mystery that follows, what is the fulcrum, the pivot on which the account turns? The cross (Mk 15:25–37) is the great "watershed" between what precedes the death of Jesus and that which follows it.

In the course of events that lead the reader to the foot of Mt. Golgotha (the condemnation by the religious authorities in 14:53–72; the condemnation by Pilate in 15:1–15; the insults of the soldiers in 15:16–24), all the figures who have a positive relationship with the Master exit from the scene. The three pericopes that follow the flight of the young man (14:53–72, 15:1–15, and 15:16–24) describe ambiguous figures who seem to be rallying themselves in support of Jesus, but who abandon him a short time later. There is the case of Peter, who follows the Master in 14:54, but denies him in 14:66–72. There is the case of Pilate, fully aware in 15:10 of the envy that animates the accusations of the chief priests, but who, in the end, prefers to consign Jesus to death. And there is the case of Simon of Cyrene, "the father of Alexander and Rufus," who carries the cross only because he is constrained to do so, without any reaction to the sufferings of Jesus (15:21). During Jesus' public ministry, the large groups to whom the he addresses himself are the disciples, the crowds, and the religious authorities. Now, one after another, these groups reject Jesus: the disciples flee and repudiate him; the crowds allow themselves to be the instruments of the religious authorities; and these last participate, at least indirectly, in his condemnation to death.

At the center of the paschal mystery (15:25–37) is the cross, the physical and theological place to which the sorrowful path walked by Jesus leads as he is progressively stripped of everything he has. The story is constructed in three temporal arcs: Jesus is crucified at nine o'clock in the morning (15:25–32), at noon darkness covers the earth (Mk 15:33), and at three o'clock in the afternoon a loud cry concludes his earthly existence (15:34–37). The evangelist does not add anything to brighten the scene. Mark's perspective is much different from that of Luke, who adds a semblance of sharing (it is enough just to think of the good thief). In the Gospel of Mark, the death of Jesus is set against a background that is utterly desolate.

Only after Jesus' death cry (15:37) does Mark offer a glimmer of hope, as a series of positive figures enter the scene. There is the case of the centurion (15:39) who seems to redeem the violence of the soldiers and the indifference of Pilate. There is the case of Joseph of Arimathea (15:43), an authoritative member of the Sanhedrin who seems to redeem the pettiness of the religious authorities. And there is the case of the women (15:40–41) who, though keeping themselves at a distance, fill the bitter emptiness left by the disciples. They are discreet presences who attest that the ministry of the Master has not been in vain. All of this can be synthesized in schema on the facing page.

Entering into the Particulars

In order to demonstrate that the schema presented here is not some arbitrary grid, we will now enter into more of the details, illustrating the

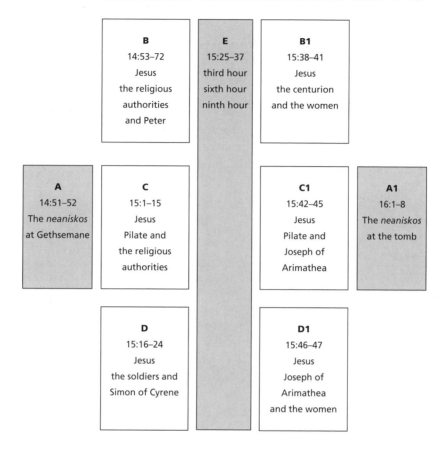

correspondences between the episodes that bring Jesus to Golgotha and the glimmers of hope that appear on the day following his death.

Mark 14:53–72 and Mark 15:38–41 (B and B1)

First, Mark creates a parallelism between the denial of Peter in the story of Jesus before the religious authorities (Mk 14:53–72), which is set in the area around the house of the high priest, and the story of the centurion and the women at the foot of the cross (15:38–41), which takes place in the area around Golgotha. The women, who observe the death of the Master from afar in 15:40, correspond to Peter, who follows Jesus from afar in 14:54. In 14:58 Mark tells us that certain false witnesses accuse Jesus of having said, "I will destroy this temple that is made with hands, and in three days I will build another, not made with hands." And in 15:38 the theme is taken up again in the tearing of the veil of the temple "in two, from top to bottom." For his part, the centurion responds indirectly to the question of the high priest, who in

14:61 asks the Master: "Are you the Christ, the son of the Blessed One?" Standing before the desolate scene of the death of Jesus, the centurion exclaims: "Truly this was the son of God" (15:39).

The parallels outlined above are reflected in the vocabulary used in the passages, as well as in the theological ideas to which they give voice. Peter and the women both evoke discipleship. Thus, Peter is the last to exit the scene before the death of Jesus, and the women are the first to come after his death. The question regarding the destruction of the temple also expresses a precise theology. Jesus speaks of a "destruction" and a "rebuilding" of the temple, but how this was to be accomplished could only be understood at Golgotha. There it becomes clear that Jesus is speaking of the "destruction" and "rebuilding" of the community, his body on this earth. At the moment the veil of the temple rips from top to bottom, a new "holy space" is inaugurated before the eyes of the centurion, a representative of the new people of God that embraces all the nations.

Finally, there is a return to the theme of the identity of Jesus, which runs through Mark's gospel like a scarlet thread. In condemning Jesus to death, the religious authorities publicly deny the unique relationship with God declared by Jesus (death on a cross was considered the death of one cursed by God). The centurion, on the other hand, attests to the profound bond of sonship that binds the condemned Jesus to the Father, declaring what, until now, no one in the whole of the Mark has been allowed to say, with the exception of the Evangelist (Mk 1:1) and the demons (Mk 3:11, 5:7).

Mark 15:1–5 and Mark 15:42–45 (C and C1)

The location of these events serves to unite both passages: we are in the environs of the residence of Pilate. The scene opens "as soon as it was morning" (15:1), and it concludes in the same general area "when evening had come" (15:42). To this spatial and temporal correspondence Mark adds that of the protagonists: on one side Pilate and the Jewish religious authorities discuss condemning Jesus to death, and on the other Pilate and Joseph of Arimathea (a qualified member of the Sanhedrin) discuss the handing over of the body. In both passages the decision rests for a moment upon a third figure who is summoned to the scene: Barabbas enters the first scene (15:6–15), and the centurion enters the second (15:44). Pilate is seized by wonder on both occasions, a peculiarity that the reader should underestimate inasmuch as Mark employs a Greek word that is rarely used in his gospel: *thaumazein*.

The theological themes embedded in these narratives expand the parallelism. The kingdom of God is at the center of the trial before

Pilate, which begins with the famous words: "Are you the king of the Jews?" (15:2). A little while later it seems as if the appearance of Joseph of Arimathea offers a response, since he is presented as one "who was also himself waiting expectantly for the kingdom of God" (15:43). It is notable that the "also" seems to imply that others were waiting for such a kingdom as well, and that the act of burial takes place within this time of waiting.

Mark 15:16–24 and Mark 15:46–47 (D and D1)

Jesus is delivered into the hands of the soldiers in the first passage (15:16–24), and into the hands of Joseph of Arimathea in the second (15:46–47). In both cases the decision comes from Pilate. We also witness a change of context from the preceding episodes. In Mark 16:24 the reader passes from the court where the soldiers have gathered to the foot of Golgotha, and in 15:46–47 the movement is from Golgotha to the sepulcher. The first scene concludes with Jesus' crucifixion (15:24), and the second opens with the taking down of Jesus from the cross (15:46). In both passages Mark focuses upon the clothes worn by the Master. They are divided and drawn for by lot in 15:24, whereas in 15:46 the body of Jesus is removed from the cross and wrapped in a sheet of linen. It is interesting to note that the evangelist makes special mention of the clothing and the shroud twice. Moreover, Mark is the only evangelist who mentions the purchase of precious fabric on the part of Joseph of Arimathea.

The two scenes are marked by the presence of one-dimensional figures whose personal agency is oddly absent in the drama unfolding in the account. There is the case of Simon of Cyrene, who in Mark 15:21 carries the cross only because he is compelled to do so. But there is also the case of the women in 15:47 who stand by and watch without taking part in what Joseph of Arimathea is doing. In both passages the evangelist describes persons whom he presents as well known to the community, which explains two parenthetical references to Simon as the "father of Alexander and Rufus" (15:21), and to the women as "Mary Magdalene and Mary, the mother of Joseph" (15:47).

Mark 15:25–37 (E)

The cross is the pivot around which the narrative revolves and to which the events lead in creating these correspondences. Its physical reality becomes a dramatic sign of humiliation and malediction, where Jesus is subjected to a radical human and spiritual stripping. The account is framed by three temporal indicators that serve to emphasize the stripping all the more: the third hour (nine in the morning), the sixth hour (noon) and the ninth hour (three in the afternoon). Such schemas are typical of Mark's gospel.

The *third hour* is the hour of total human failure. There is no positive figure around Jesus, there is no sign of compassion that comforts him, and there are no explicit references made to the fulfillment of the scriptures. In the three preceding passages, granting a certain ambiguity, Peter, Pilate, and Simon of Cyrene seem to provide a minimum of sympathetic participation in the drama lived out by the Lord. However, the message conveyed in Mark 15:25–32 goes in a completely different direction: the whole human world has abandoned and rejected Jesus.

The *sixth hour* is the hour of darkness. This darkness weighs upon the scene until the moment when Jesus dies with a loud cry. Unlike Luke (23:44b), Mark does not provide a meteorological reading of the event and, unlike Matthew, he does not provide an eschatological framework aimed at revealing a decisive intervention of God. Mark's gospel simply emphasizes the desolation experienced by Jesus. In such a setting, the darkness seems to constitute a sign of the judgment of God, a judgment that falls not so much on those present as it does on the Son who bears the human burden of sin even unto death. The exterior night expresses the interior night lived by the Master, deprived not only of all human communion, but also of the comfort of creation itself.

The *ninth hour* is the hour in which the human and spiritual drama of Jesus of Galilee reaches its culmination with a strong and lacerating cry. In the entire account of the passion, this is the only cry that directly addresses God as its object. The repetition of the expression: "My God, my God, why have you forsaken me?" first given in Aramaic and then translated into Greek, underlines the intense experience of abandonment of Jesus, confirming the incomprehension with which that abandonment is lived. The cry obliges the reader to fix his or her attention on God. If the third hour places the sundering of Jesus from every form of human compassion in relief, and if the sixth hour rips away the comfort of creation, then the ninth hour reveals how Jesus is stripped of communion with the Father. It is certainly not by chance that the cry of Jesus touches directly upon the first verse of Psalm 22, the only verse in the whole Book of Psalms that expresses separation from God in an utterly radical manner.[14] But what makes the scene even more sorrowful is that the cry is not only misunderstood by those present, but it becomes an object of derision (15:35–36).

The cry of Golgotha, as we find it in Mark, represents one of the extremely rare occasions in which the theme of abandonment by God appears in the New Testament. Paradoxically, the one who inaugurates his ministry under the luminous sign of nearness to God (Mark 1:15) exits the scene under the heavy darkness of separation from God. So dies the Master of Galilee, abandoned by humanity and by God, wrapped in the night of failure and rejection.

Turning on this pivot point, the darkest and most violent moment of the life of Jesus, the narrative slowly opens toward hope via a series of positive signs: the darkness is lifted, the veil of the temple is rent, and we see sketches of positive figures like the centurion, the women, and Joseph of Arimathea. But these follow only after the bottom has been reached.

Conclusion

We have presented, therefore, a vision of Mark's account of the paschal mystery as a unfied whole, situating the position and role of the young man of 14:51–52 as the focal point. The scene becomes not only the door through which the reader gains access to Mark's account of the paschal mystery, but the key to its interpretation. The young man who is stripped of his clothing previews not only the stages of despoilment to which Jesus is subjected, but also the sad and humiliating flight of the disciples.

In the end, no matter how much the disciples proclaim that they will follow the Master with all their strength, sooner or later such protests end in sorrowful, humiliating, but necessary defeat. For it is possible to follow the path of the Master only on the day following the experience of the paschal mystery. This is because it is precisely their experience of the life, death, and resurrection of Jesus that allows the disciples to cross the threshold of their own limitations and to overcome their own poverty. Thus, in the Gospel of Mark, the stripping, along with the nakedness connected to it, is an unavoidable dimension of the experience of following the path tread by Jesus of Galilee.

Notes

1. Among the most recent studies of this theme see: S. C. Carlson, *The Gospel Hoax: Morton Smith's Invention of Secret Mark* (Waco, TX: Baylor University Press, 2005); Stephen B. Hatton, "Mark's Naked Disciple: The Semiotics and Comedy of Following," *Neotestamentica* 35, 1–2 (2001): 35–48; P. Jeffery, *The Secret Gospel of Mark Unveiled: Imagined Rituals of Sex, Death and Madness in Biblical Forgery* (New Haven: Yale University Press, 2006); A. Rupert, "Mark 14:51–52 and Coptic Hagiography," *Biblica* 89 (2008): 265–68; A. Yarbro Collins, "The Flight of the Naked Young Man Revisited," in *"Il Verbo*

di Dio è vivo": Studi sul Nuovo Testamento in onore del Cardinal Albert Vanhoye, S.I, ed. José Enrique Aquilar Chiu, Franco Manzi, Filippo Urso, and Carlos Zesati Estrada (Rome: Editrice Pontificio Instituto Biblico, 2007), 123–37.

2. For a more detailed treatment of the subject, see Giacomo Perego, La nudità necessaria. Il mistero del neaniskos di Mc 14,51–52 nel racconto marciano della passione, morte e risurrezione di Gesù (Milan: San Paolo, 2000).

3. See Ambrose of Milan in Psalmum XXXVI enarratio (PL 14, 993); Bede the Venerable in Marci Evangelii Expositio (PL 92, 278–279); John Chrysostom, Commentariorum in Joannem: Homilia LXXXIII (PG 59, 449); Gregorio Magno, Moralium libri sive Expositio in librum B. Job XIV, 49.57 (PL 75, 1068); and Peter Chrysologus, Sermones: Sermo LXXVIII (PL 52, 420).

4. See Euthymius Zigabenus, Commentarius in quatuor evangelia in Matthaeum XXVI (PG 129, 694); Theophylactus, Enarratio in evangelium S. Marci XIV (PG 123, 658).

5. Acts 12:17; 15:13–21; 21:18; Galatians 1:18-19; 2:9.

6. W. Schenk, Der Passionbericht nach Markus: Üntersuchungen zur Uberlieferungsgeschichte der Passiontraditionen (Berlin, 1974), 209–12, 263–64.

7. H. Olshausen, Die Leidensgeschichte des Herrn nach den vier Evangelien (Konisberg, 1862 or 1837), 124.

8. M. J. Haren, "The Naked Young Man: A Historian's Hypothesis on Mark 14:51–52," Biblica 79 (1998): 525–31.

9. Bede the Venerable in Marci (PL 92, 279).

10. A. Vanhoye, "La fuite du jeune homme nu (Mc 14:51–52)," Biblica 52 (1971): 401–6.

11. Bonfante L., "Nudity as a Costume in Classical Art," American Journal of Archaeology 93 (1989), 543–70 at 569–70.

12. See also Genesis 9:20-27; 1 Samuel 19:23-24; 2 Samuel 10:1-5; Isaiah 20:1-6; Ezekiel 16; Amos 2:16; Hosea 2:5; Micah 1:8; Job 24:7-10; Luke 8:27; Acts 19:13-17; and Revelation 3:17, 16:15, and 17:16.

13. These are the only two instances of the Greek verb plēroō (to fulfill) in the Gospel of Mark.

14. L. Caza, "Le relief que Marc a donné au cri de la croix," Science et Esprit 39, 2 (1987): 171–91.

PART III

THEOLOGY

11

THE PREFERENTIAL OPTION
FOR THE POOR

CHRIST AND THE LOGIC OF GRATUITY

Roberto S. Goizueta

The preferential option for the poor is one of the most influential theological concepts of the last fifty years—and one of the most misunderstood. No sooner is the term mentioned than it is met with the rejoinder, "But what about the rich? Aren't we supposed to love them as well?" or "Why are the poor necessarily any better than the rich? Surely there are plenty of bad poor people!" or "I thought that Christians were supposed to be about harmony and reconciliation, not partiality and divisiveness." This essay will place such questions in the context of Christological reflections by U.S. Latino/a and Latin American theologians on the life, death, and resurrection of Jesus of Galilee.

Fr. Gustavo Gutiérrez, OP, of Peru, considered by many as the founder of Latin American liberation theology, has suggested that the two principal, overarching themes in scripture are: (1) the universality and gratuity of God's love, and (2) God's preferential love for the poor. U.S. Latino/a Christology, as a theology written from "the border," offers important insights into the interdependent, mutually implicit character of these two biblical themes, especially in its efforts to retrieve the theological significance of Galilee. U.S. Latino/a and Latin American Christologies help us understand how God's love, precisely as gratuitous and universal, demands a preference for the poor. Such an approach provides a way to resolve what can seem like conflicting claims regarding the nature of this preference and point to the possibility of a reconciliation grounded in an option for the poor. Building on these insights, then, in what follows I will argue that the preferential option for the poor is in fact a necessary precondition for both Christian faith and global reconciliation.

The Logic of Gratuity

What, then, have Latino/a and other U.S. theologians learned from the Latin American church about the gratuitous nature of God's preferential option for the poor and its relationship to the Mystery of God? In my own case, I have learned that, first and foremost, God's preferential love for the poor is the theological and methodological guarantee, or safeguard, of God's transcendence, sovereignty, and Mystery. It seems to me that if God is truly "Other," and thus irreducible to any human concept or construction, then logically God will take the side of the poor, the marginalized, the outcast, the victims. In other words, if God loves everyone equally and gratuitously, then God will love the poor preferentially. What at first glance appear to be mutually contradictory assertions are, in fact, mutually implicit.

This conclusion can be reached, however, only if one first acknowledges that the poor do in fact exist and if one engages at least minimally with people who live on the margins of our society and world. Here one is immediately confronted with the fact that while there are indeed poor persons, there are also non-poor persons who pay little attention to the reality of those who are defined as "poor," "marginalized," and "powerless," precisely in relation to them. Writing from El Salvador, Fr. Jon Sobrino, S.J., distinguishes those persons who take life for granted from those who cannot.[1] Tragically, we live in a divided world and society. And those in the best position to recognize this fact are the people who suffer the consequences of that division. Conversely, those of us who benefit from social divisions—whether explicitly or implicitly—are likely to either ignore these or deemphasize their significance. It is the hungry person who is in the best position to determine whether hunger exists in our society. In Sobrino's terms, the person who cannot take life for granted is in the best position to be "honest about reality."[2] In other words, the poor or powerless have a privileged epistemological perspective from which to evaluate "reality." (Note, however, that this privilege in no way assures infallible or inevitable accuracy—only a greater likelihood of such.) And the encounter of those who take life for granted with those who do not makes it possible for us to "see" a reality we would otherwise miss.

Given then that we do indeed live in a divided world that grants its victims an epistemological advantage in confronting its reality, what is the significance of this reality for our understanding of God (and for theology)? More specifically, what can it mean to say that God enters into and becomes incarnate in a world, a society, and a history that are beset by divisions between those who have power (and take life for granted) and those who are powerless (and cannot take life for granted)? In such a world, what would it mean to say that God loves all people equally and gratuitously? In such a world, what would it mean to say that Jesus Christ is the perfect expression of God's love?

For two thousand years the Christian tradition has proposed an answer that, for many, has seemed inconceivable, if not scandalous. In such a world the perfect expression of God's love is found in the utter powerlessness of an unjustly condemned criminal who, having experienced abandonment by his closest friends and even God, hangs pitiably from a cross. God's love enters history in the person of an outcast who is tortured and crucified for befriending other outcasts. God's love enters our divided society on the side of those who suffer its consequences—not because God loves the outcast more, but because in the midst of division and conflict, God's love for the victims, and God's love for their victimizers, must take different forms. Thus, God's love for the powerful will not (at least initially) be experienced as love at all, since it will take the form of challenge, confrontation, and a call to conversion, to *metanoia*.

To say that God's love is universal is not to say that it is neutral. In fact, it is to say the very opposite: precisely *because* God's love is universal, it *cannot* be neutral. If a mother finds that a fight has broken out between her strapping teenage son and his much smaller sister, the mother will not hesitate to try to "liberate" the smaller girl from the brother's clutches—precisely because the mother loves her two children equally. In that context, the mother's love for her son will take the form of a call to conversion, though he will not likely see it that way. Were the mother to take a neutral stance and not get involved because she "loves her children equally," the young daughter would not experience the neutrality as love. In a situation of division, a neutral stance provides implicit support for the divided status quo and, therefore, implicit support for the person(s) benefiting from the division, in other words, the most powerful. Neutrality, like silence, is consent.

The crucified and risen Jesus is the historical incarnation of this logic, the logic of God's universal, gratuitous love. If the incarnate God is truly Other, truly Mystery, then God will be revealed most fully among those persons who themselves are most "other," most incomprehensible, in our world. The God who is absolutely Other, and thus "makes no sense" in the context of merely human calculations and expectations, will be encountered most fully among those persons whose very existence makes no sense among the hungry in a gluttonous world, among the powerless in a power-mad world, among the insecure in a world obsessed with security. In Sobrino's words, the God who is Other will be found among those who cannot take life for granted in a world that takes life for granted. In the words of Gutiérrez, this God will be found among the non-persons in a world that identifies personhood with wealth, power, and security. In the crucified people, God assumes the most degrading, dehumanizing dimensions of victimized human existence by becoming the absolute Victim. God does not do this in order to privilege victimhood—which is always an evil—but precisely to reveal, once and for all, the absolutely gratuitous and universal character of God's love for creation. In the person of the crucified and risen Jesus Christ, God pronounces the victory of the logic of gratuity over the logic of *suum cuique* ("to each what is due him or her").[3]

Reconciliation as the Fruit of Gratuity

If the crucified and risen Galilean is the full expression of God's gratuitous, universal love, he also reveals the intrinsic connection between gratuity and reconciliation. God's gratuitous love is revealed in the person of the Resurrected Victim as the source of reconciliation. The logic of gratuity is ineluctable: (1) God loves the poor preferentially, (2) in order to reveal the gratuitous, universal character of God's love, (3) which demands and makes reconciliation possible. This logic is evident, above all, in the central Christological events: the passion, death, and resurrection of Jesus Christ. The Paschal Triduum reveals the inherently communal character of these events and, hence, the power of the God-who-is-love to create and sustain, not just life in general, but life-in-communion. The resurrection is not merely the victory of life over death, but the vindication and justification of the Victim and, therefore, the victory of communion over estrangement and alienation.[4]

What would the passion, death, and resurrection of Jesus Christ look like from the perspective of the victims, those whom the world has ignored, cast out, and abandoned—those who are "other" to the world of power and wealth? For Sobrino, the crucifixion provides the hermeneutical lens through which to understand—looking backward—the life of Jesus, and—looking ahead—the resurrection. The crucifixion is the link between Jesus' life and his resurrection.[5] Jesus' life—his words and his deeds—becomes interpretable as that which led inexorably to his crucifixion. Because he dared to welcome and accompany the outcasts of his society, Jesus was forced to either share their fate or renounce his message. The crucifixion was the direct consequence of his com-passion for the outcasts. He was abandoned to his fate as they had been (and continue to be) abandoned by society. Interpreted from the standpoint of the crucifixion, the resurrection confirms God's justification of the divine Victim of society's injustice, as well as all the other victims of history.[6] Further, the resurrection affirms the victory of reconciliation over abandonment. It affirms the possibility and hope of constructing a newly transformed community grounded in God's gratuitous love, expressed in the Victim's offer of mercy.

In the gospels, the process of com-passion → abandonment → reconciliation (the divine logic of gratuity) comes to a head and is fully revealed in Jesus' post-resurrection appearances to the apostles. Out of fear for their own lives, Jesus' closest friends had abandoned him at his time of greatest need; through their silence and inaction they became accomplices in his torture and crucifixion. As they cowered together after his death, they must have felt not just fear but also shame and guilt, for they had effectively rent asunder the community formed when Jesus called them together. This was the situation into which the resurrected Jesus walked when he appeared to the apostles.

But rather than demand justice or recompense from his former friends and betrayers, the resurrected Jesus greets the apostles in the upper room with an offer of peace: "Peace be with you!" This offer must have disarmed the apostles, not only because the one whom they assumed was dead was now alive, but also because the one they had abandoned was now returned to haunt them! Surely they would have preferred to leave the past behind and get on with their lives, even if that meant living with some regret and pangs of conscience. But Jesus will not let them forget. He forces them to remember, not by demanding justice, but by extending to them his forgiveness and mercy. "Peace be with you!" he says. Yet the offer of mercy, precisely as a demand for remembrance, includes a call for repentance and justice: "Put your finger here." The still-visible wounds on Jesus' glorified body represent the inerasable memories of suffering that forever remain a part of the resurrection. Even the Victim's offer of forgiveness cannot wish the wounds away. Thus, the offer of mercy can be *received* only if and when the wounds are acknowledged, responsibility is accepted, and behavior is transformed: "My Lord and my God!" It is not repentance that elicits justice and forgiveness, but precisely the reverse: the extravagance of Jesus' mercy compels repentance and *metanoia*—the logic of gratuity.[7]

The resurrection, therefore, is not merely the resurrection of a single, autonomous human being; it is the resurrection of a community. That community is now radically reconstituted on the basis of gratuitousness. Grounded in the extravagant mercy of the crucified and risen Victim, the transformed community demands an equally transformed praxis, one that begins when those who had abandoned Jesus accept his offer of forgiveness. That reception necessarily includes, as intrinsic to their decision to accept his offer, the apostles' acknowledgment of their complicity in Jesus' crucifixion and a commitment to carry on his mission, to a transformed praxis. Thus, the act of receptivity to the divine mercy expressed in the crucified and risen Victim's "Peace be with you" is mediated by a renewed praxis of solidarity and struggle for justice with the victims who embody God's extravagant mercy in history. To put it in Sobrino's terms, our reception of God's offer of mercy depends upon our solidarity with the crucified and risen Galilean as mediated by our solidarity with the crucified people in history, a solidarity most fully realized when we "take the crucified people down from the cross."[8]

"There You Will See Him . . ."

Christ's crucifixion-resurrection thus includes not only the empty tomb but also the upper room. There is, however, a third element intrinsic to understanding the crucifixion-resurrection from a communal perspective, namely, Galilee. In the gospels we are told, "He has risen from the dead, and behold, he is going before you to Galilee; there you will see him" (Mt 28:7, Mk 16:7). As in the case of Jesus' encounter with the apostles in the upper room, it is instructive to understand the command to "go to Galilee" as part of the logic of Jesus' crucifixion-resurrection.

After all, the receptivity of the followers of Jesus to his appearance is intrinsic to their experience of the resurrection. While we are told that the resurrection of Jesus is corporeal and takes place in history, it is not simply an empirical event like any other, for it is available only to those with "eyes that see" (Mt 13:16, Lk 10:23).[9] Like all revelation, the resurrection is by definition a resurrection *for* or *to* someone; the encounter with the resurrected Jesus cannot take place without Jesus and another. Thus, just as Jesus' appearance to the apostles in the upper room is part of the resurrection narrative, so is his appearance "in Galilee." By sending the apostles to Galilee, Jesus brings his own ministry, which had begun in Galilee, full circle; what had been initiated in Galilee will find its consummation in Galilee. Yet Galilee is not just an ending, it is also a beginning. It is the birthplace of the apostles' new community and new mission. In a very real way, Galilee is the birthplace of the new *ekklesia*, or church.

If this is the case, it is important to understand the theological significance of the command to go to Galilee and the appearance of Jesus there. If Jesus' disciples are to go to Galilee in order to "see" Jesus, what is the significance of Galilee as a *locus theologicus*, that is, a place of human-divine encounter? Here the most extensive, systematic theological work has been done by Mexican-American theologian Fr. Virgilio Elizondo, drawing upon the work of biblical scholars such as Sean Freyne, and upon his own experience as a Mexican-American son of the U.S.–Mexico borderland.[10]

For Elizondo, Galilee's theological significance lies in its geographical and historical character as a borderland region, distant from the religious and political center of Jerusalem. The geographical and historical reality of Galilee assumes a theological role in the gospels because that reality marks the ministry of Jesus. Elizondo points out, for instance, that the borderland reality of Galilee gives rise to a Jewish religiosity beyond the control of the religious and political elites in Jerusalem. As such, Galilee symbolizes a "newness" within the Jewish community that threatens established power structures. Inhabitants of the borderland cannot be adequately supervised and therefore cannot be completely trusted. (This fear of the "hinterland" is certainly not unique to first-century Palestine, but is a common human phenomenon.)

The suspicion arises not simply from the geographical distance but also from the concomitant proximity to Hellenistic and Roman populations. For a Jerusalem religio-political elite concerned with ritual purity, the regular contact of Galilean Jews with Hellenized Jews (such as Herod and his followers) and Gentiles representing religious and cultural influences from the other side of the border was a source of suspicion: "In Galilee the Jews were looked down upon and despised by the others as they were in the rest of the world. Their own Jewish people despised them as inferior and impure. Because of their mixture with others, they were marginated by their own."[11]

Elizondo argues that as Jesus was a Jew raised in Galilee and had a ministry identified with the region, he was an object of suspicion and derision. Yet—and here is the key to the good news—this same object of derision becomes, in the person of Jesus Christ, the chosen one of God, the Messiah in whom God becomes fully revealed. In Jesus of Galilee, human expectations and preconceptions about God are overturned:

> The apparent nonimportance and rejection of Galilee are the very bases for its all-important role in the historic eruption of God's saving plan for humanity. The human scandal of God's

way does not begin with the cross, but with the historico-cultural incarnation of [God's] Son in Galilee . . . That God has chosen to become a Galilean underscores the great paradox of the incarnation, in which God becomes the despised and lowly of the world. In becoming a Galilean, God becomes the fool of the world for the sake of the world's salvation. What the world rejects, God chooses as his very own.[12]

The return of the crucified and risen Christ to Galilee is simply the final confirmation of the privileged place held by Galilee as a *locus theologicus*. What Elizondo calls "the Galilean Principle," that "what the world rejects, God chooses as his very own," turns out to be both the starting point of the mission of this marginal peasant from Nazareth in Galilee, and its logical culmination: "There you will see him."

While the roots of Jesus' mission in Galilean Judaism are critically important, it is not until the end of the gospel that Galilee is revealed as not merely the origin and context of Jesus' ministry, but also the place where he founds the newly reconciled community. Only at the end is the most radical outcome of Jesus' life and work revealed. This genuinely "resurrected" community is born in the borderland. As *ekklesia*, this transformed community thus eschews at its very foundation all barriers that separate pure from impure, or insider from outsider. At its very foundation, the church is a church of the borderland and, as such, it privileges the borderland as a place of revelation, a place of encounter with the crucified and risen Christ.

The Preferential Option for the Poor Revisited

In the borderland of Galilee, the crucified and risen Christ brings the "hermeneutical circle" of the Paschal Triduum to its culmination, thereby revealing the internal logic unfolding in the passion, death, and resurrection of the one known as Jesus of Galilee. This logic, however, is accessible only to those "who have eyes to see," those open to gratuitousness in a world of *suum cuique*. It is a logic that appears foolish and scandalous to those who insist that God is on the side of the righteous and the virtuous. Thus, the crucified and risen Christ appears scandalous to those who, in the words of Johann Baptist Metz, are more concerned with sinners than with victims, more concerned with sin than with suffering. But the Galilean Jesus is moved much more by the latter than by the former; he who readily forgives sin does not easily abide the suffering of victims. Indeed, that is the scandal of gratuity.

Sin is always forgivable, but the blindness that causes and perpetuates suffering is not—precisely because such blindness precludes the possibility of receiving God's gratuitous mercy even when it is offered (as it always is). This latter is, by definition, the only unforgivable sin.

The decision to "go to Galilee," therefore, eventually unveils the intrinsic complementarity between two biblical principles that guide the thought of Gustavo Gutiérrez: God's preferential option for the poor and the gratuity and universality of God's love. In returning to Galilee, the formerly disheartened followers of Jesus discover the intrinsic and unbreakable unity of Christ's passion, death, and resurrection. In Galilee, the full import of Christ's offer of reconciliation is made present. The acceptance by his followers of the offer of reconciliation made possible by Christ's resurrection (betrayal and abandonment are not the end of the story) reconstitutes and transforms the community that was shattered when they fled at the crucifixion. Further, it includes—and demands—the extension of that reconciled existence, grounded as it is in the gratuitous mercy of Christ's "Peace be with you," to all those persons who have never been a part of our community because they live in the borderland. The command to go to Galilee is a command to understand Christ's mercy as extending beyond the upper room to the seeming chaos and uncontrollability of the borderland.

The command to go to Galilee thus affirms the ecclesiological implications of the crucifixion-resurrection. God's preferential love for the poor is embodied in the abandoned Criminal hanging from the cross, and together they reveal the utter gratuitousness of God's mercy. In the upper room that mercy becomes the seedbed of a new, reconciled community that includes the very persons who had abandoned Jesus. In Galilee this reconciled community—the fruit of Christ's resurrection—is opened to all those persons who, because they live on the margins of society, have been excluded or abandoned. In Galilee the crucified people (to use Sobrino's terminology) become the privileged locus or place for encountering the crucified and risen Christ in history.

Elizondo's Galilean Jesus

The work of Virgilio Elizondo has helped to retrieve the theological centrality of Galilee, and has thus helped broaden our understanding of the crucifixion-resurrection event itself. Elizondo reminds us that the resurrection of Jesus transforms not only his individual existence but also the relationships from which his personhood emerges. The resurrection of Jesus not only renews and transforms the bonds with

his estranged disciples, but it leads them to return to the Galilean borderland where the post-Easter church is destined to be born and to
grow, amid the marginated inhabitants of the borderland.

The mandate to return to Galilee is the final confirmation that
God's preferential love for the poor expresses and safeguards God's universal, gratuitous love, for the full ramifications of Jesus' crucifixion-
resurrection become visible only upon his return to Galilee. The scandalous and inconceivable self-communication of God in the person of
a crucified criminal reveals the extravagant gratuitousness—and Mystery—of God's love. As Elizondo has suggested, however, what Christian theology still fails to fully appreciate is that the self-communication
of God in the Galilean borderland is equally scandalous and unexpected. It is precisely because God's love is most fully revealed in the
person of the crucified Victim that God's love can be revealed to everyone. It is precisely because the crucified and risen Christ will be seen
first in Galilee that he can be seen everywhere and in everyone. Finally, it is precisely because the church is the church of the borderland
and thrives among its inhabitants as the church of the margins that the
church can be present everywhere and to everyone.

Jesus' crucifixion, resurrection, and reconciliation with the apostles
through his return to Galilee calls all of his followers to the option for
the poor and fuels demands for social justice as the natural expression
of the gratuity of God's love and the Mystery of God, which confounds
our expectations. Our solidarity with the marginalized and work for
justice—"taking the crucified people down from the cross"—are simply
the Christian mode of openness to, encounter with, and reception of a
God who is Mystery. Far from implying any reductionism or exclusivity,
which would undermine God's transcendence, God's preferential option for the poor is the only credible guarantee of that transcendence.
Likewise, our own preferential option for the poor is a precondition for
encountering the God who is Mystery.

Gustavo Gutiérrez insists we must

> situate justice within the framework of God's gratuitous love.
> Only in the perspective of the latter is it possible to under-
> stand God's predilection for the poor. This special love does
> not have for its ultimate motive the virtues and merits of the
> poor but the goodness and freedom of God, a God who is not
> simply the guardian of a rigid moral order.[13]

All is ultimately gift, including justice and communion: "Entrance into
the kingdom of God is not a right to be won, not even by the practice

of justice; it is always a freely given gift."[14] Gutiérrez contends that this assertion has always been at the heart of liberation theology:

> Despite reductionist interpretations that try to deny the fact, this conviction has been part of the theology of liberation from the beginning and has always fed the spirituality that animates this theology. The theme of the gratuitousness of divine love is therefore the point of reference for determining the ultimate meaning of the emphasis on the practice of justice.[15]

Virgilio Elizondo in turn makes explicit the significance of the borderland as the privileged place for encountering the gratuitousness of God. Insofar as borders become barriers that separate "us" from "them," the "pure" from the "impure," they become barriers to the God who, because God is Mystery, is revealed first among "them," among the "impure." In Gutiérrez's words, "the world outside the fence [i.e., the border] is the world of gratuitousness; it is there that God dwells and there that God's friends find a joyous welcome."[16] It is there that the crucified and risen Christ will be seen and will find a joyous welcome.

This joy is the fruit of our encounter with the gracious gratuity of God. It is the fruit of a receptivity that refuses to grasp even at justice, as if it were our own achievement. If the option for the poor makes it possible to encounter the God who is Mystery, it also makes it possible to rejoice. The struggle for justice is thereby undertaken not out of duty, but out of gratitude for what we have freely received, without merit. Paradoxically, it is often among the marginalized, among the inhabitants of the borderland, that contemporary followers of Jesus find an ability to rejoice and to celebrate even in the midst of daily struggles. It is often in the borderland, in the Galilees of our world, that those who despair in the church find the most vital, energized, burgeoning communities of faith. Why are we surprised yet again? It is because we live in a world that identifies joy with material wealth and security, and for which the rejoicing of Galilee is the ultimate scandal.

Notes

1. Jon Sobrino, *Jesus the Liberator* (Maryknoll, NY: Orbis Books, 1993), 85.
2. Jon Sobrino, *Spirituality of Liberation* (Maryknoll, NY: Orbis Books, 1988), 14–16.
3. Daniel M. Bell Jr., *Liberation Theology after the End of History: The Refusal to Cease Suffering* (New York: Routledge, 2001), 144–53. See also my

Christ Our Companion: Toward a Theological Aesthetics of Liberation (Maryknoll, NY: Orbis Books, 2009), 25–43.

4. Ibid.

5. Jon Sobrino, *Christ the Liberator* (Maryknoll, NY: Orbis Books, 2001), 11–15.

6. Ibid., 79–95.

7. See Goizueta, *Christ Our Companion*, 25–43.

8. Jon Sobrino, *The Principle of Mercy: Taking the Crucified People from the Cross* (Maryknoll, NY: Orbis Books, 1994).

9. Sobrino, *Christ the Liberator*, 35–65.

10. Among his numerous works on this topic, see especially *Galilean Journey: The Mexican American Promise* (Maryknoll, NY: Orbis Books, 1983), and *A God of Incredible Surprises: Jesus of Galilee* (Lanham, MD: Rowman and Littlefield, 2003).

11. Virgilio Elizondo, "Elements for a Mexican American *Mestizo* Christology," *Voices from the Third World* 11 (1988): 105.

12. Ibid.

13. Gustavo Gutiérrez, *On Job: God-talk and the Suffering of the Innocent* (Maryknoll, NY: Orbis Books, 1987), 88.

14. Ibid., 89.

15. Ibid., 129.

16. Ibid., 88.

12

JESUS CHRIST *PARAMĀDIVĀSI*

AN INDIAN *ĀDIVĀSI* CONSTRUAL OF JESUS CHRIST

Francis Minj

India has 4,635 distinct ethnic communities, twenty-two official languages, and hundreds of other languages and religious traditions.[1] As such, it epitomizes the opportunities and challenges outlined at Vatican II, which gave church leaders the mandate of "reading the signs of the times" (*Gaudium et Spes*, 4) and discerning the "true sign of God's presence" (*Gaudium et Spes*, 11) on each continent and in every culture. This essay responds to that mandate, developing an interpretation of Jesus Christ from an Ādivāsi (indigenous) perspective. While there have been serious attempts to articulate Indian Christian theologies, this is the first Christian theology developed explicitly *from an Ādivāsi* perspective, *for Ādivāsis*, and written to nourish the Christian faith of the local Ādivāsi church.

The *Ādivāsis*

The Ādivāsis are believed to be the aboriginal population of India, though the Indian government merely considers them part of India's 697 tribes.[2] The Indian government refuses to use the terms "indigenous" and "Ādivāsi,"[3] categorizing them as part of the "Scheduled Tribes (S.T.)" of India, which qualifies Ādivāsi for some limited forms of affirmative action in certain states of India. Ādivāsi also fall outside the Hindu caste system with their distinct religio-cultural, socio-economic, and political worldview, lifestyle, and thought. Etymologically, "Ādivāsi" is a compound Sanskrit word: "Ādi," which means "primordial or the beginning," and "*vāsi*," which means "dweller." Thus, the meaning of the term is "primordial" or "aboriginal" "dwellers" of a given region. This essay concentrates on the five tribes—*Munda, Oraon, Kharia, Ho,* and *Santals*—of Jharkhand, one of India's twenty-eight states. While the Ādivāsis are protected in the national constitution, they are in fact among the poorest and most exploited people of India, lacking basic necessities like electricity, education, water, and health care.

The *Ādivāsis* live a robustly community-centered life, supported by strong values of equality, sharing, hospitality, hard work, liberty, fraternity, love of nature, anti-greed, and anti-pride. But *Ādivāsis* are also traumatized by fear of evil spirits and witches and other superstitions.[4] A unified vision of God, humanity, and the cosmos shapes their worldview. Most *Ādivāsis* practice their traditional *Sarna* religion.[5] Some *Ādivāsis* have been co-opted into Hinduism through a very complex process of *sanskritization*,[6] while others have embraced Christianity. Although Christian converts feel blessed with the message of Jesus and the works of the church, other Indians view these converts with suspicion.[7] Some *Sarna Ādivāsis* question the authenticity of the conversions[8] and, together with some fanatic Hindus, accuse Christians of forcibly converting simple "Hindu *vanavasis*."[9] Such people see Christians as propagators of foreign value and Christianity as a dangerous denationalizing force.[10] While such accusations may sound baseless to the reader, they challenge local Christians to respond with a culturally appropriate interpretation of the meaning and message of Jesus Christ.

In what follows, I will respond to this challenge by outlining a few elements of a much longer treatment I have developed of an interculturated *Ādivāsi* approach to Christology. Unfortunately, previous discussions of the theory and practice of inculturated theologies start mostly with classical texts, rather than with the real life of the people.[11] Michael Amaladoss rightly observes that the "official life-cycle rituals and festivals are so unsatisfactory" in Christian churches that the common people have filled the gap by developing a whole set of "elaborate rituals at home," which are "personally and socially more significant and satisfying."[12] While these practices serve as a cultural reservoir of popular religious practices that can enrich theological reflection, several other more negative challenges confront Indian churches interested in developing more intercultural approaches to Christology.

First, earlier missionary theologies from Europe branded the *Sarna* religion as "primitive, satanic, pagan, uncivilized...and condemned [it] as devil worship,"[13] which served to isolate Christian converts from larger Indian society. Second, such thinking projected Western Christianity and culture as "civilized," emphasizing abstract "Hellenistic" theological categories that render Christian teaching about Jesus unintelligible, arcane, and much removed from *Ādivāsi* reality, as opposed to the Jesus of the gospels who feels near to them. Third, in most Catholic seminaries Indian theologians use Hindu concepts and symbols to interpret Jesus Christ, which further alienates Ādivāsis,[14] who are oppressed in the Hindu caste system where they find no place. Fourth, the reality that Ādivāsi Christians belong to multiple cultural worlds while achieving full acceptance in none[15] is embodied in the alienation they experience for worshiping God in what are regarded as "alien" terms.[16] Fifth, while the church claims that she uses "the resources of different cultures to spread and explain the message of Christ" (*Gaudium et Spes*, 58–62) and encourages inculturation "especially in the area of Christology,"[17] there is no carefully thought out, convincingly argued, and well discerned interpretation of Jesus Christ through Ādivāsi cultural concepts and idioms.

An *Ādivāsi* Construal of Jesus Christ

The prologue of the Gospel of John (Jn 1:1–14), with its Christian interpretation of Jesus as the eternal Word made flesh, is a key text for Christian doctrine on Jesus Christ and provides an appropriate starting point for an Ādivāsi Christology. In what follows, I will suggest that the polysemic term, *Paramādivāsi*, provides a culturally appropriate way to interpret this reality in an Ādivāsi context.

Paramādivāsi is composed of three words: *param* (supreme), *ādi* (primordial) and *vāsi* (dweller). The prefix *param* radically transforms the socio-anthropological category *ādivāsi*, transposing it to the realm of both human and divine. The word *Paramādivāsi* is my own creation, and most Indians would construe "*Ādivāsi*" as referring to aboriginals, so it is likely that the term *Paramādivāsi* would evoke great surprise among Indians. Designed to work as a metaphor uniting the human and the divine, the term *Paramādivāsi* echoes Karl Rahner's idea that God's self-revelation is universal yet simultaneously local and specific to each time and people, thereby transcending the Hebrew-Christian Bible and its readers.

Jacques Dupuis argues, "What is to be seen here is the Prologue's affirmation of a universal action and presence of the Word of God already in human history before the incarnation," as well as the "action of the *Logos* as such [in human history] after the incarnation of the Word and the resurrection of Jesus Christ."[18] Given this notion that God's self-revelation takes place through the action of the Logos in human history and culture outside of Judaism and Christianity, I would argue that the term *Ādivāsi* signifying the original dweller can be legitimately applied to Jesus Christ in whom God reveals himself (Heb 1:1). Just as the *Ādivāsis* are the original dwellers, so too Jesus the *Word* can be metaphorically construed as *Paramādivāsi*, the Supreme Primordial Dweller, the image of the invisible God, and the firstborn of all creation (Col 1:15).

In this way, the metaphor *Paramādivāsi* is able to facilitate an encounter for *Ādivāsis* and others with the reality of Jesus of Nazareth, which ultimately provides an experiential basis for *Ādivāsi* theological reflection on Jesus. Likewise, it opens the "ear of the mind" to the riches of the *Ādivāsi*-Christian tradition, encouraging both outsiders and insiders to reflect on metaphorical images residing there that can be used to understand Jesus.

What follows, then, is a metaphorical construal of Jesus Christ *Paramādivāsi*. I draw particular attention to the following metaphors: Ancestor, Liberator (*Agua*), Jesus the High Priest (*Pahan*), and Jesus Christ the Healer/Exorcist (*Deonra*).[19] These images and metaphors are used in *Ādivāsi* cultures to interpret Jesus Christ as the presence of the Word, as the One who lives in solidarity with them and brings healing and salvation. Jesus Christ *Paramādivāsi* liberates the *Ādivāsi* tribes through the power of the Spirit for a harmonious dance of freedom and liberation, choreographed since primordial times by the triune God.

Jesus Christ *Paramādivāsi* as the Ancestor

The metaphor *Paramādivāsi* uses ancestor veneration to interpret the mystery of Jesus Christ. According to the *Ādivāsi* tradition, God created the first ancestors from clay, infused life in them, and later established their clans and communities. The ancestors are the progenitors, founders, parents, and patrons of families and the tribe. Besides being first, they are mediators, and provide the pattern for *Ādivāsi* life. A person's integrity, evidenced by a full life well-lived, ensures entry into the ancestral community, which is granted only through solemnized rituals. The ancestor bequeaths the spiritual and material heritage needed for a full life. Those who die an unnatural or violent death (intentional or accidental), people who are ostracized by the community, women dying during childbirth, witches, and those who defy the community fail to become ancestors. According to popular belief, the souls of such persons turn into evil spirits and wander around bringing misfortune to living members of the community.

The ancestors enjoy supernatural status and proximity with God as well as with their earthly relatives. Ancestors function as guardians of family affairs, ethical life, livestock, land, and everything that involves the well-being and sanctity of their descendants. Thus, interaction with the ancestors is part of the path to God and healthy participation in community life.[20] The *Ādivāsis* tend to place such emphasis on approaching the ancestors with rituals and prayers that these actions are often misconstrued as "ancestor worship," sometimes even by the *Ādivāsis* themselves. The sacred bond between the ancestors and living members of the community is visible in life-cycle rituals, agricultural operations, and other socio-religious rituals. The ancestors mediate between God and the community. It is believed that the ancestors have attained the spiritual state because of their exemplary life here on earth, and that their presence now mediates God's blessings for the living. The ancestors are exemplary because they have lived the traditional virtues of anti-greed, anti-pride, and anti-jealousy, and have followed all the norms and taboos.

Also known as the "living dead," the ancestors receive "propitiatory sacrifices" and act as guardians for the welfare of their progeny. The *Ādivāsis* separate some food or drink at each meal for the ancestors. The ancestors eat with the living members and act like guardian angels or patron saints. These practices, devotions, and beliefs emphasize the ancestors' presence in the life of each person and the community. Although exemplary, however, the ancestors continue to exhibit their earthly imperfections and desire "food" for their survival. They "remind" the living members about their needs lest the living members incur some misfortune.

Jesus can be construed as the greatest ancestor, the firstborn of all creation (Col 1:1) through whom God speaks (Heb 1:1). Jesus is the supreme ancestor because Jesus comes from God, our origin. He embodies the qualities of the ancestors and also supersedes them through his unique mediatorship. He is not just the tradition initiator, but he *is* the tradition, the way, truth and the life (Jn 14:6). He is present in the community and beckons the living members to follow him. As the supreme ancestor, he both fulfills and critiques the *Ādivāsi* notion and practice of ancestorship through his own life, teachings, suffering, death, and resurrection. Through his violent death Jesus challenges *Ādivāsi* cultural taboos. His murder would disqualify him ancestorship, but he defies the *Ādivāsi* taboos of denying ancestorship to those who die violently. The *Ādivāsis* encounter a salvific and exemplary death of Jesus on the cross, which teaches them to value martyrdom. Because of his Sonship, Jesus is the "eldest" of all, surpassing (1 Tim 2:5) all other intermediaries.

In *Ādivāsi* parlance, Jesus can be construed as God's Son through his being the greatest ancestor. The taunt to Jesus hanging on the cross (Mt 27:43) in Matthew's gospel seems to suggest that in this gospel people believed that Jesus claimed to be God's Son. In Mark the spirits, demons, and other invisible powers hail him as God's Son (Mk 3:11; 5:7). And the epistles repeatedly proclaim him as God's Son.[21] Jesus is anterior to all others; he is the *Paramādivāsi*, the ancestor, because he is the life-giver (Jn 6:68).

This fits well with *Ādivāsi* myths that, like many from Africa,[22] describe God as the Greatest Ancestor. Likewise, Christian faith proclaims that God has revealed himself in Jesus, the firstborn (Col 1:15), in order to give abundant life to all (Jn 10:10), a life that is qualitatively new. In this way, Jesus the ancestor mediates eternal life and sustains it by his self-gift (Jn 6:35, 48). In John's gospel, Jesus embodies the words of eternal life (Jn 6:68) and manifests himself as the resurrection and the life (Jn 11:25). While ancestors are sharers of life with their posterity, Jesus the Word is *the source* of life. By becoming human, Jesus summons each individual to emulate him and his ideals on the terms he sets. He is eternal, ubiquitous, residing in each individual, family, clan, and community, transforming and transcending the narrow confines of family, tribe, or region.

Biologically, we trace our origin to our human ancestors. Matthew's genealogy presents Jesus as the descendant from Abraham. Paul calls Jesus the last Adam, drawing a parallel between the "first Adam" and "last Adam," and he presents Jesus as the life-giving spirit (1 Cor 15:45; Rom 5:12–13) in whom the fullness of divinity dwells, reconciling all things to himself (Col 1:19–20). The ancestors bestow their localized, clan specific, spiritual presence, but Jesus offers his ubiquitous presence to all peoples. In this sense, Jesus stands at the privileged place among all *Ādivāsi* ancestors. For the Word incarnated in Jesus existed before the first human couple of the *Sarna* narrative.

Like a faithful ancestor, Jesus reassures his followers of his ongoing presence: "I am with you always" (Mt 28:20). He remains present in the word of the scripture, the community, the sacraments, and wherever the communities gather in his name (Mt 18:20). By his presence Jesus does not abolish the traditions, but rather fulfills (Mt 5:17) and transforms them. He commands his audience to do to others what they would have done to them (Mt 6:12). Thus, Jesus provides a new vision of the ancestor cult: we can remember him ritually, prayerfully, personally, and as an ecclesial community until the end of age. Jesus also sets new criteria for ancestorship: the values of the reign of God, where he alone judges the living and the dead. Thus, while Jesus leaves room for the ritual "canonization" of ancestors, he also brings a message of forgiveness and repentance rather than condemnation. As the ancestor-Judge, Jesus offers his verdict on the people based on his law: "I tell you, just as you did it to one of these least of these who are members of my family, you did it to me" (Mt 25:31-45, esp. 40).

Images of Jesus as the firstborn, the new Adam, the new Moses, and *Paramādivāsi* enrich our interpretations of Jesus and make them pastorally relevant, easily understood, and explicable to common people. By becoming the "heir" to that tradition, Jesus Christ reveals God through his life, teaching, death, resurrection, and ongoing presence through the Spirit. At the same time, Jesus transcends the limitations and restrictions of kinship; as the incarnate Son and mediator, he brings believers into a new relationship with God.

The Messiah/Liberator in the *Ādivāsi* Tradition

In ancient times, the *Ādivāsis* were a close-knit and a self-sufficient community. There was no ruling authority or king, no coercion and no coercer. The people cared for one another out of a sense of righteousness prior to their exploitation by feudal kings during the fifth through eighth centuries[23] and more notoriously in later centuries. The *Ādivāsis* probably did not feel the need for a liberator. Today they hanker for a liberator to emancipate them from the clutches of enslaving forces that weaken their cohesive identity and demean their human dignity by calling them *Vanavāsis* and manipulating them for the benefit of members of the caste system. Ratnaker Bhengra observes that the "ruling classes as well as dominant society have been ignorant about the hopes, aspirations and reality of the tribals or the indigenous peoples of India. This has been [in] regard to almost every aspect of their lives, whether political, economic, social, cultural etc."[24] Those who pity them offer "development" as a panacea, conceived, planned, and imported from "developed" nations of the West. The *Ādivāsis* resent being patronized, but this attitude gets misconstrued as being anti-development.

The expectation of a liberator gained strength during the eighteenth century when myriad forms of exploitation through unjust laws and brute force utilized by landlords, the *rajas*, and the colonialists reached their zenith. In 1784, seventy-three years before the "Indian freedom struggle" of 1857, the *Ādivāsis* waged a war of independence against the British. As long as the *Ādivāsis* found some spare piece of land on which to continue their way of life, they offered virtually no resistance to the land grabbers. Quite unprepared for this invasive land grabbing, the *Ādivāsis* sought ritual solutions to reclaim their land, but these produced no success. The *Ādivāsis* felt helpless in fighting an enemy who held opposite worldviews. This contributed to their feeling of a need for a messiah.

Despite their strong ancestral tradition, the *Ādivāsis* seem to lack a historically effective memory of their painful past, due perhaps to a lack of written tradition and scriptures. This may have contributed to their subjugation, because confrontation has not been their strong point. The invasive new communities with their audacious kings maimed the *Ādivāsis* socially, economically, culturally, psychologically, and spiritually. The perplexed *Ādivāsis* wondered why their ancestors and spirits had abandoned them, though some liberation movements led by Tilka Manjhi, the Sidho-Kanho brothers, and Birsa Munda bourgeoned during this period. These movements were driven by a dream of freedom in which they would not be considered uncivilized, backward, and insignificant, but rather be treated as co-equals, representing a strong voice for their community.

Today they are among the worst victims of our globalized economy. With the vicious and complex connivance of politicians, Indian bureaucracy, business tycoons, and brokers, the *Ādivāsis* are losing their God-given land and being forcibly displaced. A popular song beckons the displaced people back to their homeland: "O Chotanagpurians, where are you fleeing? Why do you abandon your country so forlorn? Return; come back, Oh brothers, where are you fleeing? The big mountains are calling you . . . come back brothers . . ." In this context, Jesus the liberator opens their eyes to recognize their reality so that they can see, sing, discern, and act according to God's will.

A construal of Jesus Christ *Paramādivāsi* as Liberator provides one of the most captivating, empowering, and upsetting images of Jesus. Unlike the powers that work tirelessly for their own power, Jesus becomes the voice of the voiceless and inserts himself among the *Ādivāsis* because he knows them well (Jn 10:27). He regards the poor and exploited masses as his own. He never forgets them (Is 49:15–16), and he empowers and frees them. This freedom implies freedom from all distortions—ideologies, powers, socio-religious groups—that fail to award them true dignity as God's people. This freedom does not militate violently against the "Pilates" of the world, but works rather for the renewal of the cultures, ideologies, and institutions of oppressed peoples. It is a freedom that comes from a liberating conversion. Thus, these people can confidently hope that Jesus Christ *Paramādivāsi*, the revealer of the Father, will be their liberator. And this requires that the church, as the body of Christ, play a role in confronting the modern "Pilates" who feast on the blood of the *Ādivāsis*. Jesus, the persecuted and the humiliated one, demonstrates his solidarity with the suffering *Ādivāsis*, instilling hope that their daily "death" by exploitation will turn into liberation, if they follow his praxis.

Liberation means a radical emancipation from evil for the Ādivāsis. Evil brings death, but liberation entails socio-political, economic, political, psychological, and spiritual liberation, which transvalues all the other forms of liberation. Spiritual liberation frees individuals and societies from all forms of bondage and bigotry. The *Sarna* creation myths do not trace the source of evil but they depict its expression in a mythical horse that destroys the clay human figures. The horse symbolizes hostility, power, anti-life, and disharmony. It resists defeat and enjoys decimating others. But God curses and controls the horse.[25] And by controlling the horse, God safeguards God's best creation, humanity. The Ādivāsis look for freedom from contemporary "horse powers" with the aforementioned characteristics.

Jesus Christ Liberator conquers the horse. A construal of Jesus as the highest, the noblest, and the best horse tamer, the one who forces the horse to acknowledge his Sonship, seems relevant. In the gospels Jesus challenges the "horse-like" powers by calling such elements a brood of vipers (Mt 12:34) or foxes (Lk 13:32). He does not negotiate; he confronts evil. The *Paramādivāsi* as Liberator empowers the Ādivāsis with his life-giving words. In the second century Clement of Alexandria addressed Christ as a horse tamer, bridling the wild passions of the human soul.[26] Today Jesus the Ādivāsi Liberator transforms the horse into a new symbol of life, of obedience to God, and of one who lives in harmony with his creation. Jesus liberates humanity from the slavery of horse-like greed, pride, jealousy, and the tendency to destroy life in all its forms.

The horse of the *Sarna* creation myth is presented as a false image for salvation (Ps 32:17; 33:17). Echoing Origen's view, we can say that only the *Paramādivāsi*, the faithful and true Word, can sit on a white horse (Rev 19:11).[27] Interestingly, the missionaries tamed horses for their travels among the Ādivāsis, and the latter composed songs about these horses. So the metaphor of Jesus as the liberating horse tamer should draw on the semantic potential of these images. The use of such images can help nudge people toward a self-empowering liberative action against contemporary "horses" like the merchants of sin and death. Jesus calls the heavily burdened Ādivāsis to learn from him so that he, as *Paramādivāsi*, might bestow genuine freedom and rest. "Come to me, all you that are weary, and are carrying heavy burdens, and I will give you rest" (Mt 11:28).

Jesus the High Priest (Pahan, Naike) in Solidarity with the *Ādivāsis*

Christology, soteriology, and priesthood are all interrelated with the notion of sin and the mediatory functions of the priest. Drawing from the Levite tradition (Deut 33:8–11) the priestly role in Jewish tradition comprises the following responsibilities: (1) oracular pronouncements, (2) keeping the teachings of the Torah, (3) offering sacrifice, and (4) praying for the atonement of sins (Lev 16). Jesus' mediatorship is radically different from Aaronic priesthood and revolutionizes the understanding of sacred ritual with the notion that God comes to us.[28] The Letter to the Hebrews asserts that God gives Jesus the priestly role so that he can mediate on our behalf (Heb 5:5). Being the Word of the Father, as he is in John, means that Jesus becomes our way to the Father (Jn 14:6), the sacrament of the encounter with God. Where priests formerly merely offered sacrifices (Heb 10:1), Jesus brings salvation through the one, sinless, and unrepeatable sacrifice of his incarnation, ministry, life, death, and resurrection.

The notion that Jesus is the greatest priest, or *pahan* (*kalo/pahanr/ naike*), as mediator between God, ancestors, community, and the world, is crucial for the Ādivāsis. The *pahan's* functions are confined to the ritual sacrifices he offers with or without the presence of the people at community worship or other religious functions. The *pahan's* sacrifice, typically of food or animals, serves as thanksgiving, supplication, a way of warding off evil, and praise to God. The Ādivāsi sacrifice resembles an atonement sacrifice in which an unblemished cock (white only for God) or other animal is sacrificed. The victim is made to peck the consecrated rice in a sign of God's approval of the sacrifice as a way to restore harmony, reconciliation, and well-being.

There are also propitiatory sacrifices to the spirits. The Sarna religion has no savior or incarnation, as Christians understand these, but the Asur myth shows some similarity with the "exemplary" or expiatory death. Here God dies in disguise as a leprous boy in order to destroy ancestral sins. The Sarna religion has not developed a systematic reflection on this traditional myth.

Jesus as the highest *pahan* is unique in that he acts as priest, prophet, and king in fulfilling the intercessory role. This compares favorably to a Sarna *pahan* who inherits his office or is elected to it, while Jesus is the eternal priest in his unique role as mediator between God and humans. The Letter to the Hebrews is replete with references to the priestly functions of Jesus. It explains how he fulfills the characteristics of a true priest[29] appointed by God, representing the people by performing sacrificial acts on their behalf for the forgiveness of sins. He intercedes for the people and blesses them in God's name. He mediates by being God's only Son, by healing, by curing, and by other intercessory acts, inviting those who believe in him to mold their lives according to his vision.

The *Sarna* priests perform ritual actions to restore multidimensional harmony. But Jesus' sacrificial acts, through his incarnation, life, works, death, resurrection, and ongoing presence in the Spirit, invite us to discern the meaning of an *Ādivāsi* Christian priesthood. Jesus as priest, mediator, and victim enriches and revolutionizes the *Ādivāsi* understanding of the priestly task. His violent death brings a new notion of salvation to the *Ādivāsis*, and beckons them to interpret in a new way the death of the leprous boy of the Asur myth. This may require an elaborate explication, but it allows us to interpret holistically the priestly role in salvation.

Jesus Christ *Paramādivāsi* as priest revolutionizes *Ādivāsi*-Christian reflection on priesthood. A *pahan* is a servant; he is performer, peacemaker, reconciler, and mediator through his sacred actions. Without access to the ritual arena, he would enjoy no special privilege. This reality naturally inspires the power-seeking notion of priesthood. Christian priesthood revolutionizes the *Ādivāsi* notion of *Ādivāsi* priesthood. Interestingly, *Ādivāsis* address Christian priests as *saheb* or *gomke* (lord), titles transposed from the feudal system. Rajahs, *nawabs*, colonizers, police, and bureaucrats are also called *sahebs*. Why do the *Ādivāsis* use the very titles that symbolize tyranny, exploitation, and death, and have no inherent connection to priesthood?

The *Ādivāsi* noticed that the missionaries and colonizers shared the same Christian faith, skin color, food habits, and dress. But the missionaries were countercultural countersigns. The colonizers were exploiters. The missionaries became liberators; in fact, they were the first ones to treat the *Ādivāsis* as their friends.[30] Through this kind of solidarity, the *Ādivāsis* came to believe that God in Jesus cares for and liberates them from unjust and sinful situations. They recognized the true *sahebs* and *gomkes* in the Jesus-inspired missionaries, and that the official *sahebs* and *gomkes*, whether colonizers or Indians, had been exploiting them. The colonizing *sahebs* were Christians, yet they acted against Jesus' teachings owing to their insatiable quest to plunder for power, profit, prestige, and pleasure. For a long time, the British East India Company refused entry into India to missionaries for the aforesaid reasons[31] in order to protect their economic and political interests.

The aforementioned titles suggest the multiple sacerdotal roles of priests as pastors, activists, liberators, preachers, theologians, healers, mediators, and above all as disciples of Jesus. In the *Ādivāsi* milieu the priest functions like the *sarpanch*, a *parha raja*, a social activist, elder, and leader, while he simultaneously remains a *saheb* and servant. As leaders, the Christian *pahans* are called to exercise their ministry patterned on the *Saheb* Jesus. Jesus exhorts his disciples not to emulate the

Gentiles but rather to follow him as their only model for leadership by becoming servants (Mk 10:43; Lk 22:26; Mt 20:26). Jesus' priesthood inspires his true followers among the clergy and religious to be at the service of all, especially the poor, marginalized, despised, and unwanted. Christian priests are called to be brokers (*dalal*) for the reign of God.

This relatively new understanding of priesthood suggests a great shift (Lk 4:18) from a merely ritualistic priesthood. The vocation to this form of priesthood emerges through God's grace, nurtured by love of Jesus (Jn 21:15–19). Jesus' question, "Do you love me?" inspires further reflection. The teaching, prophetic, and kingly dimensions of priesthood are transformed when they are reinterpreted in the context of *pahan* as *gomke* or *saheb*. The role of priest is nourished and challenged, purified and elevated by the liberating Word of God.

Jesus Christ the Healer/Exorcist (Deonra)

Fr. John Meier, a leading Catholic expert on the historical Jesus, believes that the notion that Jesus performed healings and other deeds perceived as miraculous by his contemporaries is so "firmly supported by the criteria of historicity" that "if the miracle tradition from Jesus' public ministry were to be rejected *in toto* as unhistorical, so should every other gospel tradition about him."[32] Thus, it is natural to ask, how might the *Ādivāsi* imagine Jesus as divine exorcist or a *deonra* in their cultural context? The *Ādivāsi* worldview sees sickness and suffering as manifestations of disharmony and ethical decay. In times of sickness *Ādivāsis* seek to reestablish the triadic harmony of the natural, social, and spiritual worlds through rituals and herbal remedies. If the herbs prove ineffective, *Ādivāsis* consult with other healers, which include ordinary and expert herbalists (*vaid*), as well as *deonras* (exorcists). A *deonra* is a gifted or clairvoyant person who is believed to possess some occult quality, developed through secret nocturnal training and ascetical practices, and who has the ability to tame spirits to do good or harm to others. The common people dread such *deonras*. The missionaries branded *Ādivāsi* health management practices as superstitious, forbade Christian converts from seeking the *deonra*'s help, and asked them to turn to unfamiliar Christian saints for intercession. Thus, Christian neophytes found themselves caught between their *Ādivāsi* "past" and new Christian ways of seeking intercession.

Ādivāsis easily recognize Jesus Christ as physician, exorcist, and a new kind of *deonra*. Indeed, the gospels themselves metaphorically (Mk 2:17) portray Jesus as a physician (Lk 4:23). Demons collapse (Jn

18:5–6), obey, and run away at his words, or they acknowledge him as God's healer-exorcist Son. Like the Ādivāsis, Jesus' contemporaries associated sickness with sinfulness. Sinfulness was cleansed by forgiveness and conversion, made possible only by God, and Jesus restored natural, social, and spiritual health through forgiveness. This is expressed in the fact that Jesus touched the sick. Jesus took Peter's mother-in-law by the hand (Mk 1:31), he touched the leper (Mk 1:41), the deaf man (Mk 7:33-35), the dead girl (Mk 5:38-41), and the blind man at Bethsaida where he spit on the man's eyes in order to heal him (Mk 8:22-25). Like Elijah (1 Kings 17:19) and Elisha (2 Kings 4:33),[33] Jesus took afflicted persons aside (Jn 9:6) and touched them (Mk 10:3; 6), while sometimes those who were afflicted reached out and touched him in order to be healed (Lk 6:19).

Jesus' action of touching the "untouchables" resonates well with the Ādivāsis. Indian civilization is built on the sweat and blood of untouchables, the *dalits*, and Ādivāsis, who nonetheless remain untouchables, taken advantage of by the ruling classes. Demeaning names like *junglee* or *vanavasi* for Ādivāsis emblemize an age-old strategy of denying their human dignity and identity. For centuries the Ādivāsis have been treated like "quarantine animals." When the Ādivāsis encountered the missionaries they accepted Jesus as their healer,[34] exorcist, and the new *deonra*. They recognized Jesus as the Holy One (Mk 1:24) and the Son of God (Mk 3:11). And they largely overcame the fear of the evil spirits, quack *deonras*, and witches, replacing fear and ritualism with faith in Jesus. Their faith helped them to fight against oppressive landlords and the unjust laws that stifled their freedom as God's children.

Their struggle in Jesus' name brought "convulsions" to the oppressors (Mk 9:20). In Jesus, they recognized the healer, the supreme *deonra* who could bring healing from their ills and effect the conversion of landlords to justice (Lk 19:1–10). Through Jesus they learned how to hate sin and love the sinner (Jn 8:1–11), and how to promote love and forgiveness (Lk 7:36–50) rather than revenge. In Jesus, forgiveness and love replace punishment; reconciliation and harmony replace judgment and condemnation. While the Ādivāsis formerly emphasized sacrifice for healing, Jesus heals through faith, forgiveness, and love. Faithlessness does not produce miracles (Mt 7:19–20). Thus, Jesus the *deonra* invites us to faith in his healing power.

But what difference does Jesus make on the question of Ādivāsi suffering? Ādivāsis believe that suffering emanates from ancestral sins of greed, pride, jealousy, and related evils. Jesus brings a new dimension to the Ādivāsi notion of suffering and Ādivāsis' response to it: he embodies suffering on behalf of others in love and sacrifice. In the Ādivāsi context, charity alone is deficient; it needs justice.[35] Such love is trans-formational. Jesus demonstrates it through his own life and teaching when he invites his disciples to love to shed their blood for others (Jn 15:13). Bearing fruit requires daily death (Jn 12:24). And the mysteri-ous suffering of innocent persons can bring life. Jesus suffers and dies an unnatural death, and hangs rejected, alienated, despised, and humili-ated on the cross (Mk 15:34). Yet the *Ādivāsis* accept him as their sav-ior. Clearly, the Christian understanding of suffering and death leads the *Ādivāsis* to reassess the traditional view of martyrdom. Does this mean that the *Sarna* religion will rethink its tragic attitude toward un-natural death? Only time will tell.

Conclusion

This essay, then, has offered an initial sketch of some elements of an *Ādivāsi* construal of Jesus Christ, elements with far reaching conse-quences for a more fully developed inculturated Christology. I have ar-gued that the metaphor *Paramādivāsi* encapsulates Christian teaching on the humanity and divinity of Jesus in a form that is intelligible to Indian *Ādivāsis*. And I have explored four *Ādivāsi* images for aspects of the mystery of Jesus Christ that I believe empower *Ādivāsi*-Christians to deepen their Christian identity in culturally appropriate terms. These include Jesus as Ancestor, Messiah/Liberator, High Priest (*Pahan, Naike*), and Healer/ Exorcist (*Deonra*). In closing, let me re-mind the reader that this is the first interpretation (as far as I know) of Jesus Christ written from an indigenous *Ādivāsi* perspective, designed to nourish the Christian faith of the local *Ādivāsi* church and to share it with the outside world. As such, the conclusions presented here are tenuous, and a fuller evaluation will come only with time for reflection and dialogue between and among *Ādivāsi* Christians and the larger church.

Notes

1. Michael Amaladoss, *Life in Freedom: Liberation Theologies from Asia* (Maryknoll, NY: Orbis Books), 22–23; Sonia Gandhi, "Living Politics: What India Has Taught Me" (lecture, Nexus Institute, The Hague, June 10, 2007), http://outlookindia.com/full.asp?fodname=20070609&fname=soniagandhi&sid=1 (accessed June 27, 2007).

2. The Indian government claims that there are no indigenous people in India. The *Ādivāsis* constitute 8 percent of India's billion plus population. See Ministry of Tribal Affairs, Government of India, http://tribal.nic.in/index1.html

(accessed June 22, 2010). I use the terms "tribal(s)" and "*Ādivāsi*(s)" interchangeably but I simply mean *Ādivāsi(s)*.

3. Shashibhushan Karwar and Alex Ekka, Bharatiya, *Janaganana aur Jharkhandi Adivasi* (Ranchi: Jharkhand Navnirman Sabha, 2000), 5–7; Ram Dayal Munda and B. P. Keshri, "Recent Developments in the Jharkhand Movement," in *The Jharkhand Movement: Indigenous Peoples' Struggle for Autonomy in India*, ed. Ram Dayal Munda and S. Bosu Mullick (Copenhagen: International Work Group for Indigenous Affair, 2003), 216–31.

4. Thomas Pulloppilil, "The Values That Undergird a Tribal Society," *Vidyajyoti Journal of Theological Reflection* 61 (1997): 187–91.

5. *Sarna* has three meanings: (1) a natural and sacred grove of *Sal* trees (*shorea robusta*), a place of *Sarna* worship (*Sarnas* cannot be planted nor destroyed; they are naturally present from time immemorial); (2) the traditional *Sarna Adivasi* religion; and (3) the believers and members of Sarna faith community.

6. In Indian sociology, "Sanskritization" is a social process by which a person or community of a lower caste or even outside of it adopt the practices of higher castes but in reality never achieve those castes.

7. Christopher Lakra, "Urbanisation and Tribal Identity," *Sevartham* 25 (2000): 31–40; *Dainik Jagran*, Ranchi, October 31, 2006; February 17, 2007; March 1, 2007; March 22, 2007; April 13, 2007; April 29, 2007; April 30, 2007; May 10, 2007; May 17, 2007; *Panchjanya*, Delhi, October 30, 2004. Editor's note: *Dainik Jagran* and *Panchjanya* are Hindi language newspapers with broad circulations in India.

8. See *Daily Pioneer*, Ranchi, March 13, 2008.

9. Defying the views of sociologists and anthropologists, this powerful group of Hindus claims that *Ādivāsis* are Hindus and use a derogatory term *Vanavasi* (forest dweller, jungle bunny, rustic) for *Ādivāsis*. See Matthias Hermanns, *Hinduism and Tribal Culture: An Anthropological Verdict on the Niyogi Report* (Bombay: K. L. Fernandes, 1957), 6–40; Francis Minj, "Conversion in Crisis: A Theological Reflection on the Current Debate on Conversion in Tribal India," *Vidyajyoti Journal of Theological Reflection* 70 (2006): 486–500.

10. Sandhya Jain, "Debate: Church Wary-Red," *Organiser* (Delhi: January 27, 2005), 7; Arun Shourie, *Missionaries in India: Continuities, Changes, Dilemmas* (New Delhi: ASA Publications, 1994), 18–20; Sita Ram Goel, *Pseudo-Secularism, Christian Missions and Hindu Resistance* (New Delhi: Voice of India, 1998); Vishal Mangalwadi, *Missionary Conspiracy: Letters to a Postmodern Hindu* (New Delhi: Nivedit Good Books Distributers, 1996).

11. Francis Minj, SJ, "Jesus Christ *Paramādivāsi*: A Liberative-Inculturated Christology from an *Ādivāsi* Context of India" (dissertation for Doctor of Sacred Theology, Jesuit School of Theology of Santa Clara University, 2009).

12. Michael Amaladoss, *Beyond Inculturation: Can the Many Be One?* (Delhi: Indian Society for Promoting Christian Knowledge, 1998), 3.

13. Sudhir Kumar Kujur, "Tribal Theology and Liberation," *Sevartham* 27 (2002): 24.

14. Rudolf C. Heredia, "Incarnating Christ in India: Pedro Arrupe and In-culturation," *Vidyajyoti Journal of Theological Reflection* 771 (2007): 354–55. One cannot blame such theologians, however, because they either reflect on a general Indian context or reflect from the context of Hindu/Hinduized tradi-tions.

15. Telesphore P. Cardinal Toppo, archbishop of Ranchi and president of the Catholic Bishops' Conference of India (CBCI), declared himself a *Sarna Adivasi Christian*, http://www.prabhatkhabar.com (*Prabhat Khabar*), Ranchi, February 14, 2005.

16. Michael Amaladoss, "Theologizing in a Tribal Context: Some Method-ological Observations," *Sevartham* (1984): 3–10; Albert Van Exem, "The New Dispensation in Sarna Religion: A Theological Interpretation," *Sevartham* (1984): 75–90; "The Self-Understanding of the Sarna Man"; "The Mistake: Reviewed after a Century," *Sevartham* 16 (1991): 81–95; Michael Van Den Bo-gaert, "Communication, Community and Tribals," *Sevartham* 15 (1990): 43–55.

17. James H. Kroeger and Peter C. Phan, eds., *Ecclesia in Asia*, no. 22. The Future of the Asian Churches: The Asian Synod and Ecclesia in Asia (Quezon City: Claretian Publications, 2002), 154–56.

18. Jacques Dupuis, *Christianity and the Religions: From Confrontation to Di-alogue* (Maryknoll, NY: Orbis Books, 2001), 142. Space does not allow me to explain other theological developments on this matter.

19. Due to space limitations, I have not been able to include reflections on the metaphors of Jesus as Son of God, Lord and Master (*Gomke*), Leader, Judge, Itinerant Teacher (*Sakhi Gosain*), Rock (*Marang Buru*), Jesus in the Power of the Holy Spirit, dancer, and others that appear in my dissertation (Francis Minj, SJ, "Jesus Christ *Paramādivāsi*).

20. Similar notions of ancestorship are prevalent among African societies. See Diane B. Stinton, *Jesus of Africa: Voices of Contemporary African Christol-ogy* (Maryknoll, NY: Orbis Books, 2003), 113; Robert J. Schreiter, ed., *Faces of Jesus in Africa* (Maryknoll, NY: Orbis Books, 2002), 119–27.

21. The expression "Son of God" appears seven times in Romans, six times in the Hebrews, and sixteen times in 1 John (George Eldon Ladd, A *Theology of the New Testament* [Grand Rapids: William B. Eerdmans Publishing Com-pany, 1974], 162).

22. Diane B. Stinton, *Jesus in Africa: Voices of Contemporary African Chris-tology* (Maryknoll, NY: Orbis Books, 2004), 118.

23. Mathew Areeparampil, *Struggle for Swaraj* (Chaibasa: Tribal Research and Training Center, 2002), 4.

24. http://www.dailypioneer.com/132185/Tribals'-self-governance-meth-ods-go-into-oblivion.html, (accessed November 3, 2008).

25. Albert Van Exem, *The Religious System of the Munda Tribe* (Ranchi: Satya Bharati, 1982), 28.

26. Rowan Williams, "A History of Faith in Jesus" in *Cambridge Compan-ion to Jesus*, ed. Markus Bockmuehl (Cambridge: Cambridge University Press, 2001), 221.

27. Joseph W. Trigg, *Origen* (London: Routledge, 1998), 146.

28. Jon Sobrino, *Christ the Liberator: A View from the Victims* (Maryknoll, NY: Orbis Books, 2001), 127–29.

29. John F. Bagget, *Seeing through the Eyes of Jesus: His Revolutionary View of Reality and His Transcendent Significance for Faith* (Grand Rapids: William B. Eerdmans Publishing Co., 2008), 265–69.

30. Nirmal Minz, *Rise Up, My People, and Claim the Promise* (Delhi: Indian Society for Promoting Christian Knowledge, 1997), 9.

31. The East India Company barred entry to missionaries until 1813 and later allowed the missionaries entry only under license (Julian Saldanha, "Documents Illustrative of Christianity in British India," *Indian Missiological Review* [June 1993]: 59–63).

32. John Meier, *A Marginal Jew: Rethinking the Historical Jesus*, vol. 2, *Mentor, Message, and Miracles* (New York: Doubleday, 1994), 630.

33. Harold Remus, *Jesus as Healer* (Cambridge: Cambridge University Press, 1997), 19.

34. Ibid., 22.

35. Constant Lievens, SJ (1856–1893), a Belgian Jesuit, championed the cause of justice for the *Ādivāsis*.

13

THINKING ABOUT JESUS
IN SECULAR EUROPE

José Sols

The search for an adequate way of being Christian is a never-ending process in Europe today as it is elsewhere around the globe, an adventure that is open and dynamic.[1] Two poles challenge our thinking and push us on: the historical present, and the revelation of God in Israel and Jesus Christ as recounted in the biblical texts of the Old and New Testaments. Some argue that, while the historical present may be open, the sacred text was set centuries ago. The object of Christian faith is not the text, however, but rather the ongoing revelation to which it bears witness.

In what follows I will briefly summarize the notion of the hermeneutical circle, which conceptualizes the movement noted above and shapes much of European Christian theology today. Next I will briefly describe the cultural matrix of secularization, which both challenges and shapes European Christianity at the present moment. Then I will briefly review a series of insights arising from crises described in the Old and New Testaments and the crisis facing European Christianity today. I will conclude by suggesting how I believe these analogies may act as guideposts for the renewal of European Christianity in the years ahead.

The Hermeneutical Circle between the Christ Event
and the Historical Present

Faith as experience, and its reflective companion theology, grow at the dynamic intersection of these two poles, the historical present and the revelation of God in Israel and Jesus Christ. This is why faith and theology never stop changing, advancing, interpreting, investigating, and adapting. Likewise, Christian experience and theology never stop exploring and discovering new meanings in the initial *kerygma* of Christianity, the first preaching of the apostles about the paschal mystery, the historical life, death, and resurrection of Jesus (Acts 2:22–24).

We Christians today cannot stand with our arms crossed as if we already knew what it is that defines us as "Christians." Doing this means putting an end to faith as a living reality. Perhaps that is why many Christians today have lost their faith: people do not accept the fact that the road still has to be traveled.

This is a very old interpretive principle of Christian faith that comes from Judaism. The New Testament is filled with interpretations of the Old Testament, or what non-Christians call the Hebrew Scriptures of Judaism. The New Testament writers interpret their historical present as the fulfillment of the promises of the Hebrew Scriptures. The resurrection story of the disciples at Emmaus provides an example: "Then beginning with Moses and all the prophets, he interpreted to them the things about himself in all the scriptures" (Lk 24:27). Between "the scriptures and now," what philosophy calls a *hermeneutical circle* is produced.[2] The part of the Christian Bible that its followers call the "Old Testament" (an unfortunate translation of the expression "Old Covenant," which describes the Jewish experience of a personal God, is interpreted in light of the Christ event as a message for all of humanity. This reflects the universalizing message of Second Isaiah (Is 40–55) written during the sixth century BCE return of Israel from the Babylonian exile, which held that the savior of all nations would come from Israel. And what Christians call the "New Testament" (an equally unfortunate translation of the expression "New Covenant" is seen as historical testimony about the fulfillment of the message announced in the Old Testament. Thus, following the logic of this hermeneutical circle, the older texts cannot be understood without the newer ones, nor can the newer texts be understood without the older ones (against the claims of some Nazi theologians, Alfred Rosenberg among them,[3] who wished to reduce Christianity to the New Testament in order to free it of the "Jewish burden" of the Old Testament). Further, just as there is a hermeneutical circle between the two historical moments of Christian revelation (Israel and Jesus Christ), so there is another hermeneutical circle between Judeo-Christian revelation as a whole and the reception we make of it throughout history.

This hermeneutical dimension of faith was discovered by Judaism, specifically rabbinic traditions on the interpretation of texts. But it continued in the aforementioned New Testament interpretation of the Hebrew Scriptures. And it developed in the theology of the church fathers and throughout the Middle Ages with the four senses of scripture, literal or historical, allegorical, tropological or moral, and anagogical, which were sometimes condensed into two: literal and spiritual. A good example is found in the *Life of Moses* by Gregory of Nyssa.[4]

As theology turned more toward rational argument in the scholastic theology of the medieval schools (relying less on the authority of tradition), the hermeneutical sophistication of the senses of scripture was eventually lost. In the sixteenth century the division between Protestants and Catholics seriously damaged theology on both sides of the debate. The hermeneutical openness of Protestantism suffered (interpreting or updating the revelation of scripture was prohibited), and the social dimension of Catholicism was reduced (faith was largely consigned to individual and micro-communitary experience).

Nevertheless, the hermeneutical tradition of theology was reborn in the nineteenth century, first in Protestantism and later in the Catholic Church, as I have suggested in my book: *Quan la fe interpreta i transforma*.[5] The history of this recovery begins with Friedrich Schleiermacher (1768–1834), who relates interpretive problems in art, philosophy, religion, and history to a vigorous discussion of transcendental philosophy of mind and the analysis of subjective consciousness. Schleiermacher also introduces into the discussion the circularity between the reader-subject and the text.

Following Schleiermacher, Wilhelm Dilthey (1833–1911) attempts to "de-psychologize" hermeneutics in order to make it an instrument of the "sciences of the Spirit," which are focused on "understanding" (*Verständnis*) as opposed to the "sciences of Nature," which he says are focused on "'explanation" (*Erklärung*). For Dilthey, the object of analysis is not so much the text as it is the era or the event for which the text becomes an indispensible instrument.

Martin Heidegger (1889–1976) comes next, with his analysis of the connection between humanity's hermeneutical structure and our radical existential-historical openness; and Hans-Georg Gadamer (1900–2002) follows, with his careful analysis of the Heideggerian hermeneutical circle. Gadamer focuses on the hermeneutical circle, but he does not suggest that the reader projects his own questions on the text without respecting its otherness. Rather, he insists that good interpretation respects the otherness of the text in relation to the world of the reader. This is seen in his analysis of the function of language, which he understands as something that does not temporally follow experience, but is rather internal to experience itself. Finally, Paul Ricoeur (1913–2005) portrays all of human life as hermeneutical, since every access to the other—and ultimately to oneself, inasmuch as one is "another to oneself"—happens through mediations. These are some of the major milestones in philosophical hermeneutics currently shaping European discussion of the hermeneutical circle between the Christ event and our historical present.

The influence of this tradition of philosophical hermeneutics on Christian interpretation of the Bible (*biblical hermeneutics*) by theologians trained in Europe is embodied in figures like Rudolf Bultmann (1884–1976), Ernst Fuchs (1903–1983), Gerhard Ebeling (1912–2001), Wolfhart Pannenberg (born 1928), Johann Baptist Metz (born 1928), and Ignacio Ellacuría (1930–1989).

The hermeneutical contribution of Rudolf Bultmann (1884–1976) radically influenced the course of biblical theology in twentieth-century Europe by placing hermeneutics at the heart of theological reflection.[6] The text makes sense through the contribution of the reader; only to the extent that it provokes an experience of faith in the reader can we talk about revelation. The problem is that Bultmann, in an unmistakably European manner, makes the individual the recipient of revelation and ignores the role of society and culture. The contributions of liberation theology were necessary to amend this error. This can be demonstrated by briefly summarizing the gradual transition from the early to mid-century work of the German Lutheran biblical theologian Bultmann to the late-century Latin American liberation theology of the Spanish-born Jesuit Ignacio Ellacuría, a process that is often ignored today.

Ellacuría privileges the reading of the biblical text over going out and working toward a fairer world, while at the same time arguing that the former mandates the latter. This hermeneutical position fit well with the recent mandate of Vatican II (1962–1965) to the church on every continent "of reading the signs of the times and of interpreting them in light of the Gospel" (*Gaudium et Spes*, 4). For Ellacuría, this meant analyzing the sociopolitical and economic processes currently transforming Central and Latin America in light of the values of the gospel, an undertaking that got him killed by the Salvadoran army in 1989.[7]

Here, in light of the priority accorded to the biblical text, it is important to understand that Ellacuría and other liberation theologians interpret the Bible from within the social-political situation of the historical present, which includes the personal and social location of the theologian. This implies that every "historical present" allows for the discovery of biblical truths that remain "hidden" to other historical presents, since the concept of revelation holds that the Bible has something original to say in the life of each person, each people, and each culture.[8] Furthermore, the Bible is the fruit of a history in which human freedom confronts both protagonists and writers with options that configure the text and that have to be studied and analyzed as part of textual, historical, and hermeneutical criticism. Accordingly, Ellacuría widens the problem of hermeneutics: it is no longer just a matter of the interpretive relationship between *reader* and *text*, or even between *reader* and *historical present*. Rather, hermeneutics includes the interpretive relationship between God, *the writer*, and *the historical present*. This may be stated in partially reverse order and with greater detail as concern for the proper interpretive relationship between God, *historical present, reader, text, writer*, and *the writer's historical context*. I have placed God in the first place since God is present in both the life of the reader and the writer. For Ellacuría, biblical hermeneutics is much more than linguistics. It is "historical hermeneutics."[9]

The Cultural Matrix of Secularization

Western Europe is a desert of faith where Christianity is becoming a relic, an object of study for art historians and of occasional ridicule for the media. In Eastern Europe Christianity finds itself uncomfortably relegated to the sidelines by post-war Soviet regimes that educated two generations in an atheistic system, while the churches did not always speak out, which greatly weakened their position in society. In Asia, with the exception of the Philippines, Christianity has not taken root, mainly because it is perceived as the religion of the colonizing countries. There are problems in Africa as well. The 1994 Tutsi genocide carried out by Hutus, who in some cases were agents of the church, damaged the credibility of Christianity in this culture. Finally, in the United States and a large part of Latin America, Christianity is sometimes used as an ideology by the extreme, aggressive, racist, and classist right, as in the U.S.–based "Project for the New American Century." Many allegedly "Christian" sects have launched aggressive outreach efforts in Latin America with directly anti-Catholic messages designed to deactivate networks for faith-based social change that the Catholic Church has been developing since the late 1960s.

A proliferation of NGOs (non-governmental organizations) has largely replaced the social service role of the church in recent years so that Christianity is no longer the key player in this regard. Similarly, secular aid workers have replaced religious missionaries in educating the public of developed countries regarding the state of the Third World. Domestically, NGO experts know as much or more than church representatives about marginalized urban areas, education, hospitals, and heath care for children and the elderly, all areas in which Christians have played historically important roles. What then does Christianity have to offer to European society today? Why be a Christian in Europe?

Babylonian Exile of Israel

Approaching the biblical text from a European perspective, we will not begin with Jesus, however, but with the Jewish Babylonian exile of the sixth century BCE, starting with the invasion of Judah by King Nebuchadnezzar in 597, 587, and 582 BCE, and ending with the Edict of Cyrus in 538 BCE. The exile became half a century of religious purification for Israel. Jews found themselves in what they saw as a new deplorable reality: they had lost the land obtained in the Covenant and were now captives of a foreign people who did not believe in their God, which in turn raised questions about the power of that God. In some ways Jewish believers found themselves then as European Christians find ourselves today: exiled from the native soil of their faith. The era of European Christendom, when Christianity set the mentality, the morals, and the calendar has disappeared. While I agree with those who say that Christendom had to be overcome, few expected the devastating panorama for European Christianity that has followed.

The Jewish prophets understood the Babylonian exile as a consequence of sin. They had warned the people against the betrayals by their leaders of the Covenant with God, but few had paid attention: "Can Ethiopians change their skin or leopards their spots? Then also you can do good who are accustomed to do evil. I will scatter you like chaff driven by the wind from the desert" (Jer 13:23–24). The prophets tried to make the people understand that they had erred by allowing their leaders to trust political alliances more than the Covenant with Yahweh.

In the view of the prophets, then, the exile became a path of purification, which later Christians would see as a kind of proto-Easter, a step from death to life, from a deadened spirituality to a new, more vital and authentic one. Thus, exile turns into a "negative theophany" and the people begin to listen, *post mortem*, to the oracle of the prophets whom they had previously despised, mistreated, and even killed. They finally understand the prophets' words of hope and faithfulness as God's word to God's people. A new Jewish spirituality is born, integrating negativity and social critique grounded in oral and written traditions about God's covenant with Israel with a new perspective building on cultural material from Babylon (the source "P" who writes some parts of Genesis). This new spirituality sets the horizon for the renewal of Israel, which gathers to listen to God's word, guided by an eschatological orientation toward the kingdom of God.

Jesus and Judaism in Exile-at-Home under the Roman Empire

Jesus of Nazareth similarly lives in a time of desolation and exile. His people are subjugated to the Roman Empire, which violently humiliates and oppresses them religiously, politically, economically, culturally, and personally. Some Jews survive as best they can by avoiding contact with the occupiers, others form organized groups of clandestine resistance, and yet others become what during World War II the French called "collaborators" with the Nazi occupation, or what were known as *Sonderkommando* in the German concentration camps, that is, Jews who helped the occupiers in exchange for favorable treatment. In this connection, we should remember that before the Romans occupied Israel in 63 BCE, the Jews had lived under successive forms of Hellenic rule from the time of Alexander's conquest of Palestine in 322 BCE to the brief revival of the independent Jewish state between 140 BCE and the aforementioned Roman occupation by Pompey.

Like the Babylonian exile, the Roman occupation was experienced by many Jews as a defeat of the Covenant with God. Romans controlled the temple, the power of the Jewish authorities was severely curtailed, and the basic religious structures of Jewish life seemed unable to offer coherent explanations for the crisis, for meaning-threatening experiences. In such a context, the structures themselves—the temple, synagogues, Pharisees, priests, and the Sanhedrin—suffered a crisis of legitimacy. It was a time for renewal movements as evidenced by the Essenes and the community at Qumran, the Sadducees under the leadership of John Hyrcanus (134–104 BCE), the Pharisees, and Jesus' own critiques of the temple.[10] Jesus lived in a complex network of competing powers that included Roman occupiers; Jewish religious authorities; Jewish political, economic, and religious collaborators with Rome; and groups promoting active cultural, political, or military resistance, among others.

Given this panorama of diversity and domination, I would characterize the spiritual experience of Judaism during the time of Jesus as one of inner exile, or exile-at-home. Undoubtedly the Israel of Jesus was much more complex and nuanced than what is described here, but for our purposes it serves to raise the question, how did Jesus react to this challenging historical context?

Four New Testament Insights

The New Testament describes four very interesting actions that I believe capture Jesus' way of acting within his own historical context. In what follows I suggest that they form a coherent message when read from within the context of contemporary Europe.

Responsible Autonomy in the Kingdom of God

In the cultural milieu of contemporary Europe the rejection of religion presents itself as the logical outcome of responsible human autonomy. In this context religion is largely viewed as an example of heteronomy, the imposition of an exterior moral law that requires submission and obedience. Seen in this way, Christianity is perceived as an archaic system demanding submission to an external authority mediated through control by bishops and priests over the consciousness and actions of adherents.

When we read the biblical text, however, we find that Jesus speaks about a liberating kind of obedience to God, a God who is the source of our freedom. Paradoxically, this kind of obedience enhances autonomy rather than reducing it. As a result of their encounter with Jesus, the blind can see, the lame can walk, the deaf can hear, and sinners are forgiven. Encountering dependency, Jesus restores and enhances autonomy, as in the case of the Gerasene demoniac cured by Jesus (Mk 5:2–20). After the demoniac is healed Jesus tells him, "Go home to your friends, and tell them how much the Lord has done for you, and how he has had mercy on you" (5:19). The man returns to his normal life where the community will now accept him, since he has been freed of the demon that possessed him.

In the two creation stories of Genesis (Gen 1:26–31 and Gen 2:15–25) God gives humanity power over creation. The autonomy implied by this power comes from God who is its source. Jesus recovers this theology through actions that restore autonomy as the gift and grace of God. This is neither exceptional nor tangential to the kingdom of God, but rather lies at the core of its message and its meaning in the world. To the woman with the hemorrhage who dares to touch his robe in hopes of being cured, Jesus says, "Daughter, your faith has made you well; go in peace, and be healed of your disease" (Mk 5:34). The link between healing and restoration embodied in Jesus' response to the woman's free expression of faith affirms her autonomy as intrinsic to the kingdom of God.

The Renewal of Israel and Openness to the Other

Jesus' actions help people to recover their confidence in God. Jesus nurtures a kind of Jewish religious experience that does not isolate believers in their own community, but rather opens them up to *the other*. Tax collectors and sinners violate the law with their actions, which is why they are rejected by the Jewish authorities. But Luke tells us that "all the tax collectors and sinners were coming near to listen to him. And the Pharisees and the scribes were grumbling and saying, 'This fellow welcomes sinners and eats with them'" (Lk 15:1–2). Later we hear that Jesus even has dinner with Zacchaeus, a known tax collector. Yet Luke adds that Zacchaeus changes his life because of this unexpected meeting, going from a being corrupt civil servant to being a generous man: "Look, half of my possessions, Lord, I will give to the poor; and if I have defrauded anyone of anything, I will pay back four times as much" (Lk 19:8).

In this vein, it is a pagan, not a Jew, who proclaims at the key moment of the Gospel of Mark, after pages of "messianic silence," that the crucified Jesus is the Messiah: "Now when the centurion, who stood facing him, saw that in this way he breathed his last, he said, 'Truly this man was God's Son!'" (Mk 15:39).

My point is that Jesus provides a solution to the rigid and asphyxiating character of religious authority of first-century Israel. Jewish religious groups were divided; they quarrelled over the amount of power each should have over the people, and some accused others of infidelity to the Covenant. Yet Jesus shows that the renewal of authentic Jewish faith must pass through the door of openness and compassion toward *the other*.

Secularization and Religious Renewal

Jesus pushes the religious structures of first-century Judaism to change, adapt, and ultimately give way to new ones. This religious transformation shares certain key characteristics with the impact of secularization in modern Europe, especially regarding the loss of prestige, influence, and power by religious authorities. As an example, in Matthew 23 Jesus directs a series of condemnations beginning with "Woe to you!" against the teachers of the law and the Pharisees whom he accuses of being "blind guides," "hypocrites," and "whitewashed tombs." We must realize that Jesus has no official religious authority legitimating his right to make these accusations, given his status as what the churches today would call "a layman." And the gospels tell us that Jesus' lack of formal or official sanction was a source of contention with the religious authorities of his day (Mk 1:21–28, 1:27–33; Jn 2:18).

Interpreting these texts from within contemporary Europe, I would suggest that the religious authorities in question likely experienced Jesus' accusations as fueling a delegitimating process similar to what "secularization" has wrought in Europe. This would explain why the Gospel of Matthew follows the condemning "woes" of Matthew 23 cited above and the condemnation of the "goats" at the final judgment in Matthew 26:41–46 with the unsurprising conclusion that "the chief priests and the whole council were looking for false testimony against Jesus so that they might put him to death" (Mt 26:59).

God Is There

The gospels tell us that Jesus' fundamental message resides precisely in his presence among the people of Israel. Salvation has arrived, the kingdom of God has begun. In the beginning of Mark's gospel, after John's imprisonment Jesus declares: "The time is fulfilled, and the kingdom of God has come near; repent, and believe in the good news" (Mk 1:15). At the end of Luke's gospel two disciples leave Jerusalem and go to Emmaus, discouraged by the failure of their teacher and religious leader. We are told that the risen Christ walks with them, though they do not recognize him until the breaking of the bread (Lk 24:13–35).

In both cases, where God is apparently absent, we hear that God is actually there. God is accompanying the process, transforming the followers of the crucified Jesus into a new kind of Jewish community, even if—judging by previous religious standards—God appears absent. God shows Godself slowly within an emerging spiritual community. From the perspective of a rigid Judaism that has no place for the God of Jesus, that God seems to have disappeared, while in the experience of Jesus' followers God's gracious saving presence slowly appears as the presence of the risen Jesus and the sending of the Spirit. The disciples at Emmaus, like Mary Magdalene at the tomb (Jn 20:14–17), never capture God completely with their gaze, for when they recognize God's presence God is no longer there. Thus, while Israel continues to live in exile-at-home after the death of Jesus, and while Israel will be sent by Rome within a generation into the exile of the diaspora, we are told that God is still there.

Return to the Historical Present

Reading and interpreting these four insights into the story of Jesus from within the context of contemporary Europe, I conclude by suggesting how they can serve as guideposts for the Christian community as it navigates the jungle of secular life in the years ahead.

Responsible Autonomy and the Message of Easter

The personal autonomy celebrated by contemporary Europe has received progressively greater emphasis since the beginning of European modernity in the sixteenth century, and has been explicitly associated

with what it means to be truly human and truly adult since the eigh-
teenth-century European Enlightenment. I would suggest, however,
that this emphasis reflects an important defect of European Christendom, where Christian faith was too often experienced and preached as
something extrinsic and heteronymous. Faith was reduced to a group of
dogmas to be accepted, whether or not they were understood. Indeed,
faith was said to reside precisely in the acceptance of that which is unintelligible, becoming synonymous with the authority of tradition, ecclesiastical leaders, and one's parents and elders. Augustine's idea of
God as "*the most intimate part of my intimacy*" was slowly lost, since God
was seen as an extrinsic reality. Thus it was natural for Europeans to
believe that God imposes Godself from the outside on a subjectivity
that modern Europe experiences as internal. God's entry into the life of
the modern European subject was thereby perceived as somewhat aggressive or out of harmony with our inner life and deepest aspirations.

We have seen, however, that Jesus presented a face of God that
was quite the opposite, rejecting practices that exploited the weak and
restoring their autonomy. Meeting Jesus made people freer than before.
On the other hand, seventeen centuries of European Christendom too
often made its subjects less free, though of course there are many ex-
ceptions, including the mystics and the saints. Bishops and priests have
become the normative interpreters of revelation, a situation clearly
analogous to that confronted by Jesus in the synoptics (Mk 11:28, Mt
21:23c, Lk 20:2). The gospels remind us, however, that Jesus was a Jewish layman who confronted the religious authorities of his time with an
experience of God that seemed new and threatening.

Unfortunately, instead of nurturing followers of the Galilean Jesus,
the European church has too often sanctioned a way of being Christian
that imitates the Jewish authorities who persecuted him. In the process
European Christianity has lost track of the more universal, Isaian experience of the God of Israel who brings salvation to the nations (Is 25:6–7;
53:1–12) that permeates the experience of Jesus and the message of the
gospels (see, for example, Is 56:7; Mk 11:15–19; Is 25:6, 65:11–15; Mt
8:11–12; Lk 13:28–29; Is 61:1f; Lk 4:18). Catholic liturgies in Spain are
rarely festive, and too often rituals are led by an officiating priest who
controls everything down to the smallest detail. While there is certainly
life in many places, it has been a long time since the great church of Europe has been a vital expanding assembly of believers. Unfortunately, in
many places it has primarily become a hierarchical organizational structure operating under a tightly controlled chain of command.

Interestingly enough, secularization has simultaneously liberated
Europeans from this oppressive and fossilized form of Christianity while

promoting a kind of Babylonian exile-at-home for Christianity. While this situation is understandibly distressing to some, I would suggest that Christians tear a page from the story of the sixth-century BCE Jews of Second Isaiah who voluntarily returned from the great city of Babylon to a forsaken Israel. The historical experience of exile has opened up a moment for renewal, offering the opportunity to renew and rebuild European Christianity in a new form, more faithful to the original, closer to the style of the historical Jesus.

Just as Greco-Roman culture opened a new moment in the religious life of first-century Israel, to which Jesus responded so I would argue that the secularization of Europe has created a new moment for the church here. Ignacio Ellacuría's reflection on the life of the church at a critical moment in the history of El Salvador is appropriately entitled, *Conversion of the Church to the Reign of God*. So, too, I would argue that the church in Europe must be reconverted to the kingdom of God if it hopes to live and flourish. The church is not the gospel, but rather an agent constituted to preach it and to form lives inspired by its message. In the oft-quoted words of the great thirteenth-century European saint, Francis of Assisi, "Preach the gospel at all times, and when necessary use words."

The Jews of Second Isaiah experienced their departure from Babylonia as a time of religious renewal, just as Jewish followers of Jesus experienced Easter as the fulfillment of the promises of Isaiah and the rest of the Hebrew Scriptures. Similarly, I would argue that European Christians should embrace the recuperation of autonomy demanded by secularization with Easterly joy. The historical present offers us the opportunity to renew European Christianity in a form that frees its followers from the religious dependencies and the enervating clericalism that are the enemy of responsible autonomy in order to promote the well-being and authentic religious experience of all peoples, all communities, and all classes in a diverse church and a diverse world.

Openness to the Other

The example of Jesus considered above suggests that the renewal of European Christianity will take place through a slow process of purification grounded in opening itself to *the other*. But who is *the other* in Europe today? She is the one who is different from us, the one who complicates our identity, the one who prevents us from completing our tasks. *The other* is the one who, by definition, makes us uncomfortable, who alters our life like the man who "fell among robbers" in the parable of the Good Samaritan (Lk 10:25-37). *The other* is the one who denies Christianity, who follows any religion different from ours, or who denies the legitimacy of religious belief.

Facing radical secularization, European Christianity must avoid a reactionary posture, defending its Christian legacy at every turn, learning nothing, and continuing as we were. Rather, I would argue that secularization has taught us that the legacy of Christendom in Europe was often, if not mostly, not Christian, and therefore must not be defended. European Christianity should focus rather on recovering the value that the gospels tell us Jesus places on autonomy and freedom as gifts and graces from God, which we see both in how he debates his opponents (Mk 11:28–33, Mt 21:23–27, Lk 20:1–8) and how he speaks to his followers (Jn 1:38–39). This autonomy does not go against God, but rather comes from God and brings us to God. This is a message European Christians should proclaim today: a God who is the source of autonomy and not heteronomy.

Freedom, Autonomy, and Christianity

I have argued, then, that European Christianity has damaged its freedom. Without freedom, there is no Christianity, which may be captured in two things: love and freedom. European Christianity, unlike Jesus, has not valued freedom, and in so doing has compromised the emphasis on love. When we look at the way in which the Christian churches in Europe have governed over the centuries, both from the Vatican as well as from many Protestant palaces, we can see that there have been great empires but little love and little freedom.

The emphasis of European secularization on human autonomy provides a magnificent opportunity to renew Christian freedom. Freedom is achieved and actualized through the development of the subject at the personal level (life options), the communal level (articulating one's own freedom with that of the other members of the community of believers), and at the social and global level (through responsibility for the common good). However, the primary place for Christian activity has never been the church, but the world. Just as Jesus did when he preached the gospel, Christians act most authentically from their own free will, in community, in the service of humanity (with a preferential option for the poor), and without discriminating against people.

The problem today is that European Christianity faces not only secularization, but also very conservative ecclesiastical leadership, which does not accept (or is at least profoundly ambivalent about) the end of European Christendom. This posture is at odds with secularization: it is a posture that condemns the world, maintains the structures of clerical power while exercising them with force, and exhibits a combative attitude toward new theological insights emerging from formerly marginated populations. In this way, European Christianity is squeezed between secularization and ecclesiastical conservatism. Of course, this is what Jesus experienced, caught between Roman power, which found his message fanatical and its social repercussions dangerous, and Jewish religious authorities who considered his words about God blasphemous and his religious authority disturbing. His Jewish followers then announced a crucified Messiah that was "foolishness" for the Greeks and "a stumbling block" for the Jews (1 Cor 1:22–23). Looking back from the perspective of contemporary Europe, we too easily forget that God has no other representative on earth. God liberated and glorified the Son at the resurrection, the "firstborn of many" (Rom 8:29), understood as temples of the Holy Spirit endowed with freedom and autonomy that empowers them to become true followers of Jesus and members of the community that carries on his work.

God Is There

In short, then, I have argued that God has not abandoned European Christianity. Rather, I have suggested that secularization presents an opportunity for renewal. The biblical text tells us that Jewish religious authorities betrayed the Covenant and supressed freedom, leading into the Babylonian exile and the exile-at-home under Roman rule at the time of Jesus. But the text also suggests that what has been irresponsibly abandoned returns in the form of a crisis, which sets the stage for rebirth and renewal.

So, too, European Christians have been called to follow Jesus in freedom and love. The gospels tell us we are called to carry on the mission of Jesus to initiate the kingdom of God, and to be living signs of his message that love of God is love of neighbor (Mk 12:28–34, Mt 22:34–40, Lk 10:25–28). And our secularized culture convinces us that authentic freedom and love are grounded in responsible autonomy. I have suggested, therefore, that European Christians are called as followers of Jesus and responsible adults to reform the structures of ecclesial and secular power that abrogate human freedom and autonomy. The path of renewal for European Christianity runs through the road to mature Christian faith.

Notes

1. This paper was presented in the Catalan language at a seminar in Barcelona, Spain, entitled, "Believers in a Secularized World," organized by the "Institució Cultural CIC," March 14, 2005, and published in: José Sols, "Jesús i el seu entorn, Jesús i el nostre entorn," *Ars Brevis* 11 (2006): 233–49. I have adapted and updated the content for this publication in English.

218 ❖ JOSÉ SOLS

2. For an explanation of the term "hermeneutical circle," see Hans Georg
Gadamer, Truth and Method, trans. Joel Weinsheimer and Donald G. Marshall
(New York: Crossroad, 1991), esp. 164, 293, 267. Gadamer states, "The classical discipline concerned with the art of understanding texts is hermeneutics"
(164). He says the hermeneutical circle "describes understanding as the interplay of the movement of tradition [in the form of the text] and the movement
of the interpreter [in the form of the person trying to understand the text]"
(293). He offers the following description of the circular interplay of tradition
[in the form of a text] and interpretation [in the form of the person trying to
understand the text]: "A person who is trying to understand a text is always
projecting. He projects a meaning for the text as a whole as soon as some initial meaning emerges in the text. Again the initial meaning emerges only because he is reading the text with particular expectations in regard to a certain
meaning. Working out this fore-projection, which is constantly revised in
terms of what emerges as he penetrates into meaning, is understanding what is
there" (267).

3. Alfred Rosenberg, Der Mythus des 20 Jahrhunderts (Munich: Hohene-
ichen, 1930).

4. The best analysis of the four senses of scripture is found in the work of
the French Jesuit, Henri de Lubac, *Exégèse médiévale: Les quatre sens de l'Ecrit-
ure* (Paris: Aubier Montagne, 1959, 1961, 1964).

5. José Sols, *Quan la fe interpreta i transforma* (Barcelona: Claret, 2003).
The following paragraphs contain a few expressions taken from this study, not
always quoted directly.

6. Rudolf Bultmann, *Glauben und Verstehen*, vol. 3 (Tubingen: J. C. B.
Mohr – Paul Siebeck, 1957), 148–49.

7. See José Sols, *La teología histórica de Ignacio Ellacuría* (Madrid: Trotta,
1999).

8. Ignacio Ellacuría, *Conversión de la Iglesia al Reino de Dios: Para anuncia-
rlo y realizarlo en la historia* (Santander: Sal Terrae, 1984), 266.

9. Ibid., 267.

10. Gerd Theissen and Annette Merz, *El Jesús histórico* (Salamanca: Sí-
gueme, 2000), 160–63.

PART IV

SPIRITUALITY

14

JESUS OF GALILEE

HOPE FOR A GLOBALIZED WORLD IN DESPAIR

Mary Doak

Gaudium et Spes, the Pastoral Constitution on the Church in the Modern World issued by the Second Vatican Council (1962–1965), observed already in 1965 that the world had become more deeply interconnected, a fact that confronts humanity with the questions of how people will interact with one another and to what purpose. Will humanity develop economic systems that facilitate the sharing of the world's resources and better assist those in need? Or will humanity develop a global system of hierarchy and domination, allowing a privileged few in the world to appropriate even more of the world's resources? In a strikingly prophetic passage, *Gaudium et Spes* starkly warned that "the modern world shows itself at once powerful and weak, capable of the noblest deeds or the foulest. Before it lies the path to freedom or to slavery, to progress or retreat, to brotherhood or hatred."[1]

Although written nearly fifty years ago, this surely remains an apt description of humanity today. "Globalization" is now the common term used to describe the unprecedented human interconnectedness at the beginning of this new millennium, with economics, technology, finance, communication, and politics increasingly integrated worldwide. Foreign exchange and capital markets are globally linked, operating twenty-four hours a day and across national boundaries. At the same time, new communication technologies, including the Internet, cellular phones, and media networks, facilitate not only an international economy but also a global culture predicated on the instantaneous sharing of information and entertainment. This unprecedented degree of human interaction influencing the conditions of life throughout the world is a force that can be used for greater good and for greater evil than was before possible.[2] Globalization gives us the resources to foster human solidarity and support internationally, even while we see evidence that our interconnectedness also increases the possibility of violence and domination. The choice before us, as Daniel Groody insightfully observes, is whether we will steer our common ship toward a more peaceful and just world or be shipwrecked on the icebergs of selfishness and greed.[3]

The evidence thus far is that globalization has been anything but an unalloyed good. Inequality among nations has risen dramatically in the past fifty years: whereas the income difference between the richest and poorest countries was 35 to 1 in 1950, the income difference was 72 to 1 in 1992 (and continues to grow). As Groody has noted, "the three richest *persons* have more assets than the combined GNP (Gross National Product) of the poorest forty-eight *nations*, a quarter of the world's countries."[4] It is sobering to consider that what people in Europe and in the United States spend altogether on luxury items is almost *ninety times as much money* as the amount needed to provide basic sanitation and safe drinking water to all those in the world who currently lack these necessities.[5] The desperation of those excluded from the benefits of the global market is fueling world-wide migration, with over 200 million international migrants and nearly four times that number who have migrated regionally.[6] At the same time, international media and marketing undermine the cultural patterns that sustain local communities, and the increased proximity of ethnic and religious groups that could lead to mutual appreciation often results in violent conflict instead. The technological advances of the twentieth century improved longevity and quality of life for many, but they also made possible the horrific violence of "world" wars and genocides.

One might expect to find a positive outlook on the current situation among those who benefit most from access to the world's resources and who dominate the global economy as well as international politics. After all, this internationalized economy has brought an unprecedented standard of living to the developed nations, and globalization has dramatically increased the diversity of goods available. Yet in the United States one finds little optimism among those currently enjoying the luxuries provided by the global market. Instead, there is a widespread and fearful uncertainty that masks an undercurrent of despair. This lack of hope is manifest in the proliferation of predictions of the end of the world and in the popularity of enraged talk-show hosts whose warnings of doom deeply influence U.S. political discourse.

Perhaps we should not be surprised that fear and the politics of fear are such powerful forces among the wealthy and privileged in a period of great inequality. After all, the wealthy have much to lose. In addition, globalized economic and political systems are extraordinarily difficult to

control and seem impervious to intentional direction. Even for the afflu-
ent, the conditions of their well-being depend on complex international
systems in the face of which human agency seems insignificant.

Where, then, can people find the hope necessary to overcome fear
and to resist the temptations to selfishness amid the globalized systems
that are so hard to control even while they determine many of the conditions of life today? As a Catholic theologian, an educated U.S. citizen, a wife, the Anglo mother of a Mexican daughter, and a feminist
committed to an international ethic of care in service of the common
good, I am deeply concerned with what might inspire those of us who
benefit from the current global economy (yet seem none the happier
for our privilege and wealth) to join those without adequate food and
shelter to work together for a world of greater sharing rather than
greater selfishness. More pointedly for privileged U.S. Christians, can
we find in our Christian faith the resources to live confidently and joyfully amid globalization's complex of possibilities and problems, acknowledging the potential for violence yet placing our hope in mutual
support and community?

To answer these questions, I return to the significance of Christianity's origins in the hope brought by a Galilean rabbi to a people
and a world marked by imperial domination, also a violent and oppressive situation in which there was much reason to despair. Yet, instead
of proffering hope in our time as Jesus did in his day, established Christian churches are often as fearful as the rest of society, divided among
ourselves as we fight over how best to retain whatever privilege and position we have achieved. At the same time, newer Christian movements evince an energetic otherworldliness eschewing hope for this
world in favor of apocalyptic visions of destruction. Christian eschatology too often functions in this way: not as a source of hope for human
history but as a reason to turn away from the world and its problems. If
Christianity is to provide hope for a world in the grip of fear and despair, we need to put again at the center of Christian life the hope that
Jesus brought in his life and ministry, the hope that survived the crucifixion and was spread throughout the world by people filled with the
joy of his resurrection.

In this essay I will argue that the hope that Jesus inspired, a hope
not yet fully realized in his death and resurrection, must become historicized through forms of Christian praxis that globalize hope in the current context of globalized economics, communication, and politics.
Rather than relegating eschatology to the "last things," as arcane details
on the margins of Christian life, I argue that eschatology must be brought
back to the center of Christian life. Followers of Jesus of Galilee ought

to embody an eschatological hope that faces and resists the horrific violence and systems of violence that dehumanize all involved. This must be a hope expansive enough to encompass the many nations of the globe, yet grounded enough to attend to the particular sufferings of specific persons and peoples, especially those deemed insignificant by the power players in the global market and in international politics.

The Hope of Jesus the Galilean

Although many Christians today emphasize the promise of a personal afterlife of bliss with God, most branches of the Christian tradition officially affirm a broader and more communitarian goal for human life. This more adequate—and more biblical!—Christian hope anticipates a union of all peoples and nations in God, a union that includes not only a complete harmony among a reconciled humanity but also, as is increasingly recognized, a unity with God's entire creation. This ultimate goal is not, however, a uniformity that unites by eliminating differences; what is envisioned here is instead the unity of a good creation that celebrates its diversity. Indeed, our ultimate goal is existence within the loving relations of the Trinity, as part of a divine life enriched by the differences incorporated within this perichoretic community of love.[7]

On the one hand, the Christian tradition acknowledges that this hoped for unity-in-diversity will not be fully achieved within sinful human history. On the other hand, this Christian eschatology is not offered solely as an otherworldly hope, irrelevant to life in this world. Indeed, the unity with all in God is manifest and grows in this world, in the lives we live here and now. Thus, as noted in *Gaudium et Spes*, humanity will find perfected in the afterlife what it achieves in history, and the grace that is bringing people into communion with God also enables people to see beyond present divisions and to seek unity now with all of God's creation.[8]

The life and ministry of Jesus as a Jew were certainly formed by the hope for a just society in harmony with God and nature as envisioned in the Torah and the prophets. However, Jesus was experienced as something more than another prophet calling people to return to the Law and to a way of life consistent with hope for the reign of God. Jesus was understood instead to be the in-breaking of this reign of God in the midst of history, making possible a new degree of harmony with God and others in this life. A closer look at the life and ministry of Jesus of Galilee reveals the hope for reconciliation and harmony historicized in his life, death, and resurrection. The teaching and ministry of this

Galilean laborer inspired people with a vision of the reign of God captivating enough to cause them to leave their homes and their work, and eventually to carry this vision throughout the world. What was so attractive about this ideal and the hope that it expressed? What did people experience in their encounters with Jesus that was so inspiring and empowering?

To answer this question, we need to look more carefully at the ministry and message of Jesus in and around Galilee, where he began. As recorded in the gospels, Jesus proclaimed the advent of the reign of God in Israel, and more specifically, in Galilee. Jesus' manner of living God's reign was demonstrated in his open table fellowship, eating with all people including (most notably) the prostituted women and Roman collaborators with whom no decent Jew would interact publicly. Jesus further compounded this disregard for the social boundaries legitimated by religious laws when he insisted on healing by touching those whose skin diseases rendered them untouchable; in doing this, he made himself as officially untouchable as they had been.[9]

While there is much that remains puzzling about the reign of God in its startling and complex challenges to the ordinary assumptions of Jesus' time and of our own day, the descriptions of Jesus' teaching and actions leave no doubt that Jesus understood this reign to involve inclusive human communities that reject the normal stratifications separating the socially valued from those of little worth. Jesus lived the eschatologically envisioned harmony of the reign of God and called others to do so as well. His practice of open table fellowship embodied his message that God's reign overcomes social divisions and is centered among those usually most despised or devalued by society.

From a contemporary U.S. perspective, we may grasp more deeply the liberating power of Jesus when we consider his social location. Jesus is described as the son of a *tektōn*—a carpenter or, perhaps better translated, a craftsman. If John Dominic Crossan is right, as a craftsman Jesus came from a group that had been squeezed out of the peasant class and was only one step from being destitute.[10] In any case, John P. Meier, N. T. Wright, Gerd Theissen, and a variety of other historical scholars agree that Jesus was clearly not a member of the privileged classes, in what was undoubtedly a highly stratified society.[11] People in Jesus' vulnerable socio-economic situation could reasonably be expected to focus on maintaining whatever position or privilege they had and to distance themselves from the thoroughly vulnerable and powerless. Yet with confidence in God as his loving father and the source of all life, Jesus embraced precisely what should have been most threatening to him: fellowship with the lowest classes. Extending inclusion and dignity to the marginalized and demeaned, Jesus embodied a freedom from preoccupation with socio-economic security, from striving to climb up (as well he might have) or at least to avoid being dragged further down.

To the vulnerable at all levels, from the destitute with little to lose to the wealthy who benefited greatly from the status quo, Jesus modeled a liberating freedom based on confidence in the love of God and hope in the possibility of communities in which people care for each other. In Jesus' presence, people were empowered to believe in their own value enough to stop clinging to the norms and practices that kept them from slipping further down the social ladder. Instead of fighting to secure their own positions at the expense of others, people were inspired by Jesus to come together in celebrations that erased social location and invited all to participate equally.[12]

Yet this call to communities of mutual dependence included a recognition of the particularity of each person and his or her needs. We see this clearly in the stories of Jesus' response to women who suffered from the regulations and stratifications of their society in distinct ways. It would have been easy for Jesus not to notice the situation of women at all, since his society expected him to interact only with men. Yet Jesus publicly included prostituted women in his community, and he did not recoil from their touch, particularly when that improper touch was all the woman had to offer. Jesus gave life to the son of a widow and to the brother of sisters, ensuring that these women would not also die in a world where women depended on male relatives to survive. Jesus healed the woman with the flow of blood, restoring her to the community from which she had been excluded as untouchable. (She might well have been abandoned or on the verge of being abandoned as unfit for woman's work of providing food).[13] The inclusive community that Jesus formed was not then a gender neutral community in the sense of presuming that all people must or even can be treated as the same. Rather, Jesus embodied a concern to attend to people's differences so that his was a diverse community, as we see in Jesus' attention to the specifically gendered forms of women's poverty, powerlessness, and devaluation in a society that limited their agency yet rejected them for having to survive through prostitution.

What This Hope Means Today

Jesus' praxis of hope in the reign of God as humanity's future is deeply relevant to our current situation of globalized capitalism. In this situation, forty-five million people per year die of causes due to poverty, and a mere two days of the world's military spending would pay for the health services that could prevent the deaths of three million infants each year.[14] We live in a time in which greed, desperation, and hopelessness are being globalized, with even the winners nervous about their ability to retain their positions. Insecurity causes us to fear that if we make room for others there will be no room for us, and this fear is surely exacerbated by a competitive capitalism that determines winners and losers on a global scale. Our situation today is not unlike that of the Roman Empire which, in Jesus' time, sought to conquer the world in search of benefits for itself, allowing certain members of local communities to share its power and privilege in exchange for cooperating with the imperial system.

As the gospels indicate, Jesus sought neither to join Rome nor to take Rome's place but rather to build relationships of inclusion, appreciation, and mutual support as an alternative to the dominant practices of exclusion, rejection, and domination. By daring to be vulnerable himself, Jesus embodied liberation, and thus liberated others from the unending struggle for positions of social status and economic security. Can Jesus' example and his empowering spirit inspire his followers among the privileged classes, especially in Europe and the United States, to seek not power at the expense of others but a power shared among us, the power of acting together for the good of all? What would it mean today to live this countercultural hope as a world-wide church in the midst of imperialistic capitalism? Is it possible to construct communities of mutual dependence and diversity rather than competition and hegemonic uniformity, even while working to direct international economic and political systems toward inclusion rather than domination?

Pope John Paul II frequently and eloquently proclaimed that the human person is intended for community and finds fulfillment only in living as a self-gift to others. Yet people are persuaded less by theories than by actions. As Johann Baptist Metz has long argued, the only true defense of faith is a practical one. In other words, the way to demonstrate the credibility of hope is by living according to that hope.[15] Christians will convince others that self-fulfillment is found through the gift of the self only insofar as we Christians ourselves live in joyful commitment to others. If we are personally transformed by hope in Jesus for the reign of God, then we will stop struggling to secure ourselves (and our churches!) in a fundamentally insecure world, and instead risk ourselves in relationships of vulnerability and mutuality. As followers of Jesus, we are called to commit ourselves to developing our churches into vibrant communities of mutual support, especially for the marginalized, while also learning to put the resources of the ecclesial community at the service of rebuilding communities of mutual support in the larger society.

The emphasis of Catholic social teaching on subsidiarity provides important insights for this effort to live our hope in the reign of God in the context of globalization. The idea that problems should be solved by the most local form of community able to handle a problem adequately is especially important for ensuring in a globalized reality that people are empowered as agents to form and to act within communities in which they take responsibility for each other. People cannot support and welcome each other without community relationships that allow them to know each other. The pressures of globalization toward ever larger, anonymous systems must be counteracted through efforts to revitalize local communities.

Yet one must be careful that subsidiarity does not become an excuse for withdrawal from one's larger responsibilities. As a worldwide church in an interconnected world, Christians must not neglect the international efforts necessary to coordinate the sharing of resources between those who have an abundance and those who have less than they need. Nor do we have the luxury of rejecting involvement with the governmental structures through which global interactions can be directed toward greater mutuality and away from domination and greed. To be sure, until the eschaton arrives, the governments and international organizations of this world will remain unjust and largely in the service of the powerful. Nevertheless, it would be counterproductive and foolhardy to wait for perfect governmental systems in this interconnected world in which all affect each other. Those committed to justice must rather take advantage of whatever opportunities are available now to work toward a more just sharing of the world's resources, the alleviation of suffering, and greater involvement for all in the decision-making processes that are determining the world we live in. "Extending the principle of community to worldwide terms has become the most urgent of all the issues that face our epoch," Niebuhr argued already in the early twentieth century.[16] Only by doing so is it possible to bear witness to the hope in a universal reign of God with the power to transform every aspect of human life.

The test of whether Christians today embody the hope of Jesus of Galilee lies especially in our response to the sufferings of those deemed insignificant and frequently unnoticed in the world at large as well as in our own communities. The specific sufferings of women are often overlooked, even while women are frequently the most vulnerable among the poor. In situations where resources are limited, women and girls are often the last to be fed, educated, or given medical care (which can lead to appallingly high rates of maternal death and repro- ductive injuries such as fistulas that leave women incontinent and so- cially ostracized). In areas already affected by climate change, poor women may work harder and longer to get the water and fuel necessary for the survival of their families. In situations of war, gang-rape of women and girls has emerged as a potent weapon for terrorizing com- munities. In one of the most disturbing developments of our interna- tionalized economic system, women and girls are being kidnapped and trafficked widely so that the supply of women meets the global demand for sexual services.[17]

What do efforts of U.S. Christians to historicize our Christian hope in the world today offer these women? Jesus of Galilee noticed and responded to the specific sufferings of women in his day, so those who would continue his mission must also be concerned with the suf- fering of the women who seem to matter little to the rest of humanity. This suffering of the vulnerable in the context of globalization espe- cially challenges privileged U.S. Christians to respond both globally and locally, since every location has its own particular needs yet is part of an interconnected world. Poor women suffering from fistulas in Africa will be greatly benefited by international aid to provide medical help, but poor women in the United States also need better access to prenatal care.[18] Women are trafficked in Cambodia, but also in San Diego and many other cities in the United States.[19] Hope in the reign of God is a hope for the entire world, an insistence that all prostituted women are valued sisters who deserve other options, that all raped and torn bodies are bodies that ought to be healed. As followers of Jesus, we in the United States must join with those around the world who boldly proclaim the joy of community with all of the despised, suffering, and rejected, whether they live on another continent or in our own towns. This community is, after all, the pearl of great price worth selling all that we have to attain.[20]

The Hope Yet to Be Realized

To avoid the serious mistake of confusing Christian hope with opti- mism about historical progress, Christians committed to a countercul- tural agenda in the developed world must keep in mind the reception of this hope in Jesus' time. After all, Jesus was not successful in trans- forming the world of his day. Instead, the world violently rejected the hope that Jesus embodied and crucified him. Jesus died an apparent failure, and yet his disciples proclaimed him risen from the dead.

Though they had been overcome by fear at his arrest, Jesus' followers were empowered after this seemingly total failure with a new confidence that neither death nor the powers of this world are ultimate.[21]

To live as disciples of Jesus amid the unequal distribution of the world's resources today, we cannot forget that Jesus died in Jerusalem in confrontation with oppressive power and exclusionary authority. He opposed but did not defeat this system of domination and marginalization.[22] In our world today, this suggests that Christians must call for an end to structures of oppression, while bearing the double-edged knowledge that although another reality is truly possible, sin will not be completely defeated in this world. Thus martyrdom remains a constant possibility in Christian life. Fidelity to Jesus will not allow his disciples to remain safe with an eschatological hope confined to the margins of society, since the invitation to the reign of God is intended for the whole world. Yet Christians must be prepared for much of the world to continue to reject the reign of God and to defend its structures of power and domination with violence.

The gospels, of course, do not reduce Jesus' ministry to an entirely this-worldly reform project, and neither should we. The reign of the everlasting God is a hope beyond history, a hope that has inspired people to give their lives in witness against the ultimacy of the powers of this world. At the same time, however, the hope for the reign of God is indeed a hope involved in this world, a confidence that God's power can—and someday will—transform all aspects of human life.[23] The reign of God as the Lord of all is not limited to heaven or to earth, to now or to later, to this world or to an afterlife.

This eschatological proviso reminding us that our hope is not fully achievable in history should encourage resistance to all of the oppressive and divisive powers in this world. Looking forward to a goal beyond history frees people to risk themselves, even against the odds, on behalf of others. Knowing that failure in this world is not ultimate or final can be a source of strength especially for those who are vulnerable and weak by the standards of the world. Women who struggle to escape prostitution in a condemning society, who are healing from rape in a war zone where they may well be attacked again, or who have little hope of finding sufficient food to feed their children may find peace and courage in the confidence that the ultimate destiny of humanity in the reign of God is beyond the vicissitudes of this life. Keeping in mind that Jesus' death in failure led to the empowering victory of the resurrection ought to inspire all Christians joyfully and confidently to risk attracting the violence of the world by their commitment to the reign of God. This non-optimistic but thoroughly hopeful perspective should also inspire those of us Christians who are among the world's elite to risk the loss of our privileged position as we seek a more just and inclusive world.

The Bearers of Hope

From the perspective of a U.S. Christian striving to follow Jesus in a globalized world, living out such a hope in opposition to the forces of global oppression and exclusion and in the face of inevitable failures requires that we not forget who it was that Jesus chose to be the primary bearers of this hope in history. Jesus began his ministry of table fellowship with rough peasants and with the disreputable and devalued—with prostituted women and collaborators with Rome. As Gustavo Gutiérrez, Virgilio Elizondo, Rosemary Ruether, and so many others remind us, Jesus called despised and uneducated Galileans rather than the intellectual, religious, or political elites of his day to be the central emissaries of his mission. These "insignificant" people, disregarded by the world yet welcomed by Jesus, are the ones who continued the movement after Jesus' death and who, empowered by the Holy Spirit, spread Christianity throughout the world.[24]

Fidelity to the message of hope that Jesus brought requires, then, that those privileged enough to read and write theological articles (such as this one) learn to accept our own de-centering. Middle and upper-class U.S. Christians are not the central actors in spreading God's reign; we are not the most important among Jesus' disciples. All of humanity is invited to relinquish self-centeredness and to enter into a solidarity that shares the vulnerability of the poor, joining together in building communities of inclusion and mutual support. Yet those of us called from positions of privilege are inclined to retain the self-centeredness of believing that we are the primary bearers of God's reign in history. We thus attempt to replicate the hierarchies of this world in the reign of God, while we overlook the hope borne by the "insignificant," the powerless, the destitute, and the despised who continue to affirm life and love, to strengthen relationships and to support each other in the midst of pain and suffering.

Consider, for example, the ways that women among the desperately poor and rejected are bearers of hope as they work to rescue themselves and those around them from desperate circumstances. Some women with little education are starting businesses to lift their families out of poverty, while other women whose fistula injuries have been repaired are getting enough medical training to be able to repair fistulas in other women. Women from the untouchable caste in India who managed to get an education have returned to the slums to empower other members of their caste. Perhaps among the most courageous are the women who have been gang-raped yet continue to resist the oppression of women in their communities. With few resources and no obvious power, women around the world are doing much to overcome their own desperation and to improve the lives of others as well.[25]

The stories of these women suggest a yet deeper challenge: could the hope of Jesus be embodied in the world and brought to Christians by non-Christians—by Muslims, Hindus, and Buddhists, for example?[26] Throughout our history, Christians have repeated the gospel stories suggesting that God's reign is found especially among the poor and usually where it is least expected. Are we able to acknowledge today that the non-Christian poor might be living more fully the hope of Jesus than privileged Christians from developed nations? Such a reality should not be surprising to those who take seriously that Jesus is the incarnation of the Word of God eternally active and eternally manifest in the world. The revelatory power and grace of God remain surprising and destabilizing of our categories, perhaps no more so than when Christians find themselves being invited by non-Christians to join in efforts that Christians cannot help but recognize as continuing the work of Jesus and his disciples.

Conclusion

The church has spread the gospel of Jesus throughout the world, much as the author of Luke-Acts envisioned. The hope in God's reign traveled with Jesus and his companions from Galilee to crucifixion and resurrection in Jerusalem, and from there to Egypt and Rome, to India and China, and to major cities and small towns in the United States and around the world. The beauty of Jesus' Galilean vision and the anticipatory experience of the reign of God remain an active hope for the transformation of the entire world. This hope is crucified daily among the suffering and impoverished of the world, and it is also frequently co-opted by the privileged to support the status quo. Yet it is a hope that rises again and again as people encounter the power of God and are inspired to risk their lives, giving up security and privilege in order to build communities that recognize the value of all human beings.

In our present context of globalized consumerism, what could be more precious or more desperately needed than a hope that inspires people to strive to live together in relationships of mutual valuing and support for all? As a privileged U.S. Christian, I experience this hope as a countercultural call to seek something greater than the security of my position of privilege and the opportunity to consume more than my neighbors.

Notes

1. *Gaudium et Spes*, 9. I am deeply grateful to Robert Lassalle-Klein for his careful editing and suggestions that made this article much better.

2. Reinhold Niebuhr develops this point in *Nature and Destiny of Man*, vol. 2 (New York: Charles Scribner's Sons, 1943), esp. 315–21.

3. Daniel G. Groody, *Globalization, Spirituality, and Justice* (Maryknoll, NY: Orbis Books, 2007), 19.

4. Groody, *Globalization*, 5. See ibid. 3–10 for the statistics on income inequality, including those cited here.

5. Ibid., 7.

6. United Nations, *Human Development Report 2009, Overcoming Barriers: Human Mobility and Development* (New York: United Nations Human Development Program), 21 (available at http://hdr.undp.org).

7. See, for example, the Vatican II documents, *Lumen Gentium*, 1 and 48, *Gaudium et Spes*, 24 and 45, and the Faith and Order Commission's Paper #198, "The Nature and Mission of the Church: A Stage on the Way to a Common Statement," esp. 24-47.

8. "For after we have obeyed the Lord, and in His Spirit nurtured on earth the values of human dignity, brotherhood and freedom, and indeed all the good fruits of our nature and enterprise, we will find them again but freed of stain, burnished and transfigured" (*Gaudium et Spes*, 39).

9. Jesus' open table fellowship and disregard of social boundaries is noted by theologians, biblical scholars, and general readers of the New Testament. See, for example, Virgilio Elizondo, *Galilean Journey: The Mexican-American Promise* rev. and expanded version (Maryknoll, NY: Orbis Books, 2000), esp. 58–66; John Dominic Crossan, *Jesus: A Revolutionary Biography* (New York: HarperCollins, 1995); and Garry Wills, *What Jesus Meant* (New York: Viking, 2006).

10. Crossan, *Jesus*, 23-26.

11. John P. Meier, *A Marginal Jew: Rethinking the Historical Jesus*, vol. 1, *The Roots of the Problem and the Person* (New York: Doubleday, 1991), 282; N. T. Wright, *Christian Origins and the Question of God*, vol. 2, *Jesus and the Victory of God* (Minneapolis: Fortress Press, 1996), 147–59; Gerd Theissen and Annette Merz, *The Historical Jesus: A Comprehensive Guide* (London: SCM Press, 1996, 1998), 171–73.

12. Ibid. Drawing on and adding to the research of others, Virgilio Elizondo has developed this point especially well throughout his extensive corpus. See especially his *Galilean Journey*, 120.

13. See Lk 7:36–50; Lk 7:11–16; Jn 11:17–44; Mk 5:25– 34.

14. Statistics cited in Groody, *Globalization*, 5, 9.

15. Johann Baptist Metz, *Faith in History and Society: Toward a Practical Fundamental Theology*, trans. David Smith (New York: Seabury Press, 1980), esp. 3–11.

16. Reinhold Niebuhr, *The Children of Light and the Children of Darkness: A Vindication of Democracy and a Critique of Its Traditional Defense* (New York: Charles Scribner's Sons, 1944), 153. He further notes that this world community is not only our "final necessity and possibility" but also our "final impossibility" (187), arguing as I have here that the inevitable imperfection and even injustice in governing structures does not justify refusal to cooperate with them.

17. For an excellent discussion of some of the challenges for women in poverty around the world, see Nicholas D. Kristof and Sheryl WuDunn, *Half the Sky: Turning Oppression into Opportunity for Women Worldwide* (New York: Alfred A. Knopf, 2009).

18. For an excellent assessment of the theological implications of fistula, see Colleen Carpenter Cullinan, "In Pain and Sorrow: Childbirth, Incarnation, and the Suffering of Women," *CrossCurrents* (Spring 2008): 95–107.

19. For further information on trafficking and prostitution, see the United States Federal Bureau of Investigation's website: http://www.fbi.gov/hq/cid/civilrights/slavery.htm.

20. Mt 13:45–46.

21. Elizondo, *Galilean Journey*, 79–82.

22. Ibid., esp. 68.

23. Ibid., 1.

24. Ibid., esp. 53, 83.

25. Kristof, *Half the Sky*.

26. Among the recent books exploring this topic, see especially Peter C. Phan, *Being Religious Interreligiously: Asian Perspectives on Interfaith Dialogue* (Maryknoll, NY: Orbis Books, 2004).

15

"RAISED IN JERUSALEM"

Michael E. Lee

Two images from childhood have made an indelible impression on my religious imagination. Since I am a Christian, it is no wonder that they are images of Jesus, but what is surprising is how different the images are and how they reside together in my consciousness.

The first comes from *La Catedral Dulce Nombre de Jesús*, the church of Humacao, Puerto Rico, where my grandparents lived. I visited them on occasional summers, and I recall going to worship in that church as a saturating sensory experience. The dark restful interior was such a contrast to the sunny and often bustling plaza outside. Not that the natural world outside didn't make its presence felt—the many pigeons flying around looking for perches and the occasional stray dog strolling through an open door seemed to be mainstays of any liturgical celebration. Yet, with statuary and stained glass to catch my eyes, the smell of candles and incense, and the sounds of fluttering fans all making a bid for my consciousness, it was the crucifix that captivated me. There was *Jesucristo* hanging on a cross, bleeding profusely from his wounds, *el pobre*. He was horrifying and yet strangely comforting. He evoked sadness, compassion, inspiration, commitment, and a host of other emotions. If nothing else, going to that church would always involve coming before that cross and responding to its call in one way or another.

One thousand miles away in Miami, Florida, the chapel of St. Thomas the Apostle Church and elementary school had a Jesus of a completely different character, but who also became part of the formative vision impressed on my consciousness. He wore a billowy garment that covered his entire body, except for raised hands and extended feet that still possessed nail wounds. This was the resurrected Christ, not nailed to a cross but hovering in front of it as a reminder of what exactly was vanquished in his victory. Though perhaps less visceral, he still evoked emotions of wonder, joy, and awe.

More than any one trait or sentiment derived from these images, perhaps what strikes me most is that neither of these images stands alone in my mind, but rather they mingle together to form a unity. Moored in different architecture, prayed before in different languages, part of different cultures, these images of Jesus Christ are still part of one Christian faith in my personal, cultural, and spiritual landscape. To come before Jesus Christ, whether in liturgical prayer, meditation, or the discernment of life decisions, has always meant somehow approaching both of these images.

It is difficult to put a name to this faith. It would be too easy to play on stereotypes and talk about a Hispanic faith of the crucified Jesus and an "American" faith of the resurrected one; a doleful and fatalistic faith versus a happy if even positivistic one on the other, or even a faith of the oppressed and marginalized versus that of the "dominant" group. But these caricatures do not work—it is far more complicated than that. As a child of Puerto Rican parents growing up in the United States, I did feel that my house was different from those of other "American" kids: we had different food, a different language mixed in, different ways to pray. However, a visit to my grandparents always reminded me that I was different from my Puerto Rican cousins too. As a native-born English speaker with fair skin and an "Anglo" last name, I did not fit in there either and, to be sure, I never felt the sting of anti-Hispanic hate in ways or to the degree that others have felt it. The conflict was more interior.

As in the case of the two images of Jesus in my imagination, I have always felt the pull of two cultures, but never the feeling of being completely at home. On the one hand, I felt a need to resist the attitude that my Hispanic cultural heritage was a quaint oddity that should be left behind in order to become truly "American." Yet, on the other hand, I also had to resist the self-doubt that inevitably arose when I was made to feel that I wasn't "really Hispanic," either because my Spanish wasn't good enough, my skin was not dark enough, or my music or clothes were too *gringo*.

I cannot say that entering adulthood and the vocation of a theologian has really changed or resolved this inner conflict. If anything, a greater appreciation and engagement with my Hispanic heritage, both personally (in family life and friendships) and professionally (in ministry, research, and teaching), is always tempered by the realization that greater educational and employment opportunities now separate me from the life experience of marginalization of the majority of Latina/os in this country. The one thing of which I have become certain is that strict dualisms cannot account for the complexity of my experience of the Christian faith, nor of the two (or more) streams that make up what is more properly described as U.S. Latina/o religious experience and faith. How to think about this faith? Must I choose one source that is "truly" home? What sort of faith tradition will I pass on to my children? What implications does this bicultural faith have for how I live my life as a Christian?

This essay focuses on those whose identities navigate in and between two (or more) cultures and so bring to theological reflection a different set of questions. In particular, I would like to argue that many second- and third-generation U.S. Latina/os who feel forced to choose between the "U.S." and "Hispanic" dimensions of our identity experience this dualistic "either-or" logic as inauthentic, whether it be in the form of pressure to assimilate and surrender the "Hispanic" elements of our identities, or to reject the "U.S." side. Understood in a theological way, I would suggest that our hybrid ways of negotiating selfhood and faith are a legitimate and potentially more effective path to integrating the empowering trajectory of the gospel that "lifts up the lowly" and the prophetic one that calls power to service and solidarity.

I will begin by analyzing some social-scientific data about young, native-born, second-and third-generation U.S. Latina/os who inhabit bicultural identities that differ considerably from those of their foreign-born immigrant counterparts. To help us understand the ways in which they describe their multiple identities, communicate in multiple languages, and participate in a wider society in which they are both alien and at home, I'll turn to certain concepts of postcolonial thinkers who highlight the often subtle but powerful ongoing effects of colonial history, and the possibilities for overcoming them in what is called "hybridity."

With this naming in place, I then turn to theology and attempt to advance the groundbreaking insight revealed in Virgilio Elizondo's great work, Galilean Journey.[1] While he draws upon Galilee as a metaphor for a borderland existence, I will suggest that the notion of being "raised in Jerusalem" serves as a complement and extension of this notion, while corresponding more closely to the experience of hybridity. I will examine the ambiguous character of Nicodemus in the Gospel of John in an effort to uncover and name more precisely the cultural challenges of marginalization and assimilation that are endemic to many second- and third-generation U.S. Latinas/os today.[2] And I will suggest that this approach offers a richer way of understanding the possibilities for faith in what is increasingly a global scene of intercultural exchange. More specifically, I will describe a way of thinking about the multiple social locations that bicultural and multicultural peoples occupy today, and about the distinct demands that those various locations place on them. Moreover, I will argue that this way of thinking has implications for the way Christians understand some of the defining ideas and doctrines that shape their faith, such as how to speak in contemporary terms about the divinity and humanity of Jesus Christ.

In and Between Two Worlds

In a well-known essay, theologian David Tracy has dubbed our postmodern time the "age that cannot name itself."[3] Despite—or perhaps because of—our heightened sense of the many cultures that make up the United States, it is a time in which people from this country have trouble naming themselves. For second- and third-generation children of immigrants, the challenge of constructing an adult identity requires negotiating a particularly complex set of questions about origins and culture in a dominant society that is frequently hostile to complexity. In filling out a recent census survey, I had no problem identifying myself as Puerto Rican and my wife as Cuban, since both of our parents are from those respective locales. But what about our two boys? There is no space for Cuban–Puerto Rican–Americans.[4] And what would that designation mean for them in any case? For many, the lyrics sung by a character in the musical *In the Heights* sums up their situation, "My mom is Dominican-Cuban; my dad is from Chile and P.R., which means: I'm Chile-Domini-Cu-Rican! But I always say I'm from Queens!"[5]

In 2009 the Pew Hispanic Center conducted a survey focused on U.S. Latina/os between the ages of sixteen and twenty-five, exploring a wide range of issues including identity, demography, language use, and economic well-being.[6] It provides an intricate portrait of a population whose circumstances are summed up in the report's title: "Between Two Worlds." In the findings one sees the (literally) multifaceted identity issues facing those who inhabit this space in between two worlds, and who do so in a multiplicity of ways. I would like to focus on the findings that underscore the differences between the ways in which first-generation Hispanic immigrants and native-born second- and-third generation Latina/os work out their place in the tapestry of cultures that make up the United States. Though the findings are rich and require more analysis, they do seem to indicate important developments in the ways that Latina/os in the United States cope with the pressures of economic marginalization and cultural assimilation.

Perhaps the most surprising initial finding in the report is that, contrary to popular perceptions of Latina/os as immigrants, two-thirds of Hispanics ages sixteen to twenty-five are U.S. born. Whatever the influence of immigrant parents, their cultural heritage, and ongoing contact with their countries of origin, the majority of young Latina/os today were born in the United States and have been raised within its culture, language, and so forth.

Given this fact, it would be easy to suggest that U.S. Hispanics will march down the same road of assimilation that previous European immigrants have trod and, indeed, some of the data seems to support this conclusion. For example, Hispanics in the survey seem to embody the truism that the children of U.S. immigrants quickly grow more proficient with English and less so with language of the "old country." Thus, while 90 percent of immigrants report that they read Spanish very well or pretty well, only 68 percent of second-generation Hispanics follow this pattern, and the number plummets to 26 percent for the third generation and beyond. Conversely, while only 48 percent of foreign-born Hispanics say they can speak English well, the number more than doubles to 98 percent for their native-born counterparts.[7]

Still, it would be too easy to conclude that the proximity to broader U.S. cultural markers means a corresponding distance from Hispanic ones. Looking at the data on language use, while there is a loss of facility in reading Spanish, the language is not lost entirely. In fact, 79 percent of second-generation Latina/os stated that they speak Spanish very well or pretty well. Of third generation Latina/os, who for the most part grew up in households with English as the primary language, almost four in ten (38 percent) still retained the ability to speak and understand Spanish and almost a third of this generation (30 percent) say that at least half of the songs they listen to are in Spanish. Numbers such as these suggest a resilience in the maintenance of Spanish language skills that does not fit the assimilationist portrait of immigration.

Even this brief glance at the data suggests that though second- and third-generation Latina/os must wrestle with living between two cultures, they do, in fact, find ways to hold on to both. It is not clear that assimilation requires the loss of language and cultural patterns associated with Latin America and Spain, nor, sadly, is it clear that each passing generation enjoys a better economic standing. U.S.–born Latina/o youths are twice as likely to have ties to a gang, have gotten into a fight, or carried a weapon in the past year than those who are foreign-born. They are also more likely to be in prison. Disturbingly, while poverty, teen parenthood, and high school dropout rates are lower in the second generation, they climb in the next generation. Statistics like these help illuminate why assimilation is not the only problem that comes from living between two worlds; the ongoing problems of racial and ethnic discrimination remain part of U.S. Latina/o life. In order to think through these multiple challenges faced by Latina/os, let us turn to some concepts from thinkers who come from intercultural contexts rooted in colonialism.

In trying to understand the development of local cultures in the context of colonial power, thinkers like Edward Said have developed a crucial insight regarding the inherent power of naming. His criticism of *orientalism*, a concept that encompasses a wide range of European writings from history and archeology to fiction and poetry, is that it distorts Asian cultures by constituting them as "the East" (the Orient) in opposition to "the West." Said recognizes in this binary construction of the world in terms of East-West what Michel Foucault calls a discourse, so that orientalism represents a desire "not only to understand what was non-European, but also to control and manipulate what was manifestly different."[8]

The real power of orientalism, the power of this discourse, lies in the way that it promotes acceptance of its governing images as "the way things are." This idea, what Antonio Gramsci calls "hegemony," indicates how, despite evidence to the contrary, stereotypes have a resilience in shaping "common sense" ways of understanding whole peoples. It is not that the dominant group imposes its ideas purely by brute force. Hegemony is exercised through the much more subtle but no less dangerous forms of knowledge and culture that covertly reinforce attitudes, caricatures, and stereotypes so that they are accepted as conventional wisdom.

The notions of discourse and hegemony, and how they have shaped perceptions of peoples who were once colonized, have thus become an essential part of Latina/o studies. Just think of the way that images of the lazy Mexican sleeping under a *sombrero* or of the sultry Latin temptress have become cultural fixtures in certain genres of film. From Ricky Ricardo and Carmen Miranda to Ricky Martin and Jennifer Lopez, one can see an ensemble of attitudes and images that make up the U.S. cultural landscape and its idea of what is "Hispanic." One need only add a political topic like immigration to see how this combination of discourse and hegemony come to be expressed as real political power.

It is no wonder, then, that asserting one's own identity becomes an important strategy to overcome the problem of being named by another. From the 1960s slogans of the Chicano movement (Brown Pride! Viva La Raza!) to the recent documentary of Rosie Perez (*Soy Boricua, Pa' Que Tu Lo Sepas!*; in English, "I'm Boricua, Just So You Know!"), an important part of Hispanic identity in the United States involves countering the forces of a dominant discourse that sows a kind of inferiority complex in the mind of U.S. Latina/os. As a twenty-five-year-old His-panic female confidently expresses in the Pew survey, "I was at a T. J. Maxx with my Colombian friend, and we were talking in Spanish, and this white person said 'You're supposed to speak English in America.' And I said, 'Oh really? So you need to learn Spanish because this is a changing country. Get over it.'"⁹

This is a changing country, and the ability to move between two worlds, particularly for second- and third-generation Latina/os, repre-sents a form of resistance to the forces of assimilation; it appears to be one of the key qualities necessary to navigate the ever-shifting U.S. cultural landscape. So, while we have seen that many native-born Latina/os in the Pew survey might use the term "American" to describe themselves, a full 41 percent of the second generation and even 32 per-cent of the third generation still rely on their family's country of origin as the first term to which they turn. Despite cultural forces that would have them surrender or reject their Hispanic heritage, it appears that young Latina/os are finding the resources to resist.

Yet, while resistance to a hegemonic dominant culture is an impor-tant way for a marginalized population to retain a sense of identity, the rhetoric of opposition can become too rigid. Put another way, if Latina/o identity focuses too narrowly on opposition to U.S. (under-stood as Anglo, gringo, and so on) power and stereotypes, then it buys into the very duality of "American vs. Hispanic" that was wrong in the first place. Not only does it leave Latina/os battling to decide whether they are "American" or not, but it forces us to defend whether we are "Hispanic" enough. The use of language, dress, music, and other cul-tural markers, which at one moment can be liberating expressions of identity, can at another moment easily become new codes of exclusion that serve only to recapitulate a sense of being nobody.

The complexity of this cultural matrix has been addressed in Homi Bhabha's potent notion of hybridity.¹⁰ Recognizing the manner in which formerly colonized peoples can assert their identities in ways that only serve to reinforce divisions, Bhabha speaks about hybridity as a way to overcome these cultural rigidities. The space of hybridity is the interstitial, the in-between place that is a place of surprising power. Though often perceived by the dominant group and experi-enced by the marginalized as an empty space of victimization, the in-between place of hybridity is actually a location of hidden power that unmasks the anxieties present in harmful discourses. Though a com-plicated notion, hybridity reveals a sense of the agency and the power of bi-cultural peoples to forge their own identities.

The gift, power, and opportunity of U.S. Latina/os emerge from the way in which they inhabit different cultures *as their own*. As we have seen, second- and third-generation Latina/os do not and cannot stand outside of the U.S. culture in which they were born and raised. They need not reject it in order to pass an authenticity test of being Hispanic. However, they also need not negotiate their Hispanic cultural heritage in a passive or assimilationist way that would have them surrender another part of their complex identities.

Reflecting on this problem theologically, Latina/o theologians have brought to their readings of the Bible cultural questions that have traditionally been overlooked. While much of this interpretation has naturally focused on Jesus, the figure of Nicodemus in the Gospel of John, a person who constantly inhabits ambiguous spaces such as those between light/dark, teacher/ignorant one, and believer/unbeliever, will provide an interesting example and source of reflection on the challenges of biculturality.

Raised in Jerusalem: Nicodemus, the Ambiguous Disciple?

In his classic work, *Galilean Journey: The Mexican-American Promise*, Virgilio Elizondo captures something essential about the intercultural questions raised by the U.S. Latina/o experience of faith. By focusing on the gospels' portrayal of Jesus as being from the border region of Galilee, Elizondo opens up a whole new way of reflecting on the "border existence" of many U.S. Latina/os. In particular, Elizondo powerfully describes the "double rejection" at the heart of the Latina/o experience between cultures as "part of and despised by both."[11]

Part of and despised by both, related yet alien to both: this is a basic existential reality for many Latina/os. Elizondo's great contribution lies in declaring that the good news of Jesus reveals a God who loves that which is despised and strengthens marginalized people to resist the powers of exclusion and domination. Inspired in part by this insight, the stream of thought known as U.S. Latina/o theology has initiated rich reflection on the cultural dimensions of a range of theological topics, particularly from a location that is both figuratively and often literally the borderland.

However, U.S. Latina/os now inhabit a fuller geographical space that extends to every state in the country, and we have seen that U.S. culture does indeed find a more central place among second- and third-generation Latina/os. So it makes sense to return to the Bible for metaphors, figures, and characters to help understand the more richly nuanced hybridity that characterizes the "in between" spaces that young Latina/os occupy today.

When considering the notion of ambiguity in relation to identity issues, perhaps there is no more suitable character in the gospels than Nicodemus in John's gospel. The ambiguity of his identity and ultimately his position in regard to Jesus are topics that continue to generate much discussion among biblical scholars. What is the significance of this character? Is he the example of ignorance in John's gospel? Of unwillingess to believe? Or does he in fact represent a key symbol in John's gospel of someone coming to faith in Jesus? The very fact that scholars seem unable to reach consensus on this character caught between two worlds makes Nicodemus an intriguing point of reference in thinking through identity questions raised by second- and third-generation Latina/os.

The Gospel of John introduces Nicodemus as a Pharisee and a "leader of the Jews" (3:1).[12] He comes to Jesus by night, a fact that many scholars interpret as a symbol of unbelief, and initiates a dialog in which Jesus makes two very famous but rather curious statements. The first is the well-known declaration, "No one can see the kingdom of God without being born from above/again" (3:3).[13] The other is that "the wind/spirit blows where it chooses, and you hear the sound of it, but you do not know where it comes from or where it goes. So it is with everyone who is born of the wind/Spirit" (3:8).[14]

A common interpretation of the passage portrays Nicodemus as an ignorant straight-man who misunderstands Jesus because he chooses the wrong connotation of the words that Jesus speaks. In a text where wordplay and misapprehension are used as devices to bring out central themes, the fact that Nicodemus is supposed to be a learned Pharisee only deepens the irony of his ignorance. One could also contrast him with others in the gospel, such as the Samaritan woman at the well, who has a far deeper appreciation for Jesus' words and identity. Her confession stands in marked contrast to the apparent silence of Nicodemus.

Yet, before giving up on Nicodemus as hopelessly in the dark, it should be noted that he has chosen to come to Jesus. They do not meet by chance; Nicodemus actively seeks out Jesus to engage this dialogue. It is true that to do so at night may symbolize a present state of ignorance, but it can also suggest a sense of risk or danger associated with this seeking out of Jesus. Ultimately, the passage does not provide enough information to resolve the status of Nicodemus, but through this encounter with Jesus the author is able reveal important truths

about the nature of Christian discipleship. The next appearance of
Nicodemus in the text clearly intimates that the solicitation of these
truths might involve certain dangers.

Nicodemus reappears in John's gospel at the end of a dispute between the Pharisees and officers who, though instructed to bring in
Jesus, do not return with him because they are amazed at his speech.[15]
The Pharisees ask, "Have any of the authorities or of the Pharisees believed in him?" (7:48). The text then tells us, "Nicodemus, who had
gone to Jesus before, and who was one of them, asked, 'Our law does
not judge people without first giving them a hearing to find out what
they are doing, does it?' (7:50–51). This question draws the scorn of his
peers who ask with astonishment, "Surely you are not also from
Galilee, are you? Search and you will see that no prophet is to arise
from Galilee" (7:52).

The conflict between Nicodemus and his peers turns upon which
of them properly understands the law, and whether there is anything of
value that can come from Galilee. The question from Nicodemus
comes immediately after the Pharisees disparage the crowds as accursed
for their ignorance of the law. It is unclear whether Nicodemus is
merely arguing a point of the law or trying to create a space for hearing
and learning what Jesus has to say. Either way, Nicodemus finds himself
in a liminal place, caught between those who see nothing in the man
from Galilee and those who believe in him as "the prophet," or "the
Messiah." Nicodemus makes no confession of faith himself, but by raising this question among his Pharisee peers, he has revealed something
about himself in the light of day, something that could not be said
about his previous night encounter with Jesus. Moreover, his question
draws contempt that is articulated in striking fashion: his identity is
questioned by his peers. He is asked whether he is a Galilean.

Galilee, which is not considered worthy of producing a prophet,
functions here as a disparagement, an epithet of marginalization.
Nicodemus provides no response to this accusation, and the reader may
be justifiably puzzled by this ambiguous character. Yet, while the first
two appearances in John of Nicodemus revolve around questions, our
final glimpse involves action. He appears after the crucifixion of Jesus
to embalm his body:

> After these things, Joseph of Arimathea, who was a disciple of
> Jesus, though a secret one because of his fear of the Jews, asked
> Pilate to let him take away the body of Jesus. Pilate gave him
> permission; so he came and removed his body. Nicodemus, who

had at first come to Jesus by night, also came, bringing a mixture of myrrh and aloes, weighing about a hundred pounds. They took the body of Jesus and wrapped it with the spices in linen cloths, according to the burial custom of the Jews. (19:38–40)

The companion of Nicodemus in this scene, Joseph of Arimathea, is described as a secret disciple of Jesus because of fear. It may be a compromised discipleship, but he is a disciple nevertheless, and in coming before Pilate he no longer acts in secret. John tells us that Joseph of Arimathea comes before the authority that ostensibly authorized the crucifixion in order to ask for the body. Can we bestow on Nicodemus the same status, a kind of belief by association? It is difficult to say. However, we can note that the overwhelming amount of spices Nicodemus brings, the myrrh and aloes, were appropriate for the burial of a king. Some scholars conclude that this represents his continuing ignorance: here he comes to bury a king in the Roman sense of the word, not understanding the different type of king that Jesus is. Yet, I find more intriguing and convincing the notion that Nicodemus, like Joseph, is making himself vulnerable before imperial power. By burying Jesus in a symbolically royal manner, he is subverting the authority of the Roman emperor. Nicodemus's action can be construed as an indirect challenge to imperial power by acknowledging the authority of another.

Though Nicodemus never makes the sort of confession in John that other characters do, his words before the Pharisees and his actions before Pilate leave him open to a double rejection. His responses to the now crucified Galilean—hearing, learning, and embalming him—leave him vulnerable and, provocatively, dealing with the accusation of being a Galilean himself. By no means is the discipleship of Nicodemus established definitively in the Gospel of John. But this is part of what makes him such an intriguing character. The very ambiguity of his status leaves open a choice that readers must take up and answer for themselves.

(Re-)Turning to Galilee

Rather than argue in any definitive way for Nicodemus as either stubbornly ignorant or secretly faithful, I would contend that the very ambiguity of his status in John offers an opportunity to reflect on the location of bicultural peoples. People in this situation struggle to survive between two worlds, navigating the challenges of hegemonic discourse while resisting the temptation to embrace dangerous dualisms that leave us trapped between two worlds. In order to illustrate the possibilities raised by the character of Nicodemus, let us reverse the order of his appearances in the Gospel of John. My intention is to highlight through the figure of Nicodemus three important moments, or turning points, where Latina/o Christians and others who turn to biblical images for guidance and strength in negotiating biculturality make important decisions.

Nicodemus before Pilate

What does it mean to be a person of faith in the most powerful nation on earth? How can the discipleship of a Christian matter in the face of a globalized consumer economy that either crushes or commodifies anything that stands for alternative values? While millions of Latina/os in the United States yearn for happiness and strive toward a vision of success, that vision is fraught with ambiguities in a society so divided by disparities in wealth and discrimination due to race, gender, and sexual orientation. A system that tokenizes people in order to disguise oppression can welcome even a small measure of success from those on the margins. As more Latina/o "success stories" emerge, the story of Nicodemus challenges its readers to find the courage to render gifts that may subvert the dehumanizing ways of empire, to ask uncomfortable questions of unjust structures, and to show solidarity with crucified persons and peoples.

Nicodemus before the Pharisees

How are bi-cultural and hybridic people to negotiate the complex choices imposed on us by powerful forces exerted by those whose views of the world are too simplistic? Culture is a space of fluidity and, as we have seen, a place that offers hybrid ways of carving out identity. In empires, the dominant group exercises hegemony by marginalizing vast groups of others, and this has an internal dimension for those so marginalized. In this environment, Latina/o Christians should reject not only internalizing racist messages of inferiority but also taking refuge in hyper-racialized identity constructions that actually worsen cultural divisions, often promoting ethnic litmus tests that parody authentic cultural identity. Latina/os possess a distinctive gift as a *gente puente*, a bridge people, who embody the role occupied by Nicodemus in John's gospel as a person able to hear and understand both sides of the cultural divide. Our challenge is to maintain the capacity for compassion and the courage and ability to show solidarity with all who are marginalized. Like Nicodemus, we should risk being called Galilean, for part of us comes from and will always be tied to the Galilees of this world.

Nicodemus before the Galilean

How can the hybridic ways that Latina/os have developed to negotiate the killing dualisms of culture help us to negotiate the enervating dualisms of faith (such as those that are spiritual-material, private-public, religious-political)? In coming before the Galilean one, Nicodemus is confronted by a man whose identity he does not recognize and a God whose ways he cannot fathom. Latina/os have a deep reservoir of traditions and religious practices that nourish us, but these must not be held defensively or ossified like museum pieces frozen in time. It is precisely in the creative ways that Latina/os adapt and adopt our faith and traditional practices to the demands of reality that the Spirit truly moves where it will. The "both and" character of U.S. Latina/o cultures helps us to see the folly of relegating faith to the private sphere and to unmask some kinds of spiritualism as disguised escapism.

In Matthew, Mark, and John, the followers of Jesus return to Galilee—there they see the Risen One. And in all of the gospels his followers are invited to follow the path that Jesus walked from Galilee to Jerusalem. So, too, even for those children of immigrants who perhaps were not born in the borderland of Galilee but raised in Jerusalem, it is only fitting that the gospels should suggest that the life of the disciple is to be forged "in between" the two points on the journey. Though there is danger in taking up Jesus' path from Galilee to Jerusalem, we can do so with the hope that, like the crucified one, we too will be raised in Jerusalem.

Notes

1. Virgilio Elizondo, *Galilean Journey: The Mexican-American Promise* (Maryknoll, NY: Orbis Books, 1983, 2000).

2. Taking a cue from the Pew Hispanic Center's survey, the designation "3rd generation" will include subsequent generations, and indeed in the case of some Latina/os in the Southwest, those who never immigrated but had the border cross them as the land was appropriated by the United States.

3. David Tracy, *On Naming the Present: God, Hermeneutics, and Church* (Maryknoll, NY: Orbis Books, 1994), 3.

4. Not only are there problems with multiple ethnic heritages, but the 2008 American Community Survey Census form instructed "For this survey, Hispanic origins are not races." Thus, even though in the non-Hispanic population only 0.3 percent of respondents identify with "some other race," a full 30.4 percent of Hispanics taking the survey chose this designation. See U.S. Census Bureau, 2008 American Community Survey.

5. "Carnaval del Barrio" from *In the Heights*, music and lyrics by Lin-Manuel Miranda and book by Quiara Alegría Hudes.

6. Pew Hispanic Center, "Between Two Worlds: How Young Latinos Come of Age in America," Washington, DC (December 11, 2009). All cited statistics come from this report.

7. In addition, when asked whether they used the term "American" to describe themselves, only 29 percent of first-generation immigrants responded positively while almost nine in ten (89 percent) of second-generation and practically all (96 percent) of third-generation Latina/o youths did.

8. Edward Said, *Orientalism* (New York: Vintage Books, 1978), 12.

9. Pew Hispanic Center, "Between Two Worlds," 31.

10. Homi Bhabha, *The Location of Culture* (London: Routledge, 1994).

11. Elizondo, *Galilean Journey*, 52.

12. All biblical citations are from the *New Revised Standard Version* (NRSV).

13. The Greek verb, *anothen*, possesses both meanings ("from above" and "again").

14. Here the double "wind/spirit" reflects the multiple meanings of *pneuma*.

15. Given the awful history of Christian anti-Judaism, there are important caveats that must be made when dealing with a passage that portrays Pharisees in a negative light. The interpretation I am setting forth here operates strictly within the narrative and symbolic world set forth in the Gospel of John, a work that scholars believe came from a period in the late first century in which there was tension and competition between early Christianity and post-Second Temple Judaism. It would be wrong to read these tensions back to the life of Jesus, and history has shown the tragic consequences that ensue when Christians use the portrayal of tension between Jesus and some Jewish authorities to juxtapose Christianity and Judaism. In no way should the conflict in this gospel between Nicodemus and his Pharisee peers give foundation to arguments about the superiority of Christianity over Judaism.

16

CHRISTOLOGY AT THE U.S./MEXICO BORDER

AN ESCHATOLOGICAL VIEW[1]

Daniel Groody

Few issues today are as complex as global migration. It affects all areas of human life, making it arguably one of the most controversial issues of our time.[2] As a defining issue of the twenty-first century, which has been described as "the age of migration,"[3] immigration is what Vatican II called a "sign of the times." Approximately 214 million people, or one out of every thirty-five persons on the planet, are living away from their native lands. This is the rough equivalent of the population of Brazil, the world's fifth largest country.[4] Many of these migrants have been forcibly uprooted: approximately 30 to 40 million are undocumented, 24 million are internally displaced, and almost 10 million are refugees.[5]

The U.S./Mexico border is one of the busiest and deadliest frontiers in the world, and it serves as an apt microcosm of the problematics of global migration. Its 1,952-mile length stretches from the coast of the Pacific Ocean near San Diego, California, to the shores of the Gulf of Mexico near Brownsville, Texas. Politically, it is the boundary between Mexico and the United States. Geographically, it is the border between North America and South America. Economically, it is the dividing line between the poverty of Latin America and the prosperity of the United States. For many Latin Americans surviving on less than three dollars a day, the prospect of immigrating to the United States to earn upwards of forty dollars a day is a powerful magnet.

Each year, hundreds of thousands of immigrants try to enter the United States illegally through the southern border. Unable to obtain proper documentation for political and economic reasons, these immigrants, in their desperation, cross through desolate areas in order to circumvent long and impermeable walls, surveillance cameras, military technology, and the vigilant eye of border patrol agents. They traverse high mountains and cross waterless, inhospitable deserts to make it into the United States. Others are hospitalized with various kinds of heat-related illnesses. Still others are apprehended and put in immigration detention centers and deported. And a certain number, miraculously, make it across, only to find a whole new set of challenges awaiting them in a strange and foreign land.

But some are not so lucky. The death toll has soared exponentially due to more restrictive border control policies established in the last decades, which are designed to put immigrants at even greater risk. Since 1995 when new policies were initiated, hundreds of immigrants have died each year trying to cross the U.S./Mexico border in the hope of finding a better life and a more promising future on the other side. Today, on average, more than one immigrant dies each day trying to cross from Mexico into the United States. How can followers of Jesus think about this reality from a theological perspective?

A Theological Perspective on Migration

In addition to being a social, political, and economic affair, migration is a profoundly theological issue. It is a theme that runs throughout the Judeo-Christian Scriptures, from the call of Abraham to the promise of a spiritual homeland. In between are stories of oppression and liberation, movement and wandering, exile and return, descent and ascent, and memory and mission. The stories of God and the people of God are inextricably intertwined with migratory movement. Reflection on these biblical narratives can give us new insight into the dynamics of migration, and a closer study of the reality of migration today can give us new ways of interpreting the same biblical stories.

As an example of the way in which this approach can enrich our understanding of both ancient biblical texts and migrants today, I will take a brief look at the familiar biblical text of Matthew 25:31–46 (the story of "the sheep and the goats"), reading it through the lens of today's borderlands, a geographically and socially marginated setting with close parallels to the Galilee of Jesus. On the one hand, I will speak about the physical journey of migrants across the U.S./Mexico border, while on the other, I will interpret their reality through the lens of Matthew 25:31–46.

In this passage from Matthew Jesus imagines the final judgment, when the nations stand before God. He says that when the Son of Man separates the sheep (those who have done God's will) from the goats (those who have not), he will tell the sheep, "I was hungry and you gave me food, I was thirsty and you gave me drink, a stranger and you welcomed me, naked and you clothed me, ill and you cared for me, in prison and you visited me" (Matt 25:35–36). Near the end Jesus adds, "Whatever you did for one of the least of these, you did for me" (Matt 35:41). Some commentators characterize this passage as a "summary of the gospel" and a defining text on Christian charity. Scholars debate the original meaning of the phrase "least of these,"[6] but the parallels between Matthew 25 and the plight of Mexican immigrants to the United States are striking, reading like a story about the daily lives of undocumented migrants.[7] Such correlations invite reflective action and, as I will highlight here, a mysterious arena where we may encounter the risen Christ. I believe a closer examination of the experiences of such migrants can contribute much to the way in which we understand both Christian spirituality today and the encounter with Christ in contemporary society. In what follows I will examine Matthew 25 in light of the historical reality of immigration unfolding at the U.S./Mexico border, which I consider an "American Galilee."

"I Was Hungry and You Gave Me to Eat"

Though media headlines highlight recent violence and criminal activity at the border, federal authorities readily acknowledge that 98 percent of undocumented immigrants are not drug dealers or criminals, but most often hard-working people looking for jobs. I would suggest most are hungry in two ways: (1) for food for their families, and (2) for human dignity. At the heart of these is the search for work. With increased unemployment and underemployment, diminishing real wages, sluggish economic growth, and extensive poverty, especially in rural sectors, many families are struggling simply to survive. And as John Annerino notes, "nothing will stop these honest people in their quest for a better life, not the killing desert, and not the transformation of the 'tortilla curtain' into the Iron Curtain."[8] Gustavo from Cuernavaca, Mexico, put it this way:

> Sometimes my kids come to me and say, "Daddy, I'm hungry." And I don't have enough money to buy them food. And I can't tell them I don't have any money, but I don't. I can barely put beans, potatoes and tortillas on the table with what I make. If I am lucky, I can afford the luxury of potato chips or a piece of cake once a week. But that's it. I feel awful, but nothing is worse than seeing your hungry child look you in the eyes, knowing you don't have enough to give them.[9]

The real-life implications of the economic disparity between Mexico and the United States were clarified for me by talking with people on both sides of the border. On the Mexico side an immigrant named Moises said he came north "looking for enough money so my family has bread to eat."[10] On the U.S. side, just a few miles away, I spoke with a woman vacationing at a San Diego resort who said she came to the area "looking for specialty bread that I cannot find anywhere else."[11] The unspoken conversation between these people that will likely never take place is a microcosm of the borderlands, where two people can be looking for their daily bread from such different starting points, one from desperation and destitution, and the other from affluence and luxury. The border is a place where the undocumented immigrant and the legal resident can inhabit the same geographical space while living in what seem like two totally different worlds.

From a theological perspective, the journey of many migrants to the Mexican-American border is like that of Lazarus who comes to the gate of the rich man (Luke 16:19–31), longing to eat the scraps that fall from the banquet table of the United States. In Luke's gospel we learn the name of the poor man Lazarus, but we never hear the name of the rich man. The name "Dives," the Latin word for "rich," was added by translators to the vulgate (Latin) version of Luke 16:19 in medieval times. The rich man has no name in Luke's original, but we do know the name of the poor man. By contrast, we know the names of the rich and famous along the U.S.-Mexico border, but the poor go unrecognized. Many of those found dead in the desert are buried in unmarked graves, with only a brick reading, "John Doe" or "Jane Doe" as their headstone.[12] They hunger for bread, but also to be recognized and valued for who they are as persons, created in the image and likeness of God.

"I Was Thirsty and You Gave Me Drink"

Though many migrants leave to escape hunger at home, others die of thirst on the treacherous trek across the barren deserts of California, Arizona, New Mexico, and Texas. Thousands walk fifty to sixty miles through the Sonora Desert in temperatures exceeding 120 degrees (48 degrees Celsius) before reaching major highways and towns. The heat is so intense that, after baking in the sun, discarded plastic water jugs crumble like potato chips.

Such conditions lead migrants to take desperate measures for water. Some break open cactuses to suck water from the plant fiber. Others drink from putrid ponds or livestock water troughs, infested with diseases of every kind, including flesh-eating parasites. Some drink their own urine, or that of farm animals, in order to survive. "It's not pretty," said Daniel, "but when you are faced [with] dying of thirst, you do what you have to do."[13]

Amid such austere conditions, stories of spontaneous generosity capture the remarkable spirit of many migrants. When Roberto crossed the desert a few years ago he encountered a couple who were lost and had been walking for three days. They had run out of water and their lips were brown and purple. On seeing them wandering aimlessly in a fog and exhibiting signs of hyperthermia and dehydration, Roberto had to decide whether to share what little water he had, knowing it could leave him bereft down the road. Yet, without hesitation, Roberto offered them his water, saving their lives in the process. When I asked Roberto about this incident, he said, "It was not a heroic act. It was simply action born from the heart; it was just the right thing to do."[14]

We are impressed by heroic figures like Mother Teresa who recognize Christ in the poor. Yet in Matthew 25, neither the righteous nor the unrighteous recognize the presence of Christ in the poor. In fact, both groups say, "Lord, when did we see you hungry and feed you, or thirsty and give you drink" (Matt 25:37, 44)? What are we to make of this "blessed ignorance"? And how do the actions of people like Roberto shed light on this text? It appears, paradoxically, that the righteous have little sense of the virtuousness of their actions, and that it is not the prospect of some future reward that motivates them but rather the awareness of what being truly human requires, that the humane response is simply the right thing to do. Put another way, former U.N. High Commissioner for Refugees Saddrudin Aga Khan once observed, "The awkward truth about human deprivation is that it demeans those who permit, or ignore it, more than it does those who are deprived."[15]

"I Was a Stranger and You Welcomed Me"

Displaced from their homes, migrants often feel deeply disconnected from all they hold dear. Many have left behind husbands, wives, children, and extended family to make it to the United States, which looms in their imagination like a promised land. Yet even when they secure employment, many feel they are nothing more than arms and legs for their employers, without heart or feeling, without body or soul, valued only for the money they produce, but lacking humanity. They feel estranged on a variety of levels, from the culture, from their families, from society, from themselves, and from the church.

In the parable of the rich man and Lazarus, Luke says that even the dogs came to lick the sores of Lazarus (Luke 16:21). In a similar light, it is not uncommon for many immigrants to feel more in common with the dogs than with the human beings on the other side of the border. As Miguel said,

> One of the worst things about being an immigrant is the feeling of discrimination, of being bossed and kicked around like you are a slave and humiliated because you are a foreigner. Sometimes I feel like even the dogs live better than I do, like I am the lowest form of life on earth. There is no worse feeling than feeling like you are not worth anything as a human being.[16]

If they make it across the border, most immigrants will work at low-paying jobs that no one else wants, except the most desperate. They will de-bone chickens in poultry plants, pick crops in the heat, and build houses on unregulated constructions sites. They are willing to work at the most dangerous jobs and, though working conditions have become safer over the last decade, one immigrant dies each day in the workplace. Immigrants die cutting North Carolina tobacco and Nebraska beef, chopping down trees in Colorado, welding a balcony in Florida, trimming grass at a Las Vegas golf course, and falling from scaffolding in Georgia.[17] One of the deepest hungers of the undocumented immigrant is simply to be welcomed by others in a society that exploits their labor while reinforcing their inferiority.

"I Was Naked and You Clothed Me"

The natural elements are only one of the dangers that migrants face. Angel said that after he left Guatemala to migrate north with his brother and sister, seven mañosos (bandito gangs) attacked them, tied them up, and raped their sister right in front of their eyes.[18] Three more times during their journey mañosos mugged, robbed, and even shot at them. On one occasion thieves took all of their clothes, leaving only their underwear. They beat Angel so badly that he could not walk for four days.

Some, like Angel, lose not only possessions but also their basic freedom. In order to cross the border migrants hire coyote smugglers for $2,000 or higher. Unable to pay, they become indebted to industries involved in human trafficking and labor exploitation that prey on their vulnerability. When they get to the United States some migrants are sold to farm labor camps or prostitution rings to pay off their debt, which leaves them both naked and enslaved. After everything is taken away, many migrants say the one thing they have left is their faith and hope in God.

When I met Manuel he was standing by the side of the road, waving plastic water jugs. He had just walked sixty miles across the desert. But when he could not keep up, his friends abandoned him. "It was horrible," he said. "First I ran out of food. Then I ran out of water. Then I began to pray." When I asked how he prayed, he said, "I suddenly realized that the only friend I had was God. All my other friends abandoned me, but I realized that God was the one friend that would never leave me." As he spoke about his spiritual life, he compared himself to Job, who lost his home, his family, his possessions, his health, and even his friends. "Job's story is my story," he said. "But Job is an inspiration to me," he added. "After all Job went through," Manuel said, he never cursed God. "Somehow all I've learned in life is how to suffer, but Job challenges me to be faithful as well."[19] Like Job, Manuel and other migrants realize they come into the world naked and they will leave the world naked. It is the time in between that is the most difficult, when the search for daily bread is a constant struggle.

"I Was Ill and You Cared for Me"

Sickness is a way of life for many immigrants along the border. Most are not accustomed to extreme physical exertion or the bristly terrain. The cactus, mesquite, and other prickly trees cause cuts and lacerations, while traversing the rocky trails can cause sprains, strains, or fractures. Beyond these, immigrants are also vulnerable to venomous creatures like scorpions and rattlesnakes, which they try to ward off by rubbing themselves with garlic when they go to sleep at night on the desert floor. Such injuries in the desert can be fatal, as *coyote* smugglers often leave behind injured or weaker members of the group, even if it means they will die.

The most serious illnesses, however, result from the high temperatures, which can exceed 120 degrees in the shade. Such conditions lead to dehydration, the inability to urinate, a weak or rapid pulse, and vomiting and diarrhea. Cramping begins in the legs, arms, or abdominal wall, and immigrants experience headaches, dizziness, and confusion. The body starts to lose its ability to cool itself, and, if left untreated, the immigrant can become unconscious.

After four days in the desert heat, Caesar spoke about how sick he became:

I couldn't hear right. I started hearing this buzzing sound in my ears and began to get dizzy. My mouth became dry to the point where I couldn't salivate...I couldn't taste even the green-colored water we had. Then my vision began to blur. Everyone looked pallid. My hands and feet went numb. The blisters were so big on my feet I couldn't feel them anymore. I started getting this really bad headache, and I could actually feel my heart beat, slowly, slowly. Everything was in a haze, like it was going in slow motion. My nose began to bleed and my throat tightened up. I thought, this is it; this is where I am going to die...I didn't have any more strength to continue...but I begged for just a little more strength from God...and, miraculously, I found the strength to keep going.[20]

Caesar went on to say that the desert gave him a whole new understanding of Jesus' temptation in the desert (Matt 4:1–11). He said, "Perhaps the greatest temptation was simply to resign, to give up, and to allow myself to die in the desert. And it would have been easier to do this, but then I saw the faces of my children in the back of my head, and the memory of them gave me the strength to keep going, to keep fighting, to not give up."[21] Amid such suffering, it is nothing short of miraculous to hear immigrants look beyond their suffering to thank God for the gift of life, even though it is threatened on many levels.

"I Was in Prison and You Visited Me"

While the search for bread drives many migrants to cross the border, tragically it criminalizes them in the process. Though a kind of natural law motivates them to risk everything in order to provide for their families, the civil law prosecutes them for doing so. When migrants are apprehended by border patrol agents, they are brought to immigration detention centers where they are finger-printed, processed, detained, and deported to their country of origin. They return home even poorer than when they left, and they remain trapped between the pressure of poverty and dangers of crossing.

Beyond the risks of incarceration, however, many immigrants find themselves imprisoned by negative stereotypes, which further demean them as human beings. Since September 11, 2001, distinctions have blurred between drug dealers, terrorists, and immigrants, even though none of the terrorists involved in that crime came through the southern border, and most entered the country through legal channels. Some forms of imprisonment stem from racism, xenophobia, and aggressive nationalism.

In recent years armed vigilante groups along the Mexican-American border have emerged, declaring "open season" on trespassing immigrants.[22] Some vigilante and other Arizona militia groups have declared war on immigrants who serve as scapegoats for domestic problems not of their making and targets for those who see easy solutions to complex issues they don't understand. "If I had my way," one rancher said, "I'd shoot every single one of 'em."[23] And very little is being done to stop them. One leader named Jack Foote summed up his sentiments when he said,

> You and the vast majority of your fellow dog turds are ignorant, uneducated, and desperate for a life in a decent nation because the one that you live in is nothing but a pile of dog shit, made up of millions of little dog turds like you. You stand around your entire lives, whining about how bad things are in your dog of a nation, waiting for the dog to stick its ass under our fence and shit each one of you into our back yards.[24]

While vigilante groups represent the extreme of the anti-immigrant sentiment, many immigrants interiorize the message that they are "illegal." The term "illegal alien" speaks not only to their political status but also to the disconnectedness many feel from the usual markers that give shape to our daily lives. If anything is *alien* about the drama unfolding at the U.S./Mexico border—and would be alien to the mind and heart of Jesus of Galilee—it is this term, which marks these immigrants as threats rather than the gift they are to the church and to the United States.[25] Nonetheless, it is this experience of rejection and dehumanization that leads many to identify with a God who was himself once rejected, a God who crossed borders, who immigrated, who suffered, and who descended into hell like they descend into the desert, in order to liberate them and bring them to a place of hope, freedom, and life.

Conclusion

Today's migrants face not only social, political, and economic obstacles but a spiritual struggle as well. Their situation begs for theological interpretation, for ways to make sense of their inhuman treatment and to guide their paths in their search for God amidst a confusing tangle of injustice, suffering, and hope. In many respects their predicament is a contemporary form of crucifixion with strong parallels to the gospels. They experience an economic crucifixion in their poverty, a political crucifixion in their marginality, a legal crucifixion in their undocu- mented status, a cultural crucifixion in their displacement, a social cru- cifixion in being separated from their families and loved ones, and, for those who die, an actual crucifixion. For the undocumented, crossing the line into the United States is nothing short of a way of the cross. Catholic social teaching says the true test of a society is how it treats its most vulnerable members. Yet Matthew 25 goes further, challenging us to discern the face of Christ among those who are hungry, thirsty, es- tranged, naked, sick, and imprisoned.

As we saw in our reflection on Matthew 25 and the "judgment of the nations," the unfolding drama of undocumented immigrants along the U.S./Mexico border is not only about them. The story is also about us. And it is not only a story about our personal salvation and theirs, but it is also mysteriously and inextricably a story about the salvation and redemption of both countries. A great gulf that opened up between the social location of these migrants and us, the prosperous beneficia- ries of U.S. society, a gulf that challenges us to ponder how we might learn to see them as they really are, not as a threat but as a gift of God. Immigrants prompt us to consider the source of our own security, the depth of our dependence on God, the extent of own willfulness and self-determinism, and our willingness to depend on others in our time of need and vulnerability.[26]

In a society that prides itself on self-sufficiency, immigrants reveal our utter need and dependence on God, breaking through our clever and sophisticated ways of masking the spiritual hunger, thirst, naked- ness, and sometimes barrenness of life in the United States. In a cul- ture that prizes economic prosperity, immigrants speak of a wealth that cannot be purchased, challenging those of us imprisoned by the idols of materialism and consumerism, captive to displaced hungers that alien- ate us from ourselves and from our neighbors in need. In a nation that feels ever more insecure in the face of global terrorism, immigrants manifest a depth of faith, hope, and love and a remarkable capacity to praise God amid incredible suffering, which puzzles us who see them as strangers and threats to our common good.

Rev. Robin Hoover writes, "We see in the immigrant a critique of modernity and enlightened rationality, individualism, self-depen- dency...[Immigrants] give us a new way of understanding how to live and be in the world. Like Jesus, they critique society by the very way they live and move in the world."[27] The faith and hope that strengthen so many immigrants as they risk everything for those they love lead us to consider how the crucified peoples of today bring salvation to the world that crucifies them and to the church that leaves them bleeding by the side of the road. Lydio Tomasi has it right when he says, "It's not that the Church saves the immigrant, but that the immigrant saves the Church."[28]

Notes

1. Portions of this article initially appeared in an article by Daniel G. Groody entitled, "Crossing the Line: A Spiritual View of the US/Mexican Border," *The Way* 43, 2 (April 2004): 58–69.

2. Former U.N. Secretary General Kofi Annan summarizes the problematic nature of this age of migration in terms of the "issues of human rights and economic opportunity, of labour shortages and unemployment, of brain drain and brain gain, of multiculturalism and integration, of refugee flows and asylum-seekers, of law enforcement and human trafficking, of human security and national security" (UNDESA, *World Economic and Social Survey 2004: International Migration* [New York: UN Department of Economic and Social Information and Policy Analysis, 2004], iii).

3. Stephen Castles and Mark J. Miller, *The Age of Migration: International Population Movements in the Modern World* (London: Guilford Press, 2003).

4. Some of the most important sources on migration statistics come from the World Bank (www.worldbank.org), the International Organization of Migration (IOM, http://www.iom.int/jahia/jsp/index.jsp), the International Labor Organization (ILO, http://www.ilo.org/global/lang—en/index.htm), the United Nations High Commissioner for Refugees (UNHCR, www.unhcr.org), the United Nations Department of Economic and Social Affairs (UNDESA; see especially *Trends in Total Migration Stock: The 2005 Revision*, http://www.un.org/esa/population/publications/migration/UN_Migrant_Stock_Documentation_2005.pdf), and the Global Commission for International Migration (GCIM, www.gcim.org/en/). See in particular *Migration in an Interconnected World: Report of the Global Commission for International Migration* (Geneva: Global Commission on International Migration), 83–85, available at http://www.gcim.org/attachements/gcim-complete-report-2005.pdf (accessed May 11, 2009).

5. For more on these statistics, see http://www.iom.int/jahia/Jahia/pid/254 (accessed May 12, 2009).

6. John R. Donahue, S.J., "The 'Parable' of the Sheep and the Goats: A Challenge to Christian Ethics," *Theological Studies* 47, 1 (1986): 3.

7. Alongside the suffering of the immigrants, one does see individual and collective responses to the plight of immigrants that embody the works of

mercy outlined in Matthew 25. Groups like Humane Borders put thousands of gallons of water out each year to aid stranded immigrants. No More Deaths sends trained volunteers and medics to help the hungry and sick. Others like The Valley Missionary Program in Coachella, California, offer retreats and community support to help estranged immigrants find a home in a foreign land. Human rights groups like Derechos Humanos and others seek to break the bonds that imprison immigrants unjustly. Even with these efforts, however, undocumented immigrants remain some of the most vulnerable members of U.S./American society.

8. John Annerino, *Dead in Their Tracks: Crossing America's Desert Borderlands* (New York: Four Walls Eight Windows, 1999), 40–42.

9. Mexican immigrant, interview by author, July 18, 2003, tape recording, Sasabe, Arizona.

10. Mexican immigrant, interview by author, April 18, 2001, tape recording, Tijuana, Mexico.

11. San Diego woman, interview by author, April 18, 2001, tape recording, San Diego, California.

12. The cemetery in Holtville, California, is where hundreds of immigrants who die in California are buried.

13. Mexican immigrant, interview by author, June 15, 2003, tape recording, Altar, Mexico.

14. Mexican immigrant, interview by author, June 15, 2003, tape recording, Altar, Mexico.

15. Gil Loescher, "The PRS Project," unpublished paper, presented at Queen Elizabeth House, Oxford University, November 22, 2007.

16. Mexican immigrant, interview by author, November 15, 1999, tape recording, Coachella, California.

17. Justin Pritchard, "A Mexican Worker Dies Each Day," Associated Press, March 14, 2004.

18. "We Almost Suffocated in the Trailer Truck," *Houston Catholic Worker* 23, 4 (July-August 2003): 1, 8.

19. Mexican immigrant, interview by author, June 18, 2003, tape recording, Arivaca, Arizona.

20. Mexican immigrant, interview by author, June 22, 2003, tape recording, Tuscon, Arizona.

21. Mexican immigrant, interview by author, June 22, 2003, tape recording, Tuscon, Arizona.

22. Bob Moser, "Open Season: As extremists peddle their anti-immigrant rhetoric along the troubled Arizona border, a storm gathers," *SPLCENTER.ORG*, http://www.splcenter.org/intelligenceproject/ip-index.html:6/20/2003.

23. Ibid.

24. Ibid.

25. William P. Fay, "Catholic Social Teaching and the Undocumented," http://www.cliniclegal.org/Social_teaching/undocumented.htm:7/8/2003.

26. For more on migrants and salvation, see Diane Bergant, "Ruth: The Migrant Who Saved the People," in *Migration, Religious Experience and Globalization*, ed. Gioacchino Campese and Pietro Ciallella (New York: Center for Migration Studies, 2003), 49–61.

27. Robin Hoover, interview by author, June 15, 2003, tape recording, Tuscon, Arizona.

28. Lydio F. Tomasi, "The Other Catholics" (Ph.D. diss., New York University, 1978), 301.

CONTRIBUTORS

FR. PABLO ALONSO, SJ, was born in Murcia (Spain) and entered the Jesuits in 1986. He holds a doctorate in theology from the Catholic University of Leuven and obtained a master's degree in biblical philology at the Complutense University (Madrid) and the licentiate in sacred scripture at the Biblical Institute in Rome. He worked in Tanzania for two years with the Jesuit Refugee Service among Rwandan and Burundian refugees. Currently he is an assistant professor in the Department of Biblical Studies at Comillas University and lives and works in El Pozo (Madrid).

M. SHAWN COPELAND is an associate professor of systematic theology at Boston College from which she earned a doctorate in systematic theology. She has authored more than eighty articles, book chapters, and reviews; she is the editor of *Uncommon Faithfulness: the Black Catholic Experience* (2009) and the author of *Enfleshing Freedom: Body, Race and Being* (2010). Her theology carries out a dialogical conversation between the Roman Catholic tradition and African American culture and experience to advance a theology accountable to the "dangerous memory" of chattel slavery and the moral and social sin of racism.

MARY DOAK is an associate professor of theology at the University of San Diego. She received her B.A. from Loyola University of Chicago and her M.A. and Ph.D. from the University of Chicago. Her main areas of research include public and political theology, theological method, eschatology, and ecclesiology. She has published *Reclaiming Narrative for Public Theology* (SUNY, 2004), as well as various articles on issues in contemporary theology. She is currently working on a book on the mission of the church in the twenty-first century.

FR. VIRGILIO ELIZONDO earned Ph.D. and S.T.D. degrees from the Institut Catholique in Paris and is currently Notre Dame Professor of Pastoral and Hispanic Theology at the University of Notre Dame. Named with Pope John Paul II as one of two "leading spiritual innovators" at the beginning of the third millennium (*Time*, December 2000) and a founder of U.S. Hispanic-Latino/a theology, Elizondo has authored a dozen books—including his classic work, *Galilean Journey: The Mexican American Promise* (1983)—edited two dozen volumes, and written numerous articles. He has specialized in the study of Our Lady of Guadalupe, pastoral and Hispanic theology, and inculturation, and his recent publications include A God of Incredible Surprises: Jesus of Galilee (2003).

SEAN FREYNE is a professor of theology (emeritus) at Trinity College, Dublin, and was co-founder and first director of the Centre for Mediterranean and Near Eastern Studies at the College. On his retirement he acted as Visiting Professor of Early Christian History and Literature at Harvard Divinity School in 2007–8. He is a fellow of Trinity College and a member of the Royal Irish Academy. He is also a trustee of the Chester Beatty Library, Dublin. He has served on the editorial boards of New Testament Studies and Concilium: An International Journal of Theology and is a past-president of the Studiorum Novi Testamenti Societas. His research interests center on early Judaism and early Christianity, with a particular focus on Roman-Period Galilee in terms of its cultural and religious affiliations. He is the author of several books and many articles dealing with various issues connected with these areas of research. His most recent study, Jesus, a Jewish Galilean (2005), gathers together many of the ideas he has developed over the years with regard to both Jesus and Galilee.

ROBERTO S. GOIZUETA is the Margaret O'Brien Flatley Professor of Catholic Theology at Boston College and former president of the Catholic Theological Society of America and the Academy of Catholic Hispanic Theologians of the United States. He holds a B.A. from Yale University and an M.A. and Ph.D. from Marquette University. Dr. Goizueta has received honorary degrees from the University of San Francisco and Elms College, and the National Catholic Reporter has named him one of the ten most influential Hispanic-American educators, pastors, and theologians. The son of Cuban immigrants, Goizueta is the author of Caminemos con Jesús: Toward a Hispanic/Latino Theology of Accompaniment (1995), winner of a Catholic Press Asssociation Book Award, and, most recently, Christ Our Companion: Toward a Theological Aesthetics of Liberation (2009). Professor Goizueta teaches courses on Latin American and U.S. Latino/a theologies and is interested in the relationship between theology and culture, focusing especially on Hispanic-Latino/a popular religion as a source for theological reflection.

FR. DANIEL GROODY, CSC, received his Ph.D. from the Graduate Theological Union in Berkeley, California. He is an associate professor of theology and director of the Center for Latino Spirituality and Culture at the Institute for Latino Studies at the University of Notre Dame and has been a visiting research fellow at the Refugee Studies Centre, Oxford University. Drawing on years of work along the U.S.–Mexico border, he recently authored *Border of Death, Valley of Life: An Immigrant Journey of Heart and Spirit* (2002); *Globalization, Spirituality, and Justice: Navigating the Path to Peace* (2007); and the edited collections, *The Option for the Poor in Christian Theology* (2007) and, with Gioacchino Campese, *A Promised Land, A Perilous Journey: Theological Perspectives on Migration* (2008). He has worked with the U.S. Congress, the U.S. Conference of Catholic Bishops, the World Council of Churches, and the Vatican on issues of theology, globalization, and immigration.

FR. GUSTAVO GUTIÉRREZ, OP, received his Ph.D. from the Université Catholique, Lyon, France. He holds the John Cardinal O'Hara Chair in Theology at the University of Notre Dame, where he teaches and writes on liberation theology, spirituality, and biblical foundations. Widely regarded as a founder of Latin American liberation theology for his epoch-changing work, *A Theology of Liberation: History, Politics, Salvation*, he has also written other major books touching on issues of spirituality and Latin American history. These include, *We Drink From Our Own Wells: The Spiritual Journey of a People*; *On Job: God-Talk and the Suffering of the Innocent*; *The Truth Shall Make You Free*; *The God of Life*; and *Las Casas: In Search of the Poor of Jesus Christ*. Fr. Gutiérrez has received the Legion of Honor from the French government (1993) as well as numerous honorary doctorates and honors in recognition of his tireless work for human dignity and life and against oppression in Latin America and the Third World. He is currently working on a book that explores the historical background and continuing theological relevance of the preferential option for the poor.

ROBERT LASSALLE-KLEIN received his Ph.D. from the Graduate Theological Union in Berkeley. He was the Bannan Fellow at Santa Clara University during the first half of 2010 and is an associate professor and coordinator of Religious Studies at Holy Names University, Oakland, California. The grandson of immigrants and co-founder of the Oakland Catholic Worker refugee project, he has developed an intercultural approach grounded in the option for the poor to Christology, fundamental theology, global liberation theologies, and lay formation. He edited the June 2009 special issue of *Theological Studies* on *The Galilean Jesus* and, with with Kevin Burke, SJ, co-edited *Love That Produces Hope: The Thought of Ignacio Ellacuría* (2006). In progress are *Blood and Ink: The Jesuit Martyrs of the University of Central America* and *Jon Sobrino: Spiritual Writings* for the Modern Spiritual Masters Series (Orbis).

MICHAEL E. LEE received his Ph.D. from the University of Notre Dame and is an assistant professor of systematic theology at Fordham University, New York, where he also teaches in the Institute of Latin American and Latino Studies. His areas of special competence include Christology, soteriology, Latin American theology, and U.S. Latino/a theology. Having recently published *Bearing the Weight of Salvation: The Soteriology of Ignacio Ellacuría* (2008), he has two works in progress: a translation of essays by Ellacuría, tentatively titled *Liberation: The Task of History*, and a monograph on the theology of Archbishop Oscar Romero.

FR. FRANCIS MINJ, SJ, received his doctorate in sacred theology from the Jesuit School of Theology of Santa Clara University in Berkeley, California. He is dean and teaches theology at the Jesuit-run Tarunoday Regional Theologate near Ranchi, the capital of Jharkhand in eastern India. Fr. Minj is an *Ādivāsi* (a member of one of the aboriginal tribes that, like untouchables, fall outside the Indian caste system) and trains Jesuits from the central tribal belt of India in the states of Jharkhand and Chattisgarh. As a Christian and an *Ādivāsi*, he is doubly marginated in his own land. His recently completed dissertation, *Jesus Christ Paramādivāsi: A Liberative-Inculturated Christology from an Ādivāsi Context of India* (2009), develops the first contextualized Christology from and for *Ādivāsis*.

SR. CAROLINE N. MBONU received her Ph.D. from the Graduate Theological Union, Berkeley, California. She is a member of the Congregation of the Handmaids of the Holy Child Jesus, has taught at the Institute of Black Catholic Studies, Xavier University of Louisiana, and currently works with women and teaches in the rural Port Harcourt diocese in Nigeria, Africa. An interdisciplinary scholar, she employs scripture and African religious traditions to seek insights into improving women's participation in social processes. She is a member of the Igbo people from West Africa (Nigeria) and has recently published *Handmaid: The Power of Names in Theology and Society* (2010), a close reading of the annunciation scene in Luke 1:26–38 from an Igbo woman's perspective. In progress is *Trail Blazers and Pioneers: Women Religious in Nigeria*.

SR. SOPHIA PARK, SNJM, received her Ph.D. in Christian spirituality from the Graduate Theological Union, Berkeley, California, and is an assistant professor at Holy Names University, Oakland, California, where she specializes in biblical spirituality and cultural studies. She was born in South Korea and as an adult immigrated for graduate studies in the United States, where she joined the Holy Names Sisters. In addition to her work in Christian spirituality, she also studies the role of women in indigenous spirituality, especially in Korean shamanism. Her recent publications include "The Galilean Jesus: Creating a Borderland at the Foot of the Cross (Jn 19:23–30)," *Theological Studies* (2009); "Cross-cultural Spiritual Direction," *Presence* (2010); and a Korean translation of Sandra Schneiders, *The Revelatory Text: Interpreting the New Testament as Sacred Scripture* (forthcoming). In progress are works on "Reading a Cutlural Text: Tarot," and a book on Korean American Catholicism.

FR. GIACOMO PEREGO, SSP, a priest of the Society of Saint Paul, holds a Ph.D. in biblical sciences from the Ecole Biblique et Archéologique Française of Jerusalem. He lectured in New Testament studies at the Institute for Consecrated Life (Claretianum) of the Pontifical Lateran University and in the CICS of the Pontifical Gregorian University in Rome. He is presently editorial co-director of Edizioni San Paolo. His publications include *La nudità necessaria. Il ruolo del giovane di Mc 14,51–52 nel racconto marciano della passione-morte-risurrezione di Gesù* (2000); *Atlante biblico interdisciplinare* (2007, 4th ed.); *Nuovo Testamento e Vita consacrata* (2008); and *Temi Teologici della Bibbia* (2010, Dictionary).

FR. JON SOBRINO, SJ, received his Th.D. from Hochschule Sanckt Georgen, Frankfurt, and is now professor of theology at the University of Central America, San Salvador. A Spanish-born theologian, he has spent the last fifty years in El Salvador, where he worked closely with the assassinated Archbishop Oscar Romero and survived the murders of six Jesuit colleagues and two woman co-workers on November 16, 1989 because he was out of the country giving lectures in Thailand. His areas of special interest are Christology and martyrdom for faith and justice. He is the author of over twenty books and many articles, most recently *No Salvation Outside the Poor: Prophetic-Utopian Essays* (2008), and is currently preparing a work on Christian identity in light of following Jesus

JOSÉ SOLS holds a doctorate in theology from the Centre Sèvres, Paris. He is director of the Chair of Ethics and Christian Thought in the *Institut Químic de Sarrià*, Ramon Llull University, Barcelona, Spain, and coordinator of the international research group Laboratorio de Análisis y Crítica Social. He is a member of the Jesuit Studies Center, "*Cristianisme i Justícia*," coordinator of the Christian Social Thought Group of the Jesuit Universities of Spain (UNIJES), and a member of the Spanish Chapter of the Club of Rome. He has published *La teología histórica de Ignacio Ellacuría* (1998), *One Hundred Years of Violence* (2003), *Governabilitat Democrútica Global* (2007), and most recently *Atrapados en la violencia: ¿hay salida?* (2009).

INDEX